Henry Morford

Appletons' Short Trip Guide to Europe

1868

Henry Morford

Appletons' Short Trip Guide to Europe

1868

ISBN/EAN: 9783337148737

Printed in Europe, USA, Canada, Australia, Japan

Cover: Foto ©Andreas Hilbeck / pixelio.de

More available books at **www.hansebooks.com**

APPLETONS'

SHORT-TRIP GUIDE

TO

EUROPE.

[1868.]

PRINCIPALLY DEVOTED TO

ENGLAND, SCOTLAND, IRELAND, SWITZERLAND,
FRANCE, GERMANY AND ITALY;

WITH GLIMPSES OF

*SPAIN, SHORT ROUTES IN THE EAST, ETC.; AND A
COLLATION OF TRAVELLERS' PHRASES IN
FRENCH AND GERMAN.*

By HENRY MORFORD,

AUTHOR OF "OVER SEA," ".PARIS IN '67," ETC., ETC.

NEW YORK:
D. APPLETON & CO., 90, 92 & 94 GRAND STREET
1868.

TABLE OF CONTENTS.

	PAGE.
I.—Cost of Short European Trips,	5
II.—Time Necessary on Short European Trips,	15
III.—Steamship Lines to Europe, with a Hint for "'Round the World,"	24
IV.—Preparations for "Going Over,"	33
V.—What to Do and Avoid, on Shipboard,	47
VI.—Look-Outs and Land-Makings,	57
VII.—Entering Foreign Countries,	75
VIII.—Short Trips in Ireland,	81
IX.—Short Trips in Scotland,	97
X.—Short Trips in England,	118
XI.—Crossing the British Channel,	159
XII.—Short Trips in France,	162
XIII.—Paris to Geneva,	183
XIV.—Short Trips in Switzerland,	186
XV.—Bale to Strasbourg and Baden-Baden,	204
XVI.—Short Trips in Germany,	210
XVII.—Across the Alps to Italy,	231
XVIII.—Short Trips in Italy,	243
XIX.—Short Trips in Spain,	278
XX.—Hints for a Short Route in the East,	287
XXI.—Travellers' Phrases in French and German,	298
XXII.—European Money in American Coin,	321

ADVERTISEMENT

TO THE EDITION FOR 1868.

THE suggestion was several times made to the author-compiler, during the summer of 1867, at the French Exposition and elsewhere: "You are picking up materials for books of travel—why do you not supply what everybody wants: a short and comparatively-cheap Guide-Book to the countries of Europe oftenest visited by us hurried Americans, who have neither much time nor much money to spend? Very few of us, in proportion, can afford to travel in more than one or two countries, or three, or four; and we cannot expect to see all that is worth seeing, even in *them*. Give us something concise, in not-too-small type, simple, practical and good-humored—where we can easily find what we want to know, and avoid finding the ten thousand things that we *don't* want to know. Tell us how to see the best things in the least space of time and at the least expenditure of money; and inform us, among other things, how much time and money ought to be consumed in making the best short rounds."

The "Short-Trip Guide to Europe" is the result of that often-repeated suggestion, and it has been especially designed to meet that demand. The principal effort has been, to make it rapid, plain and practical—to fit it especially to the needs of the thousands of Americans who visit Europe for very brief periods: absent from home for from six weeks to three or four months—to point out the objects which should be seen *first*, if all cannot be seen—to show where and how, at one point and another, the short trip may be best extended a little or yet more—to make it an instructive (and sometimes amusing) pocket-companion, its size especially fitting it for that purpose—to aid the hurried, put the raw and nervous at ease, save money to travellers of limited means, and at least lay a profitable foundation of knowledge for those who may intend to travel more at length, more at leisure, and pursue more elaborate works of the same character. And in this connection it may be proper to say that while by far the larger proportion of the matter presented is the result of personal observation and diligent inquiry among intelligent travellers known to have gone over routes as yet unvisited by the writer—still there is an obligation owed to Baedeker, to Murray, and other professionals long in the field, and to the cosmopolitan Fetridge, whose "Harper's Hand-Book" is always found available by those who tarry long in the Old World, instead of merely running through the best parts of it.

As may be supposed, it is the intention of author and publishers to continue the publication of the "Short-Trip Guide," punctually every year, issued earlier in the following seasons than has been found practicable in the present—not an item of old or exploded matter left, from one issue to another, if something newer and more interesting can be found to fill its place and add to the practical usefulness of the series.

NEW YORK CITY, *May*, 1868.

THE SHORT-TRIP GUIDE.

(1868.)

I.

COST OF SHORT EUROPEAN TRIPS.

OF course the question *Whether to go to Europe at all?* underlies, with Americans, both those others : *How to go?* and *Where to go?* The distance (of which something more will be said directly,) is known to be great, between the New and Old Worlds, though it is really only about one-eighth of that around the globe.

With many men *Time* is the great object, and the want of it the great hindrance ; though they may annually spend quite as much of it as would be necessary for a summer tour, in dawdling elsewhere, around home or in places seen until they have become tiresome. With a far greater number of those who love Nature and Art to such an extent as to make travel a delight, *Money* is the anxiety, the want of it the hindrance, and the belief that a mint is necessary for anything European, the great bugbear which confines them to one continent.

A large proportion of this is a mistake, originally induced by want of intelligent enquiry, and materially added to by the exaggerations, not to call them falsehoods, of those who have been over the desired routes. While "going to Europe" was principally confined to the wealthy few or those driven by business demands, it was at once an easy and a tempting thing to do, to add to the supposed importance of what had been done, by overstating the cost as well as enlarging on the personal adventure and peril; and, truth to say, the habit has not yet quite died out, now when the many follow in the track of the few and detection is so much easier. Mr. Longbow, who supplies (as he believes) the centre at home of an admiring circle, not many members of which are likely to follow him abroad—cannot resist the temptation to show, when he returns, that he has been doing, in the way of cost, what *they* had better not attempt if they do not wish to fail miserably; and Madame La Mode, flaunting in home-circles the silks and jewelry purchased during the previous summer at Paris, *will* enlarge a little upon the cost of not only the silks and jewelry, but of getting into the "society" in which she figured in the great capitals.

Travelers tell "travelers' stories," in a pecuniary as well as an adventurous point of view: that is the truth, briefly told; and those stories frighten away many who would else enlarge their knowledge of life by seeing other continents than their own.

Not that many Americans fail to spend enormous amounts abroad: it is a shameful fact that we *do* spend more money, on an average, in travel, than any other nation beneath the sun. It is easy for the writer to recal to mind one gentleman of New York, without landed estates, the working of capital, or other resources than his own hard-working energy and talent, who, during two-and-a-half months of the summer of 1865, in England and France alone, and principally about London and Paris, spent, unaccompanied, between $7,000 and $8,000, and borrowed money in London for his passage homeward! And during the summer of 1867, a well-known gentleman of fortune, of New York, visiting London and Paris with his wife and child, and going no step beyond the latter city, found the $8,000 (gold) which he had taken with him, insufficient, and drew on New York for $2,000 additional. Very possibly these figures do not even approach the amount of money spent by each one of many wealthy or wasteful Americans during corresponding periods.: they are only given as instances happening to fall under personal knowledge.

So much for what may be spent in very brief tours, by those who can afford plenty of money, or think that they can do so : now for what may be saved, or rather for the question upon how little these brief tours may really be made, without discomfort or painful compromise of position.

There was a country clergyman, not far from one of the large American cities, who, having united a couple in marriage, some quarter of a century ago, was privately enquired of by the well-to-do bridegroom, shortly after the completion of the ceremony, as to the amount due for that performance. "Well," answered the clergyman, "I have no fixed price for such services. People generally pay me according to their means and what they think that they can afford. Sometimes I get as high as fifty dollars: twenty dollars; ten; five; and one man, not long ago, paid me—ha! ha!—only think of it!—only twenty-five cents!" "Humph! twenty-five cents! well, that was reasonable enough!" replied the new-made bridegroom, extracting a quarter from his pocket and handing it over to the astounded official, who had thus given one peep too many into the "extreme economy" of paying for wedding ceremonials!

The application of which is to say that visits to Europe *may* be made by Americans, a little on the principle of the Cincinnatian who burned his lamps all day because "lard oil was cheaper than daylight" —that they *may* go, if they will, quite as cheaply as they can remain at home, possibly a little cheaper. This, however, might be like the twenty-five cents of the penurious bridegroom, and would involve the steerage of the ships, the third-class cattle-pens of the European railways, and lodging somewhere in the back-slums of any cities visited.

Still, even in the steerage, on some of the best-appointed lines (about which something definite in due place) passages may be made with much less discomfort than most stay-at-home people suppose; and it is not at all certain that thousands of hardy persons, limited in means, who spend the requisite amounts of time and money on very questionable

COST OF TRIPS. 9

home-amusements approaching to vices, might not do well to tempt a little rugged life in the forward parts of the ships that carry over their wealthy brothers in the saloon-cabins. For on those best lines the discomforts, inconveniences and unhealthinesses of steerage-passage have all been materially ameliorated within the past three or four years : the sleeping accommodations on many of them are endurable if no more ; the food is almost always plentiful and generally excellent ; the amount of amusement enjoyed is always greater than that attainable by the "stiffer" people at the stern ; and the safety to person is necessarily the same except under circumstances of gross carelessness.

Let us see, for the benefit of those very limited in means and still desirous to see a little fragment of the Old World—what would be the absolute cost of doing what emigrants of both sexes and all countries very often do for the sake of spending a few days with friends in the places of nativity. Say that six weeks' time is attainable, and let the cost of that six weeks be measured in current greenbacks.

Steerage passage to Liverpool, $30—return $35 : total, $65. Time not on board ship, about three weeks ; board, for that time, average of $10 per week, $30. Expenses of sight-seeing about Liverpool, London and some neighboring towns, during that period, $10. Occasional necessary conveyance, the feet being principally trusted to, $25. Incidental expenses, liberally calculated, $20. Total, $150, greenbacks ! $20 more would enable the cheap-tourist to land in Ireland on the way, see Dublin,

Cork, Blarney Castle and the Lakes of Killarney; and $30 added to that would supply a run up to Scotland, a view of Edinburgh, Glasgow, the Scottish Lakes and Highlands. Grand total, $200, greenbacks; with a certainty that any economical person, in good health and temper, could reduce that sum by at least $25, or to $175. Another $30 added to the grand total, or from $205 to $230, would afford a run across the British Channel, to Paris, with three or four days' sights of that most enchanting of cities. How many comparatively-poor men are there, with longing and hopeless desires after seeing other countries than their own, who never make any calculation or effort to such an end, and yet who could and would compass it if they fairly understood the comparative trifle for which so much might be enjoyed!

One of the greatest of American travelers, Mr. Bayard Taylor, made his first European excursion under circumstances quite as illiberal as anything here indicated—"did" Great Britain and a very considerable portion of the continent on foot, except with rare instances of riding, and remained not less than six or seven months, his whole expenditure being only about $500, and the fortunate result of his travel that successful volume "Views-A-foot; or, Europe Seen with Knapsack and Staff." And it is very doubtful whether in any portion of his later experience, in all descriptions of traveling "state" up to that of Secretary of Legation at St. Petersburg, he has ever enjoyed his wanderings better than when making that first essay as a poor boy·

COST OF TRIPS.

But the figures already given represent, of course, the minimum possibility of travel in the most-easily-attainable European countries, compatible with even the decencies of life, without too many of its comforts ; and it is, equally of course, with that class of people standing midway between the possible steerage-passenger and the traveler *en prince*, that we have next and principally to do. The most important question of this paper is—*What need be the expenses, for a certain round, of a traveler going first-class and demanding all the comforts, and yet indisposed to waste money on costly luxuries?*

To answer that question, then, as intelligibly as may be consistent with brevity.

For six to seven weeks' absence from home, visiting portions of England, Ireland, Scotland and France, only.

Ticket to Liverpool and return, $180 to $300 (gold) —say an average of $225, for which all necessary comfort and quite sufficient "style" can be secured. Average board of the three weeks off-ship, $15 to $20 per week—say $60. Traveling expenses, railway and carriage fares, etc., $150. Maps, pictures, curiosities, books, etc. (not all necessary, but inevitable), $50. Incidental expenses, for which no name can be given ; money to guides, beggars, stewards and servants ; money lost and wasted, with an occasional indulgence in a luxury, *not* including costly wines or "society," gambling or other vices—$50. Total, $535 gold ; or, with gold at 140, about $750 currency. $75 gold or $105 currency may easily be saved from this, by a very careful person, leaving the expenditure $460 gold or $645 currency. For this, necessarily brief but quite satisfactory acquaintance may be made, in succession, with Cork, the Lakes of Killarney, and Dublin, in Ireland ; Liverpool, Chester, London (with its surroundings), in England ; Dieppe, Rouen and Paris (with its surroundings), in France ; Edinburgh, Glasgow and the Perthshire Highlands, in Scotland.

For ten weeks' absence, an estimate of $200 gold additional may safely be made, bringing the total outlay up to say $735 gold or $1000 currency ; and this will secure, in addition to the round already named, the Cumberland Lakes and Shakspeare Neighborhood of England, with Birmingham, Manchester and York ; a more extended examination of both London and Paris ; a rapid run through the more frequented parts of Switzerland, and so far into Germany as Baden-Baden and the Black Forest.

For three months' (thirteen or fourteen weeks) absence, another $200 gold may be added, bringing the amount up to say $935, or $1275 currency ; and with this all the foregoing may be done, with the addition of some of the principal German cities ; the Rhine ; Holland and Belgium ; the more laborious passes of Switzerland ; one or two of the French and English Channel watering-places ; the Scottish Western Highlands ; and the Giant's Causeway, Belfast and some of the other towns in the North of Ireland.

Four months will add to this another $200 or possibly $250 gold, making the total say $1170, or $1600 to $1650 currency ; and with this expenditure to all the foregoing may be added a run across the Alps to the Italian Lakes, Turin, Florence, Rome and

COST OF TRIPS.   13

Venice, with return by Marseilles and the South of France and a consequent glimpse of the Mediterranean.

At this point the phrase "short trip" may be said to be exhausted; for only people of liberal means and abundant leisure are likely to go far beyond in any one visit abroad, and to them these calculations possess no interest whatever. Added to what has been already named, Spain and Portugal in one direction; Eastern Germany and Austria in another; Greece, Turkey and the Asiatic and African East in another; and Sweden, Norway, Russia, etc., in yet another—constitute tours not often entered upon by those who have no special interest calling them there, and who have yet occasion to count time and money before starting.

The foregoing figures are certainly not startling, and yet they have been all liberally as well as carefully made, and all of them verified by reliable experience. Twice as much can be *thrown away*, on either route; and a considerable amount above the estimate may be *frittered* away, if due diligence is not observed; but there is no occasion whatever of going beyond the computation, if gross negligences do not allow, or costly luxuries or yet more costly vices do not induce, the additional expenditure.

Common sense, without even the aid of experience, will indicate that there are always possibilities of sickness, accident, or some other cause of detention, levying extraordinary expense—and that, therefore, it is always best to have a little "margin" of money in pocket or within reach; but the chances of either are scarcely one in an hundred, and on most of the routes specified careful men can save enough from the figures given, to supply themselves with even that "margin," while there is always the option, in the event of unforeseen embarrassment, of *shortening the trip contemplated* and hoping for "better luck next time."

II.

TIME NECESSARY ON ORDINARY EUROPEAN ROUTES.

A CONSIDERABLE portion of what might have been said in this paper, has found place in the one preceding—as in that the round that may be safely attempted within each of certain given periods, has been incidentally mentioned.

But there is room and even necessity for something more, if this little volume is to be made to fulfil its full purpose. For it is especially designed for Americans; and Americans sometimes need to be reminded of their own characteristics, quite as much as others to be informed of them.

There are two misunderstandings, on this question of *Time*, both of which need to be corrected. The first is an impression that *everything* can be done within a limited space, and the other that *nothing!* Americans generally fall into the first error; those who attempt to guide without understanding them, tumble into the second. Not even the most incarnate American can rival Puck and "put a girdle" (even one of travel) "round the earth in forty minutes;" and yet he certainly can go farther and faster with a fair appreciation of what he sees and hears, than any other created being.

The Money obstacle, which keeps at home so many of those who desire to travel and who would travel but for its existence, has already been alluded to. The obstacle of *Time* is only secondary in importance and scarcely secondary in its effects.

"Oh, there is no use of my going to Europe, with only such a little time at my disposal!" almost pettishly says the prospective possessor of two or three months of leisure. "Think that I am going to cross the Atlantic, without being able to see the whole of it when I *do!* No—wait!"

He does "wait," and one of two things is the result. Either he defers going, until growing entanglements make it impossible, or he rushes over, at last, under the impression that he must repay himself for waiting by going over the whole continent, with all its islands, in the one visit and at railway speed—the last result being that he "conglomerates" everything, even if he sees it, and brings away a dim doubt whether St. Peter's is not on the top of Jura and the great clock of Strasbourg stowed away somewhere in Westminster Abbey or the Madeleine.

Meanwhile the European, or the man of any other country whatever than America, scoffs and sneers at the idea that he can see anything whatever without staying a month in each particular place, and the American obtains a reputation for "rushing too fast" when he is really behaving very sensibly in that regard. It is for the purpose of getting at the truth and the "golden mean" in this special particular, that the present paper is written—for the purpose of inducing less of that fatal "waiting," less of that crowding too many countries together and exhausting energy in seeing things that are really of no consequence when others of the kind have been sufficiently seen and studied.

Assuming the fact that the cause of intelligent travel would be materially subserved by people going over oftener, for special routes and without the weak variety of "the grand tour or nothing!"—assuming this, which is a fact appealing to health, intelligence and common-sense, just as does the propriety of spending one day in every week on the sea-shore at enervating midsummer, instead of working every day for the three hot months in order to find time for two weeks there at the end—*What are the spaces of time really needed by Americans for certain special objects of travel?*

Let us dissect some of the routes already named, as the most intelligible mode of arriving at the time which they really need occupy, to a quick-witted and intelligent traveler.

For the trip of six to seven weeks ($535 gold—$750 currency). Time consumed on ship, going and returning, three weeks, leaving three to four weeks ashore. At and about Cork, 1 day. Cork to Lakes of Killarney, and at Lakes, 2 days. Killarney to Dublin and at Dublin, 2 days. Dublin to Liverpool, ½ day. Liverpool and Chester, 2 days. Liverpool to London, ½ day. London and suburbs, 6 days. London to Paris, with stop at Rouen, 1 day. Paris and suburbs, 5 days. Paris back to London and on to Edinburgh, by York, with lay over of one train there, 2 days. Edinburgh and suburbs, 1½ days. Glasgow and going there, 1½ days. From Glasgow through Perthshire Highlands to Stirling, 1 day.

Stirling to Burns country of Ayrshire, and stop there, 1 day. To Liverpool and return-ship, ½ day. Total, 27½ days—four weeks; some abridgement of time in London or Paris, or the dropping off of some minor excursions being necessary, if the return home within six weeks is peremptory, while within the seven all can be accomplished without difficulty or unpleasant hurry.

(Parenthetically, English rural scenery, among the most beautiful on the globe, is also the least varied, so that one excursion through it affords, with rare exceptions, a type of all, and neither time or money need be expended in dull repetitions. To some extent, the same remarks will apply to old churches and old buildings, when there is no historical interest involved: after seeing the most magnificent or the most noted, the remainder are, to a man without full leisure, rather dull than the reverse.)

For the ten weeks' trip, take same figures, 28 days ashore, and add to them as follows: From Liverpool to the Cumberland Lakes and return, with time there, 2 days. Liverpool to Birmingham and through the Shakspeare neighborhood of Warwickshire, taking the London line at Rugby, 3 days. Paris to Geneva, Berne, Interlaken, Strasbourg and Baden-Baden, and back to Paris, 12 days. Additional time at London and Paris, each 2 days, 4 days. Total on shore, 49 days, or seven weeks.

For the three months' trip (13 to 14 weeks), a different arrangement of time is advisable, as follows: Cork, 1 day. To and at Killarney, 3 days. To Dublin and there, 2 days. Dublin to the Giant's

TIME OF TRIPS. 19

Causeway and across to Belfast, 4 days. Belfast to Greenock and Glasgow, 1 day. Glasgow, 1 day. From Glasgow, through the Highlands and by Stirling to Edinburgh, 3 days. Edinburgh, 2 days. Edinburgh to Ayrshire and stop there, 1½ days. To the Cumberland Lakes, ½ day. At Cumberland Lakes, 2 days. To Liverpool, ½ day. At Liverpool, Chester, &c., 2 days. To Birmingham, Coventry, Stratford-on-Avon, Warwick, &c., 3 days. To London, 1 day. At London, 6 days. Brighton and Margate, 2 days. To Paris, by Rouen, 1½ days. Paris, 6 days. Paris to Geneva (with excursion to Chamouni), Berne, Interlaken, Lucerne (the Rhigi), Bale, Strasbourg and Baden-Baden, 14 days. Baden-Baden, down the Rhine, and across Germany, Holland and Belgium, returning to England at most convenient point, 8 days. To Liverpool, 1 day. Total, 65½ days—nine weeks and a fraction.

For the yet-more-extended trip of four months, all the last preceding figures may be used, with the option of employing the remaining 25 to 30 days in either of the following modes:

Cross the Alps into Italy, by either the St. Gothard, St. Bernard or Mt. Cenis passes, see Lakes Como, Garda, Maggiore, etc., and so many of the cities of Turin, Milan, Florence, Rome, Naples, Venice, etc., as may be attainable within the remaining limit of time and expense (the 30 days and about $200 gold), recrossing the Alps to Switzerland by one of the other passes, and thence pursuing the route last-named, through the remainder of Switzerland, Germany, etc.; or—

Abandoning, for this tour, Germany and all beyond that point of Switzerland reached at the time of crossing the Alps, expend the whole remaining, say 40 days and $275 to $300 gold, in visiting more of the Italian cities, the Bay of Naples, Vesuvius, etc., and "doing" Rome more thoroughly, taking steamer on the Mediterranean at some one of the Italian ports for Marseilles, catching a glimpse of Spain and seeing the southwest of France, crossing nearly the whole length of that empire in running back to Paris and a Channel port for the return to England ; or—

Pursuing generally the course last marked out, abandon, again, something of the Italian opportunity, and substitute one or two of the towns and a portion of the Mediterranean coast of Spain, still making Marseilles the objective point, and crossing France to Paris and the Channel, as before.

There are, of course, many other options, as well as many other comparatively-brief routes, than those which have now been hurriedly discussed—especially one which should branch off into Eastern Germany and Austria, leaving out Italy and the south altogether ; but it is believed that these include the probable preferences of most Americans, and it is beyond question that this understanding and allotment of time and expense will be found, in the main, correct, practical and worthy of study.

And now one or two particulars, with reference to the employment of time, in response to certain questions almost sure to be asked by any foreigner reading the preceding, and quite likely to be put even by Americans :

TIME OF TRIPS. 21

"*Such brief spaces have been named for some of the most important and interesting places on the globe: how is it possible, for instance, to see anything of either London or Paris in the six to eight days allotted to each ?*"

To which the answer is :

First : there are in both cities certain prominent objects, which all need to visit, and beyond which only persons of leisure care to go. In and about London, the Tower ; Westminster Abbey ; St. Paul's ; the Houses of Parliament ; Windsor Castle and Park ; Buckingham and the other royal palaces ; the British and South Kensington Museums ; the Crystal Palace ; Hyde and the other London parks ; Richmond Hill ; Kew Gardens, etc., the most interesting objects being all really named. In and about Paris, the Boulevards ; the Seine, its quays and bridges ; the Louvre ; the Tuileries ; Notre Dame, the Madeleine and other great churches ; the Tuileries Gardens, Place de la Concorde, and Champs Elysees ; the Arc d'Etoile and other great monuments ; the Bois de Boulogne ; the Bourse ; Pere la Chaise ; Versailles and Sevres ; the Hotel des Invalides ; the Cathedral Church of St. Denis ; some of the concert-gardens, cafes, etc., the leading objects being again named.

Now, to get to one-half of these, on foot or with any arrangement existing in an American city, would be simply impossible, at any moderate outlay. But both London and Paris have cab systems worthy the admiration of the world, and it is in the use of *them* that sight-seeing becomes so easy, cheap and rapid.

Take London, then, the cabs understood, and another fact also understood—that not all the time *desirable* is to be used, but enough for very intelligent views. For Westminster Abbey, St. Paul's and the Houses of Parliament, 1½ days. For the Tower, ½ day. Crystal Palace, 1 day. Windsor Castle and Park, ½ day. Richmond, Kew, Hampton Court, etc., 1 day. British Museum and Guildhall (with the Temple), 1 day. Through London Parks and streets, with the Royal Palaces (outside views), the Horse-Guards, Mansion House, Bank of England, Monuments, &c., 1 to 2½ days. Total, 6½ to 8 days, the theatres being visited in the intervening nights by those who choose, and a much better general idea of London being thus acquired by an active and intelligent traveler, than many obtain in months of residence.

Take Paris (not in an "Exposition" year). For Versailles and Sevres, with glimpse of St. Cloud and ride through the whole length of the Bois de Boulogne, 1 day. For Pere la Chaise (cemetery), ½ day. For St. Denis, ½ day. For the great churches, the Pantheon, Notre Dame, St. Roch, the Madeleine, St. Eustache, St. Etienne du Mont, &c., 1 day. For the Tuileries Gardens, Champs Elysees, along the Seine, the bridges, &c., 1 day. For inside the Louvre, with glimpses of that and the other palaces, outside, 1 day. For the Hotel des Invalides, the Champ de Mars, &c., ½ day. For the Hotel de Ville, Place de Greve, Palais Royal, Hotel Cluny, etc.—any or all of them— 1 to 3 days, at will. Total, 6½ to 8 days. The Boulevards will necessarily be seen in passing along them on special visits; and so of the great monuments, the Arc d'Etoile, Arc du Carrousel, Colonne de Vendome, Colonne de Juillet, &c.; while the theatres and the concert gardens (Mabille, &c.,) naturally fill the evenings.

Such a distribution of time would inevitably appal the slow and steady Englishman; but not so with the vivacious, quick-moving and quick-seeing American; and nothing more than these two extreme instances can be necessary, it is believed, to demonstrate that the "short-trip" plan and division of time are not only practicable but reasonable, however much even the most hurried might *prefer* to have unlimited time and money at command!

III.

STEAMSHIP LINES TO EUROPE, WITH A HINT FOR "'ROUND THE WORLD."

Most persons, not taking especial thought on the subject, fail to recognize the immense proportions to which the steam navy, carrying passengers between the port of New York and four ports of the Old World (Liverpool, Glasgow, Havre and Bremen) has reached; and partially to afford a glance at its proportions, as also to remind tourists what facilities for choice are placed at their disposal, a brief glance is here taken at the most reliable lines, their ships, performances, and the advantages they offer.

LINES TO QUEENSTOWN AND LIVERPOOL.

Cunard Line. (British and North American Royal Mail Steamship Company.) ·

This line, which may be said to stand among the first of its class in any service in the world, and which makes the proud boast that it has never lost a passenger by any accident since the day of its establishment, besides having carried the mails with a speed and regularity almost wonderful as the result of human skill and forethought—this line has now employed, in the service between New York and Liverpool, no less than twenty ships — seven mail steamers, carrying only first-class passengers — the

Scotia and Persia (paddle-wheelers), the Russia, Cuba, Java, China and Australasian, screws; besides the Siberia, Malta, Hecla, Palmyra, Tarifa, Marathon, Kedar, Olympus, Tripoli, Aleppo, Morocco and Sidon, extra steamers, carrying first and third class. The average time of the runs of the mail steamers from Queenstown to New York, during 1867, was 10d. 5h. 40m.; from New York to Liverpool, including detentions at Queenstown, 10d. 5h. 11m. The two most rapid runs of the year were those of the Scotia to Queenstown in 8d. 9h. 26m., and of the Russia to New York in 8d. 10h. 34m. The Commodore of this line is the veteran Captain Judkins, of the Scotia; and its notabilities are good fare, fine accommodations, sharp discipline, and reliability as to performance.

Inman Line. (*Liverpool, New York and Philadelphia Steamship Company.*)

This line comes second in order of establishment, and only second in the number of ships employed. It is claimed to have done more to "bridge the Atlantic," by good accommodations at moderate prices, than any other line on the ocean; and it has lately so shown the justice of that demand on the British Government, as to have been accorded a division of the mail service, besides that exclusively to Halifax. It also deserves the credit of having seen and depended upon the merit of the screw-principle, at an earlier day than any other; and its voyages have been remarkably successful and safe. Its fleet of steamers now comprise the splendid mail-boats (City of) Paris, Antwerp, London, Boston and Baltimore (also the Brooklyn nearly finished), with the New York, Washington, Manchester, Limerick, Cork, Kangaroo, and several others, on the Halifax branch, running to Liverpool as extra steamers, or held in reserve. The Commodore is Captain James Kennedy, of the City of Paris, whose average of passages, from April to August, 1867, between New York and Queenstown, was 9d. 5h. 3m., while the Antwerp, London, Boston and Baltimore followed close, and the City of Paris made the extraordinary run, in November, of 8d. 4h. 37m., the shortest westward on record. Officers courteous—fare good—ships and line excellent.

National Line. (*National Steam Navigation Company.*)

This line comes third in order of establishment, and has risen to assured and worthy success on the specialties of large and roomy ships, good fare, good accommodations at exceedingly low prices, and general courtesy. It has now in employment the fine steamers France, England, Denmark, Helvetia, Pennsylvania, Erin, Virginia, and others, receiving a constantly increasing share of the large transit between the two countries, and entitled to the credit of having gone a step beyond the Inman line in demonstrating the practicability of cheap carriage without the sacrifice of either comfort or safety. The Commodore of this line is Captain Grace, of the France, the latest-built of the fleet, and which vessel has already demonstrated her capacity to compete with the best

STEAMSHIPS TO EUROPE, ETC. 27

of the mail-steamers, while the sea-going qualities of all the vessels have been proved to admiration. All the saloons on deck form a pleasing specialty of this line, as well as abundance of room in state-rooms and saloons.

Williams and Guion Line. (Liverpool and Great Western Steam Company.)

This is the youngest of the great lines to Liverpool, but is rapidly becoming one of the most popular. Its specialties are ships of immense size, splendid model and great strength, built on the Tyne (instead of on the Clyde, as most of the other lines), adopting the brig-rig entirely, offering the greatest possible amount of room per passenger, with state-rooms and saloons all on deck (as half-an-hour's inspection of the so-far latest-finished, the magnificent Colorado, will abundantly show), and supplying, like the National, excellent transit at very low rates. The ships now in service are the Colorado, Nebraska, Manhattan and Minnesota, all of about 3,000 tons, while the Nevada and Idaho are being rapidly finished and will have place on the line during the summer. The Commodore is Captain Cutting, of the Colorado, who only heads his brother captains and the other officers of the line in "taking care of his passengers," and showing the true courtesy of sea-going.

28   SHORT-TRIP GUIDE.

LINE TO LONDONDERRY AND GLASGOW.

Anchor Line. (*Henderson Brothers, Glasgow.*)

From comparatively small beginnings this line has been for years increasing in the number and size of its ships, in efficiency of management, arrangements for the comfort and pleasure of passengers, and consequently in popularity. The vessels now employed are the splendid new vessels, the Europa, Columbia and Hibernia, in all of which the science of pleasing passengers seems to be carried to full perfection, even to the extent of supplying them with pianos,—and the Caledonia, Iowa, Britannia, United Kingdom and Cambria, with all the other comforts, and soon to have that exceptional one. The courtesy of the officers of this line is proverbial; and as the ships make the "North About," avoiding the British Channel, securing the most splendid of approaches to land, and booking passengers to Liverpool at the same price as to Glasgow, it is not strange that hundreds of those who wish to include Scotland in their tours are bending in that direction. It should be noted, in addition, that the same company run steamers from Glasgow to Lisbon, Gibraltar, Malta, the Italian ports and Alexandria, making a convenient connection in that direction.

LINE TO BREST AND HAVRE.

French Line. (*Compagnie Générale Transatlantique.*)

The withdrawal of the American line to Brest and Havre (the Fulton, Arago, etc.), while painfully impressing Americans, still leaves the consciousness that what remains is the very best. No line, in the same length of time, ever made such a reputation as the ships of the General Transatlantic Company, for safety, speed and elegance, and it may be said that none carries so many first-class passengers per ship. The vessels now employed are the Pereire, Ville de Paris, St. Laurent, Europe, Napoleon III., Lafayette, Washington and Europe. The ships seem to be built and run "regardless of expense" and with French fare and courtesy. The Pereire, during 1867, made five passages between New York and Brest, averaging 8d. 20h., and the Ville de Paris and St. Laurent averaging 9d. 11h.—among the best performances known to ocean service; and there is no doubt that '68 will see the equal of '67, in speed, comfort and popularity.

LINE TO SOUTHAMPTON AND BREMEN.

Bremen Line. (*North German Lloyd.*)

This line, always the most popular of those between Germany and America, is making rapid strides towards engrossing the whole transit—through the number, speed and excellence of their ships, and their general management. The vessels now employed are the large and powerful America, New York, Hermann, Hansa, Bremen, Deutschland, Union and Weser; while no less than three others, the Rhein, Main and Donau, are nearly completed. They have also a line, just established but promising to be very popular, between Bremen and Baltimore. With a brief average, there have been some remarkably short passages during the year—as that of the Union, eastward, in 9d. 10h., and the Weser, westward, in 9d. 3h. For passengers desiring to go direct to Southampton and London, they offer the very first attractions, combined with fine fare and most courteous treatment; and their growing popularity is no matter of wonder.

FOR CALIFORNIA, CHINA, INDIA, AND "'ROUND THE WORLD."

A few hints have been promised, for that "'round the world" which used to be a wonder, will one day be a common thing to do, and even now is entirely and easily practicable; and these hints are offered for the consideration of tourists who may be induced to "broaden their views" when they are reminded how much of the world they may manage to see in a brief space, if they will but set about it.

It is known to perhaps a majority of persons, that the Pacific Mail Steamship Company run a noble fleet of first-class steamers on the Atlantic end of their line (the Arizona, Henry Chauncey, Ocean Queen, Northern Light, Ariel and Alaska), to Aspinwall, their passengers crossing by the Panama Railway to Panama; and that from Panama a second fleet (the Colorado, Constitution, Golden City, Sacramento, Golden Age, St. Louis and Montana) carry them up the western coast and land them, generally with the very best opinion of sea-going and the company supplying the transit, at San Francisco, in about 22 days. And a proportion of the public, at least, are aware of the great enterprise recently inaugurated—that with those steamers, at San Francisco, connect yet another fleet, scarcely less in number (the New York, Costa Rica, America, Celestial Empire, Great Republic and Japan), landing passengers at Yokohama, Japan, in about 26 days from San Francisco, or 48 from New York,— and at Hong Kong, China, in about 32, or 54 from New York.

So much as this is pretty generally understood; but it is an interesting question how many persons of means and the desire to travel, remember the connections with this great line and the European steamers already named, that may so easily be made, and that coveted " 'round the world" accomplished within four to five months, or even in a less period if connections happen to be hit throughout! Say from New York, by San Francisco to Hong Kong, as already noted. From Hong Kong by the British Peninsular and Oriental Company's steamers, to Point de Galle, Ceylon (where there is also an Australian connection made, for those who desire it). Point de Galle to Bombay, with an opportunity for a brief glance at British East India, as there has before been at Japan and China. Then by the P. & O. steamer again, to and up the Red Sea, to Suez, with railway transit across Egypt to Cairo and Alexandria. Thence by the connecting P. & O. steamers from Alexandria to Marseilles (by Malta); across France to the Channel, and homeward to New York from Havre, Liverpool, Southampton or Glasgow, by some one of the European lines already named.

The contemplation is almost enough to take away the breath; but nothing in travel has ever equalled that or the splendid reality; and how long before, without waiting for the Pacific Railway (which the Union Pacific people are hurrying through so rapidly)—how long before the hint is taken and acted upon by hundreds who can well afford the time (the four months) and the money (not over ($900 to $1,000 gold), and who waste both in summer dawdling at home ? For it should be remembered that the route may be precisely reversed, by those who prefer first seeing Europe—and that while life is short, health transitory, and opportunities often pass away unexpectedly, no such chance for "rounding the circle of the globe," with little bodily fatigue, almost no danger, and the retention of luxury throughout, has ever before entered into the calculation of man.

IV.

PREPARATIONS FOR "GOING OVER."

There may need to be another reminder that the following paper, like some of the others to come after it, is especially intended for those who have never before crossed the Atlantic, and that, consequently, some of the advice tendered in it may seem very "A. B. C-ish" to those who have already taken their degree, however low a one, in the academy of travelling experience. To this the suggestion may properly be added, that even some of those who have taken that degree may find themselves none the worse for reading over these hints, even if they do so to dissent from them. An apology may need to be made, too, for the direct and conversational style adopted in this and some other papers ; the aim of the author is, in this regard, to come as near as possible to the words and manner that would be used in a personal conversation, with one of the parties doing much more than half of the talking.

One word as to the mode in which whatever of "wisdom" may be here contained—has been acquired. Or let the words be two, and embody them, after the mode of a late lamented dignitary, in a "little story." Once upon a time, when the Shrewsbury river, in New Jersey, was more of a throughfare for passenger-steamboats than it is to-day, a "hard case" of a river boatman made application to the head of one of the companies for the command of a new boat just launched and about to be put into service. "Why, good heavens!" exclaimed the owner, throwing up eyes and hands in astonishment, "what reason can you possibly give for thinking that I would trust you with a boat? Every one who knows you knows that you have been ashore on every shoal and mud-bank in the river, even when piloting for others." "Precisely the reason why I am the man to take command of the new boat!" replied the incorrigible. "I *have* been ashore, I believe, on every shoal and mud-bank in the river; consequence, I know where they all are, now, and you see I can keep clear of em." The application of which is, that the writer has "been ashore" on most of the "shoals and mud-banks" of rashness, ignorance and comparative poverty, in his experiments at foreign travel, and "knows where they are," now! And if there are some upon which he has *not* been ashore, he has seen others stranded on them and laid up the experience for himself and others.

1st. Decide whether you can afford time and money to go at all, taking into consideration the before-urged opportunities for economy. Also, decide whether, in going, you leave too much of anxiety, personal or pecuniary, for fair enjoyment; for there is an old adage about the absentee who "drags with each remove a lengthening chain," and there are not charms enough, even in the natural scenery and artistic glories of the Old World, to make such a trip "pay" when the heart or the business-powers must be left at home. So much decided, and in the affirmative, then

2nd. Having made up your mind, stick to the resolution. Arrange your time of going and make everything work to accommodate *that*, not leave that to accommodate itself to everything. Generally in this as in everything else in life, too long anticipation is not the healthiest or the most profitable, and a voyage not canvassed over for five years in advance is likely to yield more pleasure than one submitted to that length of speculation. Above all things, never boast that you are going, when you have merely *thought of going* and made no definite decision, as friends may remember the farce of "Ladies Beware!" and Mrs. Vavasour's saying: "Lady Ossulton has been talking of going to Italy ever since I can remember; if she intends to go, *why don't she go?*" And there is an instance on record of a young New Yorker of good family, who went to Europe under the influence of as much personal fear as he might have felt in going to his execution—simply because, while trying to "screw his courage to the sticking-point," he had boasted of his intended trip until all his friends began to make it, and *him*, a by-word, and the lady to whom he was engaged finally declared that "if he didn't go and thus prove that he was not afraid to do so, she would never marry him until she was grayer than Methusaleh's grandmother!" Rumor said that he was on the point of being set ashore at Sandy Hook, or taken off by the pilot-boat, after proceeding down the bay, but that the fear of ridicule deterred him and he made a voyage of continued torture, simply because he had "declared his intentions" too widely.

3d. Having resolved upon time of going and probable duration of trip, and selected the line of steamers by which the outward voyage is to be made (a selection which may be a little aided by the perusal of another paper in this connection), do not permit the paltry folly of wishing to keep a certain number of dollars for a few days longer in pocket, to prevent the early taking of a passage. The best state-rooms on any favorite steamship are likely to be first taken up ; and even in the event of any accident occurring, rendering an alteration of plans necessary, there is rarely any difficulty in disposing of a well-located berth, while most of the companies, at any time before the "eleventh hour," will transfer the passenger from one steamer to a later one, if a change of time is all the deviation from the original plan rendered necessary.

4th. If suddenly-occurring events happen to have changed the calculation in the other direction, and the plan of going is formed almost at the very moment when some favorite steamer is about to sail, never heed the stories so likely to be told, that "the steamer is full and you cannot get a place!" There is nearly always room for "one passenger more," as there is in an avenue-car, though without the discomfort ; and if the worst comes to the worst, it is a very rare case when some one of the officers of the ship cannot be found ready to give up his room for the run, at the inducement of no-very-large addition to the price of the passage-ticket. These are suggestions for extreme cases, however : as before said, passage had much better be taken early, whenever possible ; though Mr. William J. Florence, the actor, who makes many and pleasant voyages across the Atlantic, has the reputation of never engaging a berth until the day of sailing, when he goes quietly on board, plumps down his big trunk, and calmly advises the officers of the ship that "he is going over, and the sooner they arrange to find him a comfortable room, the less trouble they will be likely to have !" a hint always acted upon at once.

5th. In selecting berths, when a good opportunity for choice remains, always aim to get as near as possible to the midships of the vessel—a consideration of not much consequence to old voyagers with strong nerves, but of great importance to landsmen, as every foot of distance from the waist increases the amount of motion in a heavy sea; and not only is the danger of sea-sickness less amidships, but the chances of having sleep broken by the "pitch" of a "head" or "following" sea are proportionably decreased when so located. The same principle applies, in a less degree, to the question of outside or inside rooms (those inside or outside of the gangways). There is much less effect from the "roll," in a "beam" sea, for those occupying inner berths; but there is always much less light for reading or any other purpose, and the one advantage will probably balance the other, except in winter passages, when the inner rooms are altogether preferable.

6th. No guide-book, probably, ever contained a hint of the advice to be embodied in this paragraph ;

and yet there is no word of advice, of the whole, more important. Unless that miserable being, a "man of letters," and thus compelled to be always reading—there are few intending voyagers, male or female, who will not be the better for a little "reading up" as to the countries about to be visited. A fresh glance at the atlas, to see how they lie and the relations which they bear to each other, is almost indispensable, even to some of us who flatter ourselves (before we think the second time) that we learned our geography and have kept pretty well up with it ever since. And there is not one in fifty who would not be the better qualified for enjoyment abroad, by running over some comprehensive history of each of the principal countries. To freshen up in English, Scottish and Irish history, is almost indispensible on the eve of a trip merely to Great Britain; and the same may be said, or very nearly, of French history, especially that of Napoleon and the Revolution, if the Channel is to be crossed for anything more than the merest glance. For England, too, a running over of Shakspeare is never out of place, whether for London or Warwickshire; while some knowledge of Scott's leading novels, the "Heart of Mid-Lothian," "Bride of Lammermoor," "Rob Roy," &c., of the "Lady of the Lake," and of Burns' simpler songs, makes half the charm of a run over the Border and through the Scottish Highlands; and there is at least policy in knowing something of Lever's novels ("Charles O'Malley" and "Jack Hinton") of Moore's poems and some of the simpler legends and stories of the peasantry, before setting foot in Ireland. This

PREPARATIONS. 39

advice would not seem so far-fetched or of so little consequence, had all readers heard what the writer has done: people of wealth and supposed intelligence, on the point of airing their money and position by European tours, and asking friends, covertly, on the very verge of departure, to "tell them some of the most important things that had happened in England, France and a few of them countries"—or buttonholing chance-met acquaintances, in the stable yard of the Red Horse, at Stratford-on-Avon, to ask "who that Shakspeare was, that the people made so much fuss about?—if he fit, or writ, which was it?"

7th. Avoid the nonsense which may be so easily put into the mind, of trying to learn any of the languages of the non-English-speaking countries to be visited, in the brief space intervening between arrangment and departure. Those who have some acquaintance with French, German or Italian, as the case may be, will be all the better and none the worse for "rubbing up" as much as possible, through reading, translation or conversation; but for those who know nothing of the languages, to attempt mastering them, is simply nonsense. There are English-speaking people, now, almost everywhere on the Continent—English servants, guides, couriers, etc., and often English-speaking landlords; and for those not linguists, the best plan is to arrange for joining company with those who do speak the languages of the countries about to be visited, or to depend upon chance-met speaking of English. There are a certain set of enquiries and answers, however, connected with buying tickets, taking trains, hiring cabs, finding lodgings, making small purchases, discovering directions, etc., which may be committed to memory without much trouble and without the miserable affectation of supposing that this is "learning a language;" and for the benefit of those who prepare themselves to that extent, a few of these phrases are set down, at the close of the present volume, with their meanings in English, and the instances in which they are likely to be found useful.

8th. Another "rubbing up" is advisable though not absolutely indispensible. Thousands of questions about America, its physical appearance, wealth, working of government, industrial aspects, etc., are constantly asked of Americans on their travels, supposed to be of the average intelligence, by foreigners whom they chance to meet; and it is decidedly pleasant as well as proper, not to be three or four thousand miles from home, unable to answer the simplest questions with reference to things at our own doors at home. The more we know about our own land, the more intelligent and agreeable travellers we shall make, unavoidably; and in this connection,

9th. Throw overboard two false impressions, together, before émbarking for Europe. Overboard with the idea, at once, that the land you are leaving is better than all others in every regard, so that nothing can be learned abroad; and with it give the go-by to the alternative impression that we have nothing worth asserting and even boasting about, and that what you are to learn abroad will stand in place of the previous experiences and prides of a life. America has many things, to-day (and the last pages of the present volume may be overhauled for reminders of some of them,) unequalled by the world and matters of legitimate pride to her citizens; then she has errors and deficiencies which may well be corrected by observations among older if not necessarily wiser people. Every American, going abroad, should carry with him all practical knowledge of his own land, and all well-founded pride in it; and at the same time he should travel with eyes and ears open and power to divest himself of ridiculous national vainglory prejudically shutting away all beyond.

And now to a few minor particulars, belonging to the very eve-of starting, and still important enough to deserve place and number:

10th. Start with a confident expectation of returning, and yet leave property-interests disposed of as if no return was likely to be made. There is really less danger, in a given number of days, in going oversea than from Chicago to Boston, or New Orleans to New York, by rail; but European absences are generally longer than those on the American Continent, except the latter involve California or the very far South-west, or North-west; and if we are commonly neglectful, there is no reason why these instances should not be an exception. "No man dies the sooner for making his will," they say; and certainly no man travels less comfortably for leaving affairs at home in such a shape, that if he does not return, his absence will cause the least possible inconvenience to those left behind. And in this connection, again,

11th. There is nothing wiser for the departing "family man," whatever the status of those dependent upon him, than an investment in a moderate *life-assurance*, with an additional *assurance against accident*. Nothing of an earthly character (the religious questions will naturally suggest themselves) adds more comfort in a storm at sea, or danger in some distant land, than the reflection that there would be at least one benefit from the risk terminating unfavorably : *the dear ones at home would be pecuniarily the gainers by it.*

12th. Arrange baggage compactly, and not too extensively. For each person (male—the ladies *will* make rules for themselves), one stout leather or wood-and-leather trunk of 30 to 36 inches by 16 to 20 inches, and one convenient valise for carrying in the hand, is always sufficient, for anything less than carrying over the whole personal effects with a view to residence. The trunk for deposit in the great cities, in the event of expecting to return along the same line— if not, unavoidably to be carried along. The valise for short excursions from those great centres, having this advantage—that it can be carried in the railway-carriage or cab, (*en voiture*, as the French designate it), while the trunk must be looked after, with trouble and expense. Both trunk and valise should be plainly marked, with name and residence—initials not always enough for either safety or convenience. If the trunk is small enough, for the sea-voyage, to find place in the state-room, all the better ; if not, care must be taken that before it goes into the hold all articles are taken out from it that will be needed before landing on the other side. The valise will always find place in the state-room, of course. And this brings

13th. The important question of clothing, in which the liberty will be taken of quoting from a work by the same writer ("Over-Sea") issued last year, a few bracketed words being added to the advice there embodied:

"My point of view is for the male sex, but the female will find it easily varied to their requirements. For crossing the North Atlantic, to return in [two or] three months, the first requirement is a suit of thick clothes, so old and valueless that one can lounge upon the deck in them, with no fear of damage. (Dandyism is at a discount, at sea—a lesson quickly and surely learned). Clothing thick, because sea air is nearly always damp, and generally cold. Then as thick an overcoat and gloves as can well be procured, the use of which will become patent, either among the fogs and possible icebergs of the Banks of Newfoundland, or on the Irish coast. A thick blanket, or, what is still better, a rough buffalo-robe, to make lounging upon deck the easier and warmer. For even midsummer wear in England, Ireland and Scotland, a neat travelling-suit of thick cloth [stout Melton or cassimere, the best], which will scarcely ever be found too warm ; while in all these a light summer overcoat [water-proof tweed, best], will be found a convenience, and often a necessity. For southward of the British Channel, a suit of dark summer-cloths or flannels, useful occasionally, but by no means to be depended upon, and never to be worn without heavy under-clothing. Heavy wool under-clothing at sea, with courage enough to double it if comfort so requires. A dress suit, if there is plenty of room in the trunk, not otherwise, as there is very seldom occasion for it on a tour of this character [and for full-dress occasions, purchase or hire is always available in the large cities where such a demand is likely to arise]. Plenty of linen and white goods, to avoid being at the mercy of the washer-women at times of sudden transit,—though the fact may well be remembered, that all the latter description of goods can be laid in much cheaper at Liverpool, London, or even at Paris, than in America under the present *regime*. * * A low-crowned tourist hat, of felt ; and for England, (first of indispensibles), an *umbrella*." To this list add a good opera-glass, almost indispensible, both by sea and on land, for catching views rapidly and correctly.

14th. Make such arrangements, if possible, that a little longer absence than that contemplated, will not work serious business or other inconvenience, as the best calculator cannot always be quite sure of nondetention through some influence or action beyond himself.

15th. Arrange (as before suggested) to take a little more money abroad than is supposed to be necessary for either time or distance ; but

16th. Carry in actual money, (English gold, by far the most convenient, except for going directly to France—then French gold,) only so much as will pay expenses on ship-board and last during the few days that may happen to elapse before reaching the point at which the first draft is made payable. All beyond this should be taken either in bills-of-exchange on bankers in one or more of the great cities to be vis-

PREPARATIONS. 45

ited, or in circular letters-of-credit to corresponding houses in those cities. Only the very first class of banking houses, at home, should be dealt with, in procuring exchange or letters-of-credit, if the painful possibility of finding oneself abroad without funds, is to be avoided; and all information as to details can be procured, as well as the funds, at any one of the houses whose announcements are to be found at the close of the present volume.

17th. Procure passports, by making application to an authorized Notary or Dispatch Agent, at least a week or ten days before the time of departure. A separate passport is necessary for every adult male, and for every woman travelling *femme sole*: when husband, wife and minor children are travelling together, a single one is sufficient for all. In Great Britain no passports are necessary, though, in the present troubled Fenian days, they may at any time be found convenient, and sometimes indispensible as means of identification; in France, of late, they are seldom demanded, though the law requires them; beyond France, it is never safe to be without them, in due form and properly viséd; and even in France, if not demanded, they have their use in securing certain privileges and furnishing some guarantee of identity.

18th. Take some letters of introduction, when tendered, and to the *right persons;* but depend very little upon them, except in some business point of view. If there is sufficient influence to procure letters to the American Secretaries of Legation at London, Paris, &c., they may often be found valuable, as those Secretaries generally do the wheel-horse work of the legations, and may pay an amount of attention beneath the time or state of the Ministers.

19th. Create as little impression as possible, on the verge of departure, of feeling that some event, moving half the world, is taking place in your first leaving your native land. A sea-voyage, now, no further than Europe, is about equivalent to a trip up the Sound to Boston, fifteen years ago,—and not much more than was the transit across Sandy Hook Bay at the distance back of thirty or fifty years; and the observing world is generally coming to regard it in that light.

20th and last. If possible, go on board before the last moment of sailing, and have any heavy baggage on board even earlier. Also, if possible, make any extended tender farewells earlier and elsewhere than on the crowded deck of a steamer, at the last moment, when everybody is in the way of everybody else, when the officers naturally wish to throw overboard all the whiners, and when there is a probability of the grief of departure being added to by the worry of having wife, sister, child or friend tumbled into the dock in the sudden removal of the gangplank.

V.

WHAT TO DO AND AVOID, ON SHIPBOARD.

THE advice in this paper, too, will be set down didactically, and much of it will be considered A B C-ish by those who have once or oftener crossed the Atlantic. In the meantime, not even to some of them will the maxims be found unprofitable, if attended to—judging by the very large number of habitual travellers who seem to happen upon the very conditions of discomfort and imprudence, as if seeking them. No attempt will be made to arrange the items in groups or any regular succession, though they will be numbered, for convenience, like those in the last paper.

1st. Perhaps the first condition of comfort in a sea-voyage, is to avoid making up the mind as to any positive time at which the voyage must be concluded. An old Dutch farmer, of Long Island, who sometimes gathered corn alone in a field of twenty or thirty acres, being enquired of as to how he escaped being discouraged at the prospect of finishing his labor, replied that "he *would* be, if he thought of it; but he simply went in, each day, to do a day's work, and in that way the field got finished, eventually, almost before he knew it!" To look across the three thousand miles of the Atlantic, and think over the days necessary to travel it, even on the swiftest vessel, is rather discouraging than the reverse; but by simply avoiding any definite calculation, and considering the ship and her officers and crew as doing their "day's work," the amount of impatience may be very considerably reduced. Creeping ahead a little every day, the whole voyage will soon be accomplished : that is enough to know and enough to feel, no matter what anxieties may be at the end.

2d. Perhaps the next desideratum is to avoid any considerable anxiety as to the voyage being a prosperous one, by first remembering that more than an hundred runs are made without a single accident, and more than five hundred without the total loss of a vessel,—and then falling back upon that pleasant recollection that you have not the affair in charge, any way— that (Providence over all and always to be remembered, of course,) the officers and crew of the ship have their duty to do and are very likely to do it, for the sake of their own lives and the property committed to their skill. It may be straining a point, perhaps, but there is really some philosophy in getting into the state of mind of the droll fellow who settled up one of the "anxious" in a storm off the coast of Ireland, not many years ago. The storm, which was very heavy, had lasted for days, and seemed to be growing heavier and heavier, until the "landsmen" began to doubt whether the ship *could* live in such a terrible sea, and one of them approached the model passenger and enquired: "What he thought of it?—if the gale lasted much longer and the sea rose much higher, wouldn't they founder?" "Why, what the deuce is that to us?" replied the droll. "Haven't you paid your passage?" "I? cer-

ON SHIPBOARD. 49

tainly!" "The company, then, have contracted to take you from Liverpool to New York, for so many pounds, haven't they?" "Of course they have—but what then?" "What then? Why, everything, then! You don't sail this ship—you are a passenger; and it is their business, not yours, whether the ship sinks or floats." This may not have much reassured the frightened man, but it certainly silenced him; and there no doubt was more than a grain of earnest in the old traveller's philosophy of *remembering that he did not steer the ship*, as there was undoubtedly comfortable laziness in it.

3d. It is wise not to expect too much on shipboard, either in the way of luxury or even of positive comfort. Ships, at the largest, are small as compared with hotels, and at the steadiest are "shaky," as compared to private dwellings, except when the latter have *very* St. Thomas earthquakes to throw them off the perpendicular. Plenty of good food, respectable though confined sleeping-quarters, and attendance fair but by no means that of a first-class hotel—these are all that ought to be expected; and a very little philosophy makes them enough. It has before been said that "dandyism is at a discount, at sea;" so is, or ought to be, *finickiness*. What if neither shaving, nor dressing, nor any of the other offices of civilized life, can be done quite as well as at home? Nobody notices whether they are scrupulously performed, or not; and some of the neatest of men when on shore, when they have become old travellers, consent to be slovenly for those few days without serious suffering. The golden rule on going to sea, is : *Expect very little and be prepared to put up good-humoredly with it* ; then, if " all the modern conveniences " should happen to prevent themselves, as is not at all likely, they will afford double enjoyment, and the want of them will not entail misery.

4th. Determine to be as jolly as health will allow, and as companionable as is at all consistent with the temperament. Join in all practical harmless amusements and exercises, with the result of making your own days less tedious, and producing the same effect on those of others. One jolly fellow, sometimes, seems to leaven up a whole ship-load: one or two glum faces act like a wet-blanket on all concerned. There is a comradery in sea-going, scarcely second to that of the army; and some of the pleasantest friendships of years originate on the deck filled with comparative strangers. Quoits, shovel-board, chess, draughts, backgammon, social games at cards, all these supply amusement to those who will take any of them ; and there is room for any amount of table sociability, at meals, not marred but rather increased by the little accidents to which breakfasting or dining in rough weather is certainly subject.

5th. Make friends, early, with the captain and other officers of the ship, so far as they will permit ; but take no liberties with them, and carefully avoid compromising any one of them who may have shown any peculiar favor, by speaking of it to others of the ship's company or passengers. Strictly observe those cardinal rules which forbid going upon the bridge, talking with the officers when on duty, or distracting the attention of the quarter-masters at the wheel. Avoid getting in the way of the officers at the compasses, or hindering them when engaged in that most important event of the day—" taking an observation." Don't enquire, any oftener than is unavoidable, where the ship is at any particular moment, what a certain movement on deck means, what kind of weather it is going to be during the next twenty-four hours ; and don't ask the men, when they are heaving the log, how many miles an hour the ship is going, or don't expect them to tell the truth if you do ! Don't get in the way when hawsers are being overhauled or yards braced ; and don't wonder if, getting in the way when some evolution of hauling ropes is going on, you occasionally trip and so learn what times and places are dangerous. Don't attempt to "help," at any time, except in the rare event of an accident ; and thus "keeping out of the way," without losing any chance of observation and enjoyment, secure the friendship of the officers, the respect of the crew and the gratitude of all concerned.

6th. Make friends with the stewards, at once, not only by treating them respectfully, but by speaking to the two in charge of your particular table and state-room—requesting their attention and promising them the due *douceur* at the end of the voyage. Half a sovereign each to the saloon and lower-saloon stewards, and say a crown to the "boots," with half-a-crown for beer to the captain of the watch who first "chalks" you when you break the rules of the ship by going forward, and perhaps half a dozen shillings to persons who do errands for you during the run— this, reaching eight to ten dollars altogether, is quite sufficient to grease the wheels of service and make welcome then and afterwards.

7th. Avoid attempting to read much, at sea, however interest may tempt in that direction. There is a motion and jar of the vessel, making the letters swim and damaging head and optic-nerves to a degree needing days for recovery. Some persons can read steadily, almost without injury; others cannot: it is never best to try the experiment when it can be avoided. And there is rarely much occasion: it is a poor passage-list in which more amusement cannot be found than in books, for the short period consumed in crossing the Atlantic.

8th. Keep on deck, all that is possible. Half the charm of going to sea lies in the pure, fresh air, except in very stormy whether. The air of lower-cabins and state-rooms is necessarily more or less confined, and consequently unhealthy; while the healthiest atmosphere in the world comes fresh to the lungs from blue water. There is far less danger of sea-sickness, too, on deck than below, when actual illness does not enforce confinement to the berth; and the thousand sights and sounds of sea-life—sunrises, sunsets, moonlight, storm-waves, whales, porpoise-shoals, passing vessels, observations, log and lead-heaving, making and taking in sail, signalling, etc., are only to be enjoyed by those who keep the deck as persistently as possible. The writer saw a young lady go below, off the point of Sandy Hook, in the summer of '65, and come up again for the first time at Liverpool bar: she had the *quietest* passage over of any one on the ship, but scarcely the *most enjoyable!*

ON SHIPBOARD. 53

9th. Dress warmly—quite as warmly as comfort demands, and err on the safe side if at all. Sea-air, though healthy, is damp and deceptive as to temperature. Never mind the appearance; put on the clothes.

10th. Take much exercise. Want of occupation induces long sitting at table and hearty eating; and the system must be a strong one which can endure this for days, without exercise, and yet suffer no injury. When there is not too much sea to make it possible, at least a mile or two should be walked every morning and a corresponding space in the afternoon—the long cleared decks, or the gangways, of most of the best steamers, rendering this *amusement of exercise* easy and convenient.

11th. Put confidence in the ship: believe, for the time being, that the ship is the best afloat. If you go down into the fire-room (which, by the way, is quite as well kept out of), don't fall into the fancy that so large a mass of fire in the midst of a vessel must inevitably burn her: vessels are especially constructed to guard against that danger, and iron does not take fire easily. Don't be alarmed at the noises continually coming from the fire-room, or think that some calamity has happened there: firemen are normally noisy as well as grimy, and they need to speak loudly, to make themselves heard. Don't fancy, in short, that everything will go wrong unless you attend to it, except in one particular; and that is,

12th. Join the fire-police of the ship, and stick to the organization. Take no combustible materials below in your baggage—neither matches or dangerous chemicals; take no light of any kind below the decks, for better reason than because there is a severe punishment for any proceeding of the kind—the all-powerful reason that such an act may destroy your own life and the lives of others. On this point, watch your own conduct and that of others, and no harm is likely to result from the close surveillance.

13th. Never go forward when the ship is pitching into a heavy sea: there is always danger of injury, in such an experiment by a landsman, and very often of being swept overboard, at times when even sailors can scarcely keep footing on the wet and slippery decks. Never stand at or very near the taffrail (extreme stern) in correspondingly heavy weather, as there is always danger of the ship "jumping out from under you"—an accident which sometimes happens to experienced seamen who stand unguardedly in that dangerous position. Never climb upon the bulwarks, however calm the sea; for there is no knowing at what moment there may be *one* roll —enough to finish your individual voyage or delay the ship for the purpose of picking you up in a very damp condition!

14th. Never attempt to go up or down one of the companion-ways (stairs), or along one of the gangways, or the decks, when the sea is heavy, without making as much use of the hands as the feet—holding on firmly to the nearest convenient rail. Broken ribs or limbs are sometimes the consequence of forgetfulness or bravado, on this point.

15th. In the event of illness (other than sea-sickness) don't take nostrums, or trust to anything in your private "medicine-chest." There is always one surgeon, or more, on each ship; they are paid for attending to the health of passengers, without charge except for costly medicine; they are particularly familiar with the treatment prudent at sea; and it is very often the case that medicines upon which dependance can be placed when on the more stable element, prove injurious in the abnormal condition of never being entirely quiet.

16th. If sea-sick, don't fancy the disease is a mortal one. Few people die of it, though many (it is to be feared) are rendered vastly uncomfortable. Keep the bravest heart and the "stiffest upper-lip" possible, against the great foe; and above all, do not join the noble army of those who ask to be mercifully "thrown overboard" as a means of escaping the torture. Nobody dares obey the request—not even your worst enemy, who wishes that he could; and if it *should* be obeyed, the chances are ten to one that before you had gone down ten fathoms in blue water the cry might be a very different one.

17th. Berths, in sea-going ships, are mostly single; and yet it is best, especially in heavy weather, to have a *bed-fellow*. This is easily found in the valise or well-filled carpet-bag, which packed closely in against the side-board, the would-be sleeper lying on the side in the inner part of the berth, will generally enable him to lie without rolling, even when the ship is doing her worst in that direction, and secure sleep when it would be otherwise impossible from the constantly-waking motion.

18th—and more important than any of the preceding. Remember, oftener than when the service is read on Sabbath morning, that there is a Hand, wiser and stronger than that of any officer of the ship, ruling not only the vessel but the waves upon which she rides and the winds and other elements which may place her in peril.

VI.

LOOK-OUTS AND LAND-MAKINGS.

A LARGE part of this paper, like much of the last, has especial value for those who have never before crossed the Atlantic, though it is possible that some of the matter-of-fact information which it contains may be found beneficial, if studied and remembered, by many of those who have already been "chalked" in one or more passages.

The advice to remain as long a proportion of the time as possible on deck, at sea, has been given in the previous paper; and one of the motives has been stated as the natural desire to see passing ships and witness the novel details of the sea, the sky, and ocean-life generally. This applies to the whole crossing; but there are especial look-outs to be kept when leaving land, and yet more when approaching it, which must not be neglected if one of the greatest pleasures of the voyage is not to be lost.

No first-trip passenger needs urging, probably, to "keep an eye out" for last glimpses of his native land—to see (if leaving New York, as do ninety-nine one-hundredths) the blue Highlands of Navesink fade gradually away under the evening light, the shores of Long Island disappear, and to utter, in one shape or another, that sentiment which Byron embodied in
"My native land, good-night!"

We are all prone enough, without urging, to look a little "spoonily" on the last speck of the land we are leaving ; to think what changes and what accidents may occur before we next set eye and foot upon it ; and to feel, for a brief period, what they say that nearly every man (and perhaps quite every *woman*) feels on the morning after marriage—a sort of indefinable *wish that they had waited*. So these farewell points will be looked after, earnestly if not always understandingly, even if, as in the marriage case, the feeling soon wears away and the attention is engrossed by something that lies in the present and future instead of the past.

There is not much of an out-look, connected with the American coast, after getting fairly away from port. There may be a glimpse of the light on Fire Island, dropping behind, if the hour of departure has been late ; and a day later there may be a flicker of light or a distant view of the dark speck that supplies it, on Nantucket shoals ; but that is all, as of the land covered by the stars-and-stripes, and nearly all as of the continent. In those days, already grown old, when the steamers carried the news, there was a lookout to be kept for the approach of Cape Race, Newfoundland, where the last telegraphic intelligence was to be picked up for carrying over. But all that is changed by the cable, and Cape Race is avoided now, as entirely out of the calculation. Sometimes, however, even avoiding that, there is the loom, to the northward, when three days out from port, of a long, low-lying line of coast, not much more than a rough sand-bank, which is really Sable Island, at the southeastern point of Nova Scotia. Bound to or by Halifax, Le Have or Liverpool, (lights) are likely to be the points first made, 48 to 50 hours from New York; and in that case, running up to Halifax harbor by Sambro and Chebuctoo Heads, entering and leaving it, there are many interesting glimpses of the rough coast of Nova Scotia, and of one of the finest harbors of the continent, well worthy of attention even from those who are soon to see the more-interesting shores of the Old World. Bound for Europe direct, now, Sable Island, if seen at all, may be safely set down as supplying the last peep at the Western Continent.

It is the approach to the European Continent which naturally supplies the most interesting of look-outs and land-makings to the American making his first run over-sea. This is not the place to enlarge upon the fact, so full of romance and feeling; but small prospect must there be of that man finding much enjoyment in travel, who does not thrill at the first sight of that Old World of history and long descent, so different in every regard from the New. It is always pleasant to "make land," after the briefest and pleasantest of sea-voyages, as many a man has fully proved since the day when Columbus and his crew watched so wearily for the West Indian Islands; and no number of times crossing the Atlantic takes away the satisfied feeling at having done it once more. But no man sees the same headlands with quite the same eyes, twice; and it is all the more important, for that reason, that the approach to the European coast, by whatever line and route it is made, should not be lost by the traveller on his first voyage. Only less important is it that the *old* traveller, certain to be enquired of by those who lack his experience, should be able to answer their questions a little more readily and correctly than most non-sea-faring men find convenient.

The preliminary understanding being established, that when nearing the European coast, as shown by the greening water, gulls, and increasing number of vessels, the traveller should keep as bright a look-out, by day or by night, as if the safety of the ship depended on his vigilance—berth to be quitted at night, or table by day, the moment that "light" or "land" is whispered—this being understood, the following somewhat-extended resumé of the prominent points made on approaching the Old World, by steamer, by each of several different routes, will be found instructive as mere reading and highly-useful for reference at the critical juncture. It should be remembered, meanwhile, that the principal land-marks are light-houses, or the head-lands or rocks which make them necessary,—and that if approached by night, the light itself is the only object seen—if by day usually a white light-house with the surroundings indicated.

UP THE IRISH OR ST. GEORGE'S CHANNEL TO LIVERPOOL.

First point made, usually, on the Liverpool route, are the sharp and dangerous-looking Skellig Rocks, soon followed by Dursey Island, with the head-lands and mountains of Kerry beginning to loom dimly behind them, on the extreme south-westerly point of Ireland, the main-land adjoining being a mountainous tongue or peninsula, between Kenmare Bay on the north, and Bantry Bay (scene of so many of the invasionary landings of the French and others) on the south. The point is worthy of especial notice, from the fact that probably more voyagers from the Western World have first looked upon Europe in those little specks, than in any other one point of view. The Skelligs lie some fifty miles, and Dursey Island and its "Bull," "Cow" and "Calf" rocks, some thirty, north by west from Cape Clear, towards which the course of the vessel is shaped from the moment of making them.

The next object of special interest, the coast being rapidly approached and the mountains of Munster beginning to loom, is Fastnet Rock, a pyramid rising out of the water at some five or six miles from the high, dark, rocky shore, just before reaching Cape Clear—the whole crowned with a white light-house, and the picture (by day-light) one of desolation surrounded by a strange beauty. Here, and at the doubling of Cape Clear (an island) immediately following, by taking Fastnet on the right and the Cape on the left—here the entrance is made into St. George's or the Irish Channel; and here, too, the peculiar character of the green, treeless Irish high lands may be observed, with first glimpses of the bold rocky coast, with surf breaking white against it —the cabins from which Paddy emerges, nestling among the hills—the little round martello-towers crowning them, speaking of smuggling prevention and by-gone invasions—the peculiar tan-colored-sailed fishing-boats, and luggers that fly about like sea-gulls,—the vessels (steamers and others) dropping into and out of the Channel, etc.

It is at near Cape Clear, and after passing the bold head-land of Mizen Head,—near a little hamlet called Crookhaven, snugged away behind the hills, that the telegraph station is located, at which arriving ships are reported; and it is from this place, really, that the announcements are made of steamer-arrivals at Queenstown.

Beyond this, and commencing to run up the Irish coast, the next point of any importance, reached within a few miles, is the bluff headland, crowned with a light, known as the Old Head of Kinsale, and doubly famous as the spot where the American packet Albion was lost many years ago, with so large a number of passengers (among whom was Napoleon's Marshal Lefebvre, Duke of Dantzic)—and as the place which gives name to the one nobleman, the Baron of Kinsale, who is allowed to wear his hat in the presence of the British sovereign, that favor having been accorded the family many generations ago, as a reward for a Baron of Kinsale having overcome, by his personal strength and prowess, a continental champion who overcame all others.

It is perhaps an hour after passing Kinsale, that Daunt's Rock and its bell-buoy are reached—near the entrance to Queenstown harbor, and the spot on which the fine steamer City of New York was lost a few years since, though without any sacrifice of life. Five miles beyond, Roche's Point thrusts out, with its light, forming the southern lip of Queenstown harbor (Cove of Cork) not unlike the New York

LAND-MAKINGS. 63

Narrows in general conformation. Here, in fine weather, a steam-tender takes off passengers and mails for Queenstown and Ireland generally, while the ship merely stops power and lies off the harbor long enough to discharge the two kinds of " baggage." Sometimes, when the weather is rough and transfer more difficult, the ship steams into the harbor (as she always does to take on mails and passengers when coming west); and then, whether entering to land or come out again, a view is caught of a very handsome land-locked harbor, rather narrow of entrance but very commodious within, with the town of Queenstown (so named in place of the old " Cove of Cork," in honor of the Queen's visit, fifteen to twenty years ago,) lying on the sloping hill at the back or north-west extremity, and the beautiful river Lee sweeping round behind it, south-westward, to the city of Cork, which lies at some miles distance.

Supposing that the passenger does not land at Queenstown, and that he comes out of or away from the harbor with the ship (the Channel-pilot now on board) the next prominent point made is the rocky island and light of Ballycotton; then that of Mine Head; then the Hook Tower (nearly off Waterford); then Conigsbeg Light-ship; and finally the tall white light of Tuskar, which concludes the run directly up-Channel.

So far, the Irish coast has been kept very near, the character of its scenery widely varying from bold and barren to low and fertile, and distant glimpses of mountains almost all the while. But from Tuskar the ship "squares away" across the Channel towards Holyhead and Liverpool, and the Irish coast is soon lost to view, through the Wicklow Mountains linger long on the sight.

It is ten to twelve hours after leaving Tuskar, generally, when the bold, rocky headland of Holyhead, in Wales, is made, ahead to the right, with its strange cleft and bridged rock, its white light-house, and the wonderful break-water defending the harbor. Beyond that point, and curving round it south-eastward towards Liverpool, the high Welsh lands are seen to be thrifty farms, with neat farm-houses and many wind-mills. Behind, the far Welsh mountains rise; and in very clear weather distant views are caught of the peaks of Snowdon and others of the highest mountains in the southwest of Great Britain. An object of great interest is found, not long after passing Holyhead, in the piles of rocks known as the Skerries, two or three miles from the Welsh shore— of course dangerous and lighted. Then come, as prominent points on a coast all rough and bold, Point Lynas, the pilot-station of Liverpool; and Great Orme's Head, a rough promontory, with one of the most powerful Fresnel lights in the world. Glimpses may be caught of little Welsh villages nestled at the feet of the high lands, and Llandudno and some of the other watering-places.

But the mouth of the Mersey and Liverpool are almost in view. Vessels, bound out and in, steamers, bound to and from Channel ports, odd-looking steam-tugs (to an American eye) and odder-looking pilot-boats, all begin to thicken, and the evidence is plain

LAND-MAKINGS. 65

of approach to the most important seaport of either continent. The Northwest Light-ship is the first point marking the nearer approach; then the great Bell Buoy on the bar clangs its warning as it rocks and rolls; then Formby and Crosby Light-ships are passed; at the right the Rock-Light at New Brighton, nearly opposite the city, closes the list; and the passenger is within view of the forest of masts and the wonderful long line of docks, showing on the left and revealing the great port and city of Liverpool.

It may be proper to say, here, and the truth applying to other places as well as this—that *the approach to the port should never be lost*, especially if there is daylight in which to catch it. Many *do* lose it, in the anxiety to look after baggage, change clothing, etc., but this should never be done. Baggage should have been looked after, if at hand, before; that in the hold can be looked after as it comes up, when the ship is at anchor; and there is no occasion whatever of coming out in "full fig" in the way of coscostume, until reaching the hotel and washing off the grime of the voyage.

Once more : travellers who desire both to learn and enjoy, should never permit themselves to lose the first approach to any new coast or any great port, even if a little broken rest and discomfort should be found necessary to secure it. In no other way can the general situation and bearings be so well attained, and to miss the opportunity once may be to miss it finally.

UP THE BRITISH CHANNEL TO SOUTHAMPTON OR LONDON.

The Irish coast is not made at all on the voyage to London or Southampton. The first point sighted, if no error occurs in calculation, will be found the Scilly Rocks—small islands, with the light on St. Agnes, the largest of them, a little south of the Land's End (Cornwall) the extreme southwestern point of England—at all times a dangerous point, and painfully famous in history as the spot where the whole fleet of Sir Cloudesley Shovel, the English admiral, was ground to pieces and all hands perished, in the terrible gale of November 26, 1703, said to be the heaviest ever known in England, destroying the Eddystone Lighthouse, burying the Bishop of Bath and Wells under the ruins of his palace, wrecking and drowning eight thousand sailors, blowing down seventeen thousand trees in Kent alone, and eliciting a description from Defoe, the author of "Robinson Crusoe."

The next point, some three hours later, is the appearance at the left of the high bluff and light of the Lizard Head (commonly spoken of as the "Lizard") the first glimpse of the main land of Great Britain. In some two or two-and-a-half hours after, if the weather be particularly fine, a distant glimpse may be caught, far away to the left, of either the tower or light of Eddystone Lighthouse, perhaps the most noted erection of its class in the world—standing on a single rock, miles from the shore, dashed against by the sea in every storm, two or three times carried away and rebuilt, and one of the best existing proofs

LAND-MAKINGS. 67

of man's power and determination in fighting wind and wave. The next light and land mark are those of the Start Point, reached within the next one-and-a-half hours; and the next and far more important, is the Bill of Portiand, (so named from its resemblance to the bill of a bird) about forty miles beyond, and stretching out from below Dorchester and Weymouth.

From this point, if on the way to Southampton, land is scarcely lost again, as very soon comes St. Albans Head, at the other or eastern extremity of Weymouth Bay,—of which, and most of the other points made on the way up-Channel, it is almost needless to say, to those at all acquainted with geography, that the prevailing character of the coast is bold, rough and rocky, with chalk (giving name to the "white cliffs of Albion") commencing to show freely and never losing that appearance until the mouth of the Thames is really entered. Not long after leaving St. Albans Head, the appropriately-named Needles and their light are made—on the west point or head of the turtle-shaped Isle of Wight, forming the south lip of the sound between Wight and the main, called the Solent. Up the Solent, then, with the beautiful wooded and villa-studded island on the right and the main land on the left, and sheering sharp to the left or north-and-by-west when off Cowes and its roads, (the right flipper of the turtle) catching a distant glimpse of Portsmouth, Gosport and the great naval station of Spithead, at the right— not much of additional interest remains, except the first shore-views of fertile Old England, until the twenty or thirty miles of Southampton-water are measured, and all the aspects before noted in the approach to Liverpool are more or less duplicated in nearing Southampton, a great seaport in and of itself, and still greater as supplying a cross-country and railway port to London.

If the destination is London instead of Southampton, all the points before named are made, up to Portland Bill and possibly St. Albans Head, after which the next, instead of the Needles, on the west, is St. Catherine's, on the extreme south point of the Isle of Wight (the left flipper of the turtle as Cowes was the right).

There is a long stretch of Channel running between St. Catherine's and the next point made on the London route—Beachy Head, twenty or thirty miles beyond Brighton, and famous for the allusions to its height made by the British sailors in the old nautical romances, who had a habit of speaking of anything extra large as "looming like Beachy Head in a fog." The chalk cliffs have now assumed such height and prominence that the whole coast, whenever seen, seems to be entirely white and perpendicular, though there is really an increase in their height until past Dover. The next prominent point after Beachy Head, is Dungeness; and very soon after passing this head, first Folkestone and then Dover may be seen at a distance, while to the right the French coast breaks into view, lower than the English though something like it in boldness and chalky character.

The South Foreland is made and passed at near Dover, and the Channel then becomes the Downs—

those waters commemorated in the old song of
"Black-Eyed Susan:"

"All in the Downs the fleet was moored,
Their streamers waving in the wind," &c.

After Dover, Deal, Ramsgate (celebrated as the greatest of all summer-bathing-places of the middle classes); then the North Foreland and those Goodwin Sands on which so many ships have been wrecked and so much of life and property lost in the terrible quick sands. Rounding the North Foreland, comes Margate, the rival of Ramsgate in summer-bathing and boarding; and at this point the Channel, or Downs, becomes the Nore, actually the broad mouth of the Thames, though many miles are yet to be traversed before the Thames proper is entered and the ascent commenced at Sheerness, by the great Chatham Dockyards, Gravesend, Deptford, Woolwich, &c.,—points which may properly be said to belong to London proper and its environs, and consequently out of the province of this paper.

TO GLASGOW, BY THE "NORTH ABOUT."

Nearly all the steamers bound from America for Glasgow, direct, now-a-days, take the course known as the "North About"—pass around the north of Ireland instead of making it at the south end and passing up through the Irish Channel. Their port of call, in Ireland, is Moville, the port of Londonderry, in the entreme north; and the points made and the courses pursued are briefly as follows, before and after touching at Moville:

The first European land made, by this route is Tory Island, on the extreme northwest coast of Donegal. Then with perhaps a distant glimpse of the terribly rocky and threatening main-coast, at Malta Head, the next point is the Island of Instrahull, off the extreme northern extremity of all Ireland. Then, coming southward, Glengall Head is made at the right, with Innishowen Head not long after and forming the north lip of the entrance to Loch Foyle, on which stands Londonderry.

Moville, a tumble-down old town, stands just behind Innishowen; and beautiful views of the peculiar northern Irish scenery, and over the broad Loch, or bay, may be caught from the anchorage off the town. Here conveyance is taken to Londonderry, and rail thence southward, by passengers leaving the steamers.

Leaving Moville, for Glasgow, the course is nearly northeastward, for a time, leaving the Giant's Causeway at no great distance on the right, until Rathlin Island is made; then the bold promontories of the Mulls of Kinnoul and Cantire are passed, again on the left; then Sanda Island, at the southeastern extremity of Cantire. From this point the passage is sometimes made through the Sound of Kilbranna, between Cantire on the left and the rocky, treeless, heath-covered island of Arran on the right,—while much oftener the run is made up the right side of the island of Arran, in which latter case, especially, a peculiarly fine view is caught, in fine weather, just opposite Sanda and some distance away to the right, of Ailsa Craig, one of the most remarkable of all the projections of this beautifully wild coast. Ailsa lies at perhaps twenty miles distance from the Mull of Cantire, eastward, and about fourteen or fifteen from Sanda; —it rises a fearful mass of rock, more than a thousand feet above the sea that breaks white at its base, cone-shaped and apparently inaccessible, while thousands upon thousands of wild fowl make it their nestling-place, wheel, circle and scream around it—the scene one always remembered by the traveller who has witnessed it.

Assuming that the run is made eastward, up the east side of Arran, (the westward passage through the Sound of Kilbranna having little interest until the north end of the island is rounded and Bute comes into view, as in the route now to be noted)—the next point of interest, after passing Ailsa Craig, is Pladda light, on a little rocky island at the southeast point of the island of Arran; and then Arran is for some time in full view at the left (its characteristics of scenery before mentioned) until the attention is distracted by Holy Isle, another of its small islets, larger than Ailsa Craig and almost as wild looking. Lamlash harbor and Brodick town and watering-place, are both passed on the left, on Arran ; then come the small and rocky Cumbrae Islands, with light, on the right, with the Isle of Bute on the left, much softer and better cultivated than either Arran or the mainland previously passed. Toward light comes next, on the sound called the Kyles of Bute, between Bute and Toward.

The remainder of the brief passage up the now-entered Firth of Clyde, to Greenock, may probably vie with the approach to any port in the world. For the scenery, on both sides, is softened and beautiful; and ahead, at a distance, the Highlands of Perthshire lift themselves in fine weather, Ben Lomond crowning all. On the left, half way from the Kyles to the mouth of the Clyde, Dunoon watering-place shows picturesquely at the left, with Clough light at the right and the Gaunt Duck Rocks and beacon just off Dunoon. Then Kempach point is passed to the right, and Gouroch; and the smoky, manufacturing, ship-building town of Greenock is seen at the right or south bank of the Clyde River, where it empties into the Firth and forms Greenock Roads, lying at the foot of the Whin Hills (whence its frequent rains), with the watering place of Helensburg on the opposite promontory, between Loch Long on the left and the little Gare Loch on the right—up the latter of which, for some reason not yet explained, all the Clyde-built ships always go to adjust their compasses! At which point the province of the present paper ceases.

UP THE BRITISH CHANNEL (FRENCH SIDE) TO BREST AND HAVRE.

The first point ordinarily made, on this route, is Ushant, a very high rocky island with lighthouse crowning a literal pile of rocks, on the extreme northwestern corner of France (Brittany). Thence the course is about southeast, three or four miles, to the entrance of the harbor of Brest, displaying the usual long high piers and shut-in port, usual to French Channel towns, with the addition of very extensive

LAND-MAKINGS. 73

and formidable fortifications. Here passengers who wish to hurry direct to Paris, land and proceed by rail, only some six or eight hours being consumed in reaching the capital.

Proceeding onward from Brest to Havre, however, by ship, Ushant is again made, and rounded to the north and west. Some five hours later, steering almost due east, the island of Guernsey is sighted at the right—an island of singular conformation, with little wood, high in the centre and drooping at either end. In good weather, Alderney, another and yet smaller island, will be sighted next, at the right; while it is only in exceptionally clear weather that the island of Jersey, lying further behind, comes into view.

Some three or four hours after passing Guernsey, Cape La Hogue comes in sight, famous for one of the great naval battles—the cape backed by very high bluff lands, while the light stands low. Cherbourg is made next, some three or four miles beyond La Hogue; and in a good atmosphere a very fine view of its great breakwater (one of the finest in the world) and immense and formidable fortifications, may be caught, as also of the distant heights which relieve the low character of the coast.

After Cherbourg the next point made is Cape Levi, showing the peculiarity of two lighthouses, one above the other. Then Cape Barfleur, with very high lighthouse on long peninsula, while the grounds behind rise high at a little distance. Next, in fine weather, Cape La Hague is seen, the course being now nearly southeast-by-south. Then Cape La Héve, with two lights on the top of a formidable and almost perpendicular hill; then, and finally, about three miles from La Héve, the opening of the splendid port of Havre, one of the oldest and finest in France, with its long pier, light-house at end, and other characteristics before noted as common to all French Channel ports. Here (at the mouth of the Seine) a splendid old city presents itself, with a strange blending of commercial and historical importance ; and here again, rail communication opens to Paris and the opportunity for continental rambling generally.

VII.

ENTERING FOREIGN COUNTRIES.

THERE are a few pieces of advice to be given to short-trip travellers, with reference to entering foreign countries, highly important if very brief.

Stepping off the ship that has borne the American abroad, he should heed one especial dictate of prudence—to *remember* that he is abroad, not necessarily beyond the protection of his own flag (though a little too often), but where governments different from his own hold sway, and where much is to be lost and nothing gained by mixing himself up with the local quarrels of any one of those nations. He may have allowed himself to talk Fenianism, or ultra-British hatred of the idea of Irish nationality, on ship-board, up to the very hour of landing—though even then he had often better kept silence, to guard against spying that may place him under suspicion after landing; but be that as it may, from the moment of touching any foreign soil, if he is a prudent man, he will "keep his tongue between his teeth" as to what he believes to be wrong or right, governmentally, in the countries visited. He may believe, say, in the propriety of setting "the Green above the Red" at as early a day as possible; but that is no reason why he should utter imprudent words, on landing at Queenstown or Belfast, calculated to get him into just such scrapes, all the way from mere temporary arrest to imprisonment and possible trial, as scores of Americans have run into, without really meaning anything, during the troubled years since 1865. If he should happen to be "down on the Irish," there is no greater reason why he should declare his faith too loudly and run the risk of getting mauled or killed by the hottest of the descendants of Brian Boroihme.

When in England, too, no absolute necessity exists for abusing the Queen and vaunting the superiority of American institutions, in a manner calculated to work discomfort to others and inconvenience to self; beyond the Channel, on French soil, even if Napoleon the Third is believed to be a tyrant, it is wiser not to say as much where a government spy may hear and heed at any moment; and the same remark will apply, even more forcibly, to touring in any of the other monarchical countries of Europe, Prussia, Austria, Italy, Spain, etc., not to mention Russia, the most dangerous of all. In one country—Switzerland, itself a republic, republicanism can be talked with both safety and pleasure ; and it is prudent to run over to the Alps for the purpose of "letting off steam" in that direction, if the pressure becomes too great for safety.

There is another thing to be avoided, commencing in Ireland and scarcely ending throughout Europe. Most of the European countries likely to be visited by short-trip Americans, are Catholic, and all of them (Great Britain not excepted) part-Catholic. Most Americans who go over are either Protestants or Nothingarians—no lovers of Catholicism, either of the classes; and the habit is somewhat too general of speaking disparagingly of the forms of the Catholic worship, and of the Catholics themselves, under the roofs of their magnificent edifices, within which are gathered many of the very objects of art most strongly calling the traveller's attention and affording him most delight. This course is unwise, in one point of view, and cruel in another: unwise, as it involves ill-feeling and possible personal discomfort—cruel, as it needlessly pains others who hold differently. *It is rudeness as well as folly to go into any Church, in any land, without, while remaining there, observing its rules of conduct and refraining from any offensive act or comment.* "If things do not suit you, here, well enough to allow you to act as gentlemen and friends *while* here, be kind enough to remain away!" might be very often said, with propriety, to those Americans who start out from home with the determination to insult the world if they cannot proselyte it.

So much for the *preparation of conduct*, on entering foreign countries. Of another preparation—that involving a proper understanding of American national resources and due knowledge what in American institutions can and cannot be improved—something has already been said. And it only remains to deal a moment with one or two of the national regulations connected with persons and property, some of which may be vexatious while all must be submitted to with the best grace possible.

The advice has already been given—have passports, useful in all countries, indispensable in some. In some of the European countries they will be demanded at short intervals by government officials, taken away to be *viséd* (examined and compared), and sometimes kept longer than may seem necessary to the traveller. For this there is but one rule: give them up calmly, and wait with what patience can be summoned. The arrangement is *not*, as it may appear at the first glance, a personal insult to *you:* others suffer in the same manner, and live through the suffering.

Again, in all the despotic countries a requirement will be made, immediately after registering at the hotel, for the name of every member of the party (at least every male)—age, place of birth, country, habitual residence, occupation, last previous stopping-place, and the number of the room to be occupied! All this to be communicated to the police, immediately; and it really does seem quite the equal of any inquisitiveness displayed even among the sharpest Yankees of the Eastern States. Nothing is gained by swearing over the espionage, however; and suspicion may be excited by any reluctance, when there is no ground whatever: "when in Rome, do as Rome does," even to obeying the police in the most absurd of their requirements. It may even happen that before leaving the city *you* are advantaged by the record, in the recovery of something lost or the detection of some wrong to yourself.

As to taking in baggage, at the ports or on crossing the frontiers of different countries. Very large amounts of baggage require very large amounts of examination by the various custom-house authorities, *unless golden spectacles are put on their eyes*, when they generally see with great readiness and do not always tumble out the *bijouterie* as well as the dirty linen. From America, not many things likely to be carried in a trunk are dutiable at the European ports, except liquors, perfumes, cigars and tobacco. Of the first two there is no occasion to carry any through a foreign custom-house; they have better than we, at all times. As to cigars, tastes differ; at all events there is not much to be gained, either in cost or quality, by carrying more than the few (of which the officers of any ship will advise the passenger) allowed by law without duty. Tobacco is different, however: there is no decent tobacco in Europe, except as Americans carry it over; and inveterate tobacco-users should take plenty, and either prevent its quantity being known, by the use of those *golden spectacles*, or pay duty on the overplus, like men and citizens of that great nation which can certainly out-chew and out-expectorate the wide world!

In passing from one European country to another, whether by crossing the Channel or a mere frontier, there are constant vexatious stoppages. But they can be endured, too, pretty easily, if the rule is always observed to *have the baggage ready for examination whenever approaching a custom-station,*—so that if it *is* wanted no time will be wasted, and if it is *not*, nothing will be lost. It really seems, sometimes, that the delays occasioned will lose the connecting trains, but such things never occur. Avoid having anything contraband; have keys ready and instantly unlock when ordered; make no attempts at concealments that if detected would cause trouble; and so may the terrible *douaniers* of the Continent be passed with comparative ease, safety and celerity.

Close mouths, as to imprudent topics; observant eyes and ears, as to everything occurring; constant but judicious bribery, believing none to be above the temptation; and good temper under all circumstances—these are the four rules of travel in foreign countries; and with them, and advice previously embodied, there can be no excuse for detaining the short-trip traveller a moment longer from the commencement of his sight-seeing and adventure.

VIII.

SHORT TRIPS IN IRELAND.

ASSUMING that advice previously given will be often taken, and that the greater proportion of short-trip travellers, on their first voyage, will leave the steamer at Queenstown, on the Liverpool route,—it will be proper first to take a hurried peep at Ireland, reminding the reader that the commencement is at the extreme south, working northward, and that those who cross from Scotland to Belfast or other ports in the north, to take homeward passage from Queenstown, need only to reverse the paper to derive the same advantage. Another reminder may also be given,—entering upon the legitimate business of a guide, ashore—that much ground is to be gone over, in this and succeeding papers, and that consequently the glances at different places must be of the briefest.

QUEENSTOWN TO CORK AND KILLARNEY.

QUEENSTOWN, the port of landing from the steamer, has little to commend it to the attention of travellers, except the fine harbor which it supplies to Cork. The harbor and fortifications are well deserving the view they are certain to receive, especially from those who there first set foot in Ireland. The town lies somewhat stragglingly at the west side of the harbor, climbing a side-hill. Southward and westward, round behind the town, to the left, the river Lee sweeps away, to Cork, some ten or twelve miles distant by it, though only six by direct course by land.

Three modes of proceeding from Queenstown to Cork present themselves. The *First* enables the traveller to make acquaintance with that oddest and most dashing of conveyances, the "jaunting-car," without which Ireland could not possibly exist, just as it never could have originated elsewhere than in Ireland,—with its two seats lengthwise, passengers back to back, driver sulky-mounted, two wheels and one horse, and general arrangements for what one writer has graphically described as "going it at a gallop and everybody holding on." A very pleasant ride up the banks of the Lee may be thus obtained; but that mode of transit has a rival in the *Second:* railway, by which the passenger is whisked up, on the north side of the Lee, in a few minutes; and that by the *Third:* steamboat up the Lee, decidedly the pleasantest of all in fine weather, with the capital views afforded of the junction of the Lee with the harbor; the small villages that stud the banks; and the public grounds and fortifications on the left, and larger shipping of the port on the right, approaching the city itself. These little iron paddle-wheel steamers run frequently, in summer, and they often carry music, making the run more pleasant and less tedious.

CORK, built on both sides of the Lee, and spanning it with nine bridges, is one of the handsomest cities in Ireland, as well as one of the largest—being only second to Dublin in size and to Belfast in trade. It is also second to Dublin in dirt (no high praise); and many of the best streets are well built and handsome, but of the "back-slums" the less said (and observed) the better. To see the town hastily but to best advantage, an open jaunting-car should be taken, if the weather is fine, and a close one (another institution of Cork, covered, closed in front and open behind) if rain falls or threatens. The driver, in that case (there as elsewhere), will supply the best of guide-books. Several of the churches demand attention—among others the Cathedral, St. Patrick's, St. Ann's, and the very old Church of Shandon, with its sweet bells (the chiming of which should be heard), referred to by Father Prout in his

> "Sweet bells of Shandon
> That sound so grand on
> The pleasant waters of the river Lee."

There are also the Mansion House, the Royal Cork Institution (with a Museum said to be worth visiting), some of the Banks, etc. ; while above the main body of bridges the banks of the Lee are very beautiful, and one public walk on the south side, the Mardyke, is very pleasant, handsomely shaded and attractive. Half-an-hour's call at the Court-House will show the dingy assize-rooms in which most of the Fenians of the South have been tried, and quite suffice as a type of Irish courts. Cork has a considerable number of manufactories, in woollen, etc.; and no small amount of ship-building is carried on on the north side of the Lee, below the bridges. Before leaving Cork, one or two excursions must be made, especially one to

BLARNEY CASTLE, LAKE AND GROVES. These may be reached in a pleasant ride of five or six miles, by jaunting-car, southwestward, first glimpses of plenty of the Irish rural cabins, with their whitewashed walls, thatched roofs, turf-smoke and poverty, being also caught on the way. The Castle is a fine old ruin, with the donjon-keep still more than an hundred feet in air, much better preserved than most ruins, and said to have been originally the home of the royal M'Carthys. The original "Blarney Stone" hangs from the vaulted ceiling of one of the chambers, and only fools risk their necks in trying to kiss it, especially as there is another quite as "real" and powerful, to be kissed ("for a consideration"), on the lawn below. The Lake, lying near the Castle, is very small and very pretty; and the "Groves of Blarney" are all that they have been called of umbrageous beauty. The second excursion (optional) in point of importance, is to

Cloyne, an old town, now in ruins, a few miles from Cork, east of Queenstown, seaward, with a fine view, in passing, of Roskellan Castle, the splendid family seat of the O'Briens, Earls of Inchiquin and sometime Marquises of Thomond, rendered doubly interesting to Americans from the near connection with that family of the late Fitz-James O'Brien, poet and soldier, who fell during the rebellion.

Leaving Cork for Killarney, by rail, much handsome scenery is to be enjoyed, with, among other views, a fine one of the Castle and Groves of Blarney at some distance to the left; but nothing of special interest breaks the journey until the arrival at

Mallow, a thriving town, at two hours' distance, where the passenger changes cars from the train direct for Charleville and Dublin, to that for the cross-road for Killarney and Tralee,—and where he hears the old song of the " Rakes o' Mallow " continually sounding in imagination. There are some manufactories at Mallow, and much of Irish rural life and character may be observed at and around the station; but there is nothing to tempt the laying over of a train, when the reputation of the Lakes is calling.

It is a run of perhaps two hours (often made three or four, by the miserable railroad delays) from Mallow to Killarney; and the ride would be a tedious one, but for the opportunities of enjoying the bare, desolate scenery of the Southwest, studying the cabins squatted under the edges of the hills, seeing plenty of peat-bogs and heaps of the fuel piled to dry, and at last finding the beautiful mountains of Kerry lifting themselves ahead and to the left.

Killarney (Village) is prettily situated, a mile from the north-east point of the Lower Lake; has a population of five thousand, principally on a single long street; is picturesque (as are many of the blue-cloaked peasant-girls) and dirty (as ditto). The Nunnery, in the midst of the town; the Cathedral, to the north; and some of the hotels, supply all the features worth note, though no visitor to the town should fail to ride through it at some leisure. Of course *the* attraction of the visit is found in

THE LAKES OF KILLARNEY, three in number, called the Lower (or Lough Leane), Middle (or Mucross), and Upper. They are charmingly situated, at the very bases of the fine hills, with Macgillicuddy Reeks and Purple Mountain prominent at the western extremity; Torc Mountain and the Devil's Punch-Bowl prominent objects south and east; and such a variety in rock, shade and winding water as cannot well be matched elsewhere in the world. They are somewhat small and "band-box-y" to an American, and are (as will later be discovered) something like, though wilder and rougher, the English Lakes of Cumberland, with a distant resemblance to Lake George at home. In some features they are unequalled—in the bloom of the broom or heather surrounding them; the size and beauty of the arbutus groves on many of the islands; and the wonderful prevalence of detached rocks thrust up out of the water—especially in the Lower Lake. As is well known, too, they have both poetic and legendary charm in a rare degree, as they are the scene of all the O'Donoghue legends, out of which so many Irish stories and dramas have been formed; while Moore has immortalized one of the most charming portions of the Lower Lake in his "Sweet Innisfallen," and Lover (appropriate name) clustered round them the most mischievous of memories in

"———Kate Kearney,
Who lives on the banks of Killarney."

Of the two-days' sojourn at Killarney, the most

prudent division of time is into two portions—one day each for boat and jaunting-car. In the day by boat (when he must be accompanied by a bugler and take along lunch) he will pass through all three of the Lakes, besides visiting the island and ruined Abbey of Innisfallen, and Ross Island and Castle (the last of Cromwell's holds in Ireland) on the Lower— calling at Glena Cottage (Lord Kenmare's) under Glena Mountain, passing under Brickeen Bridge, going through the Long Range (between the Lakes) and the Meeting of the Waters, and hearing the wonderful bugle-echoes of Irish melodies under the Eagle's Nest. Boats, rowers and guides, as well as jaunting-cars, can be procured at any one of half-a-dozen excellent hotels; and there is nothing in the way of legend that the guide-bugler by boat, or the driver by car, will leave untold.

On the second day, by jaunting-car, the whole round of the Lakes may again be made, with the Ruins of Aghadoe, the wild Gap of Dunloe, etc.; while, on the return, there will be an opportunity to visit Torc Waterfall, a beautiful wild cascade under the edge of Torc Mountain, to observe much of the scenery made immortal in the "Collegians" (Gerald Griffin's novel) and its after-thought, the "Colleen Bawn"—to see the handsome house and grounds of Mucross, with possibly the village of the same name —and to spend an hour at

Mucross Abbey, one of the very finest mediæval ruins in Ireland, standing near the eastern side of Mucross Lake (Middle), with an ivy-grown square tower of wonderful beauty; the tombs of O'Donoghue, McCarthy More and other Kings of Munster yet remaining in the chancel; a wonderful old yew-tree filling up the whole court; old cloisters; ivy to any extent; and a history dating back to 1140.

The traveller should be duly advised that at and around Killarney, "Paddy," male and female, may be found in full glory; that the district is magnificently rebellious—very many of the Fenian prisoners and convicts of 1866-7 having come from about Killarney and the Gap of Dunloe; that roguery and beggary equally abound (male and female again); and that if he buys all the curiosities offered, from carved wood to potheen whiskey, he will have no money left at the outset and will need a ship of his own to freight home his purchases (not including the whiskey, which may be carried internally).

KILLARNEY TO AND ABOUT DUBLIN.

Travellers at greater leisure would be likely, after seeing Killarney, to go farther south and west to Bantry, Kenmare and Dingle Bays, all following in succession from the extreme southwest point of Ireland, northward, and affording very fine coast scenery; then by the Shannon to Limerick, still farther north, and the finest town in the west; and possibly yet farther north, out of Kerry and across Clare, to Galway Bay and Galway, where the rough-riding description of Irishman is yet said to exist in the greatest perfection, with the best potheen and the most jolly recollections of the novelist Lever.

But the short-trip traveller will only be likely to turn back on his road so far as to return by rail to

Mallow, and there changing cars again take the train direct by Charleville, Limerick Junction and Portarlington, to Dublin, the capital and chief attraction. Very much of interest, to lovers of character and scenery, will be found on the way up, in the loungers at the stations, in some of the way-passengers, and in the glimpses caught of rural scenery, turf-bogs, cabins, ruins, and distant mountains. For many miles, some two-thirds of the way up from Mallow, the railway runs through the far-famed Bog of Allen, in and over which may be seen every variety of the turf-bog, the moor, the very desert. And yet farther on, if the right side of the carriage be occupied, some very fine views will be caught of an immense furze-dotted upland, once famous as a race-course, in the shape of the Curragh of Kildare, and well worthy of a visit, now, for the sake of the large number of troops continually encamped there in summer, and the "Wrens" (human of a certain female order) said to nest there like ground-birds. Only an hour's ride beyond, by Naas, and then,

DUBLIN, the capital of Ireland, and well worthy of a visit both for its present and its past. It lies on both sides of the river Liffey (so well commemorated in the jolly old rhyme as

"―――The Liffey,
That runs down by Dublin's swate city so fine"),

some ten or a dozen miles from the splendid breakwatered harbor of Kingstown (Dublin Bay), of which the famous Hill of Howth, the traditional oath of every true Paddy, forms the bold northern defence against the Channel. Dublin, well known as the capital of Ireland when a nation, and the vice-regal seat since the Union, is at once one of the handsomest and dirtiest of cities, with very many fine public buildings, charming public grounds, and poor-quarters so much fouler even than those of the ordinary European cities, that they make a sort of celebrity of themselves. It is said to have something more than a quarter of a million of inhabitants.

To the short-trip traveller, of course, the jaunting-car will come into requisition, in and around Dublin, quite as well as in any other locality. There are very few places actually demanding internal examination, though several would repay it; but of, outside views there are an extraordinary number worth remembering. One day "at a pinch," and two at comparative leisure, will do the city comfortably, the best of guides being found, as elsewhere in Ireland, in the chatty, smoking driver of the car.

Of public buildings, those best demanding attention are the Castle, famous in both history and romance; the Bank of Ireland (once the Parliament House); Trinity College, from which so much of fun and true learning have gone out to the world; Conciliation Hall, where O'Connell made his great speeches, and on the steps of which his statue still seems to be hurling defiance at the Union and its supporters; the Custom-House; Post-Office; the Four Courts (law building); the Crystal Palace; and some of the churches, with St. Patrick's Cathedral far the most interesting of them. Some hours should be spent in the latter fine old building (restored), whatever the religion of the visitor,—as it is within it that all the Knights of St. Patrick are (or used to be) installed, their seats and banners showing prominently; while some portions of the edifice show an antiquity of seven or eight hundred years, and the tombs and monuments of Dean Swift, Curran, Archbishop Whately and several others, lend it a profound interest. The Cathedral (Catholic) is also said to contain many interesting monuments— among others that of Strongbow (De Valence, Earl of Pembroke), the first English invader of Ireland.

There are some very fine bridges over the Liffey; some splendid monuments, the inevitable Nelson leading off with the finest, in the neighborhood of the Post-Office; some very handsome streets, among the pleasantest of them Lower Sackville and Frederick Streets; while those who wish to find the opposite can be handsomely accommodated by taking a short drive through St. Patrick's Close, Bull Alley, and a few of the other "back-slums" behind St. Patrick's.

Of public grounds, within the city, the only ones of interest are Merrion Square, showing all around it the faded gentility of what was once the "rale ould Oirish arishtocracy"; and Stephen's Green, equally well known as a place of meeting and one of execution. Without the town,

Phenix Park, the boast of every Dubliner, is well worthy of its reputation, from its extent; the shaded beauty of part of it; its high location overlooking the city and harbor; the droves of fine cattle that find pasturage there; the Vice-regal Lodge, with its handsome grounds, on the northern edge; the great parade-ground (the "Fifteen Acres"), etc.; while

Glasnevin Cemetery, the "Greenwood," "Mount Auburn" and "Laurel Hill" of Dublin, supplies one of the finest of rides to the gates and one of the sweetest of walks within. In quiet beauty of natural scenery, and exquisite taste in arrangement, Glasnevin may vie with any other cemetery in Europe; and in the wondrously-sweet perfume of its many lime-trees will be found another marked charm in midsummer. The tomb of O'Connell lies in a tastefully-bordered raised circle in the centre; and within the grated door may be seen the coffin, every day covered with fresh flowers by reverent hands—though the intention is said to be, soon to remove the body to the Tower overlooking the cemetery and the city, because "O'Connell must have no tomb that cannot be seen from the sea."

A leisure evening in Dublin may be well and wisely spent at the Theatre Royal, where the acting is generally good and the merriest and most appreciative audiences in Europe are said to be found.

Of excursions from Dublin, the one which should be most surely taken if time permits, is to the wild scenery of the River Dargle, a few miles southward of the city, in the County Wicklow—in some regards among the wildest and finest on the "tight little island."

At Dublin the very brief southern Irish tour terminates, the tourist running down by rail the few miles from Dublin to Kingstown, and thence taking steamer to Holyhead (Wales) for Liverpool or London. With either of the longer tours already sketched, in view, a satisfactory glimpse can be caught of the north, as follows:

DUBLIN TO BELFAST AND THE GIANT'S CAUSEWAY.

Leaving Dublin for the North, the route will be by rail direct to Belfast, much of the lower part of the route lying near the sea, and the whole extent of it crossing successively the Counties Dublin, Louth, Armagh and Down; while of places of interest on the way, Drogheda, with the crossing of the Boyne ("Boyne Water") near it, and its historical recollections of Cromwell and James the Second; Dundalk, where Edward Bruce, brother of Robert the Bruce, was crowned King of Ireland; Newry and Lisburn, will be found the principal.

The special "linen-district" of Ireland is reached in thus running north, and while scenery roughens to become the "Black North," the white-striped bleaching-greens and large linen-factories become a new feature in the landscape, all the way from Drogheda to the capital of North Ireland,

BELFAST, at the head of Belfast Lough, with something like an eighth of a million inhabitants; the most extensive linen-manufactories in the world (in and around it); a Linen Hall, Queen's Bridge and several public buildings of interest, including the Cathedral, Post-Office, etc.; an extensive coasting and Channel trade, and more commercial importance than can be found elsewhere in Ireland, outside of Dublin and Cork. A few hours of leisure will be very well bestowed in visiting the Linen Hall (great bazaar of the trade), and some of the flax-mills and weaving-shops, the number of which seems to increase the wonder of *Ram-Rusti*, in the "Happy Man," that so small a bit of linen as Paddy Murphy's shirt-bosom can make a man so blest!

From Belfast, north for the Causeway, the best route is to take the rail by Carrickfergus to the little town of Larne, at the sea-end of Lough Larne, where the rail ceases and the long journey by jaunting-car begins. Mail cars (of the "jaunting" pattern) run thence, by various connections, all the way to the Causeway, the breaks being at Cushendall and Ballycastle, and the scenery splendidly compounded of the rough coast and the North Channel at the right hand, and the mountains of Antrim at the left; while dirt and beggary seem to swarm in the miserable villages, even worse, if possible, than at the south. One day to one and a half (according to connections) should be consumed between Belfast and

THE GIANT'S CAUSEWAY, one of the most stupendous and wonderful of Nature's freaks, lying at the extremity of the County Antrim and almost at that of the island, nearly in a northerly line with and some twenty miles distant west from the lowest point of the Scottish Mull of Cantire. It consists of nearly one-fifth of a mile (1,000 feet) of upright basaltic columns, stupendous in size, varied in shape (as to the number of sides of each crystal), and so fitted to each other as no hand but that of the Divine Architect could have arranged them. They should be walked over, boated round (and into the caves) when the weather and a sea smooth enough will allow, and laid up in memory with Niagara, the Western prairies, and the Alps,—whether the legend is or is not received, that the Causeway was built by Finn McCoul, the Irish giant (original Fenian — properly "Finnian"), to allow a Scotch giant to come over and be lathered by him! Such things may be; for what American does not know that our own Sandy Hook, at the entrance of New York harbor, was originated by one of *our* giants, walking across from Navesink Highlands to Long Island, stopping and pouring out the sand from his shoes?

N. B.—The Giant's Causeway has the reputation of drawing more shillings from unwilling pockets, in the way of fees to guides, for curiosities, and in other swindles, than any other place in the world except American Niagara. Once for all, elsewhere as well as here, on this point the cheap-tourist must "keep his weather-eye open:" the millionaire or the fool may scatter money as they like.

The return from the Causeway should not be made by the same route as the approach. A short car-ride takes the traveller to Portrush, whence the railway carries him directly back to Belfast within three to five hours. But if a few hours extra can be spared, it is very well bestowed in merely running down from Portrush to Coleraine (where "Kitty of Coleraine" is supposed to have abode), and thence by rail to

LONDONDERRY (or Derry), on the river Foyle, at the head of Lough Foyle, where a very handsome little town of twenty or thirty thousand inhabitants may be seen, remarkably well built, lighted and paved, with a central Diamond Square (palpable contradiction, in terms, to any one who does not remember that all New York squares are triangles!), charming suburbs, and a wonderful historical recollection of the long siege which it stood against James II.'s forces in 1689.

From Londonderry there are two routes by rail back to Belfast: by return to Coleraine (much the nearer); or taking the line so far southward towards Enniskillen or Omagh, and branching then eastward to Portadown, striking the road from Dublin at Lisburn. In either event the traveller is once more at Belfast; ready to take steamer to Glasgow, and the more-or-less brief Scottish tour.

[For those Americans who take Ireland *last* instead of *first*, of course the previous hints will need to be precisely reversed. Landing at Belfast from Glasgow, the run will be up to the Giant's Causeway and back to Belfast; then down to Dublin; thence to Mallow and Killarney; returning by Mallow and changing there for Cork and Queenstown and the home-steamer.

Leaving out the North, in the yet shorter trips, and landing at Dublin (Kingstown) from Holyhead, the course will be to Mallow and Killarney from Dublin; then back by Mallow and change there for Cork and Queenstown, as before. For time necessary to be consumed in the different Irish routes, see paper at commencement, on "Time of Trips."]

IX. SHORT TRIPS IN SCOTLAND.

THERE are two directions of the most ordinary progress, in Scotland, just as there are two principal land-approaches. Those who reach Edinburgh first, take more or less of the Highlands on their way to Glasgow; and *vice versa*. The point of view to be followed, in the present paper, is based on the assumption of Glasgow being first visited: of course, in the alternative case, the order here adopted simply needs reversing.

Assuming, then, that the tourist has reached Glasgow first, whether by steamer or rail, the first matters of interest are to be found

IN AND ABOUT GLASGOW.

GLASGOW, situated on the Clyde, is second in importance of the cities of Scotland, and in some respects the first. It has a population of between three and four hundred thousand; is busy and thriving in every detail of commerce and industry; and is probably a little more like New York than any other city of the Eastern World. It, in connection with Greenock and the banks of the Clyde between the two places, carries on an immense business in iron shipbuilding, and no small amount of interest is to be found in visiting the great yards, with their founderies. It seems legitimate, by the way, that these "Clyde-built steamers" should supply nearly half the world, as they do—as the first steamer ever built in Europe is said to have been launched here (in 1812), and James Watt, the great applier of steam-power to vessels, was born here. It has also a very extensive shipping and coasting trade, as is well known.

Architecturally and in public grounds, it has many beauties and much historical and romantic interest.

The Cathedral, dating back to the 12th century, and containing, with the yard, many fine monuments (among others that of John Knox), is a very proper boast of the Glasgow people; and the Royal Exchange commands very general admiration. It has five handsome bridges crossing the Clyde, and splendid quays down the river front; that portion of the wide drive which they supply being known as

The Broomielaw, certainly one of the finest riverside drives in Europe. No one can pretend to have seen Glasgow without driving down it.

Kelvin-Grove Park, the great public ground of Glasgow, lies on the Kelvin Water, a small stream running into the Clyde at the west end of the city, and is very beautiful, though the little stream itself, poisoned by the mills above it, is foul enough for Cologne. The other most notable public ground is

St. George's Square, lying in the centre of the town, surrounded by the principal hotels and many public buildings, and containing monuments to Scott, Nelson, etc. Among the special "lions" of Glasgow may be reckoned

The Salt Market, now nothing but a shabby quarter adjoining the City Prison (between the columns of which Pritchard, the wife-murderer, was hanged in 1865), but immortalized by Scott as the residence of Baillie Nicol Jarvie, in "Rob Roy"— many other quarters of the town, too, being sacred to similar memories, real and romantic, of the great freebooter and others of his class who made Glasgow a resort from its proximity to the Highlands.

Glasgow should be driven through and around in one of the open cabs plentifully supplied; and the tourist should not fail to be taken from the Salt Market up through the town by the High Street (where the worst mobs in Europe often gather), with a view of the dingy but celebrated old University, the tumble-down antique (and some shockingly dirty) houses, and many other objects of interest which the driver may always be depended upon to point out.

With even one day to spare before pushing on to the Highlands, one excursion from Glasgow should certainly be made, one day being occupied in that and the return.

AYR AND THE BURNS NEIGHBORHOOD.

AYR lies some forty miles southwest of Glasgow, on the North Channel, and immediately opposite the Isle of Arran. It may be reached by rail in two hours, after passing, only a few miles from Glasgow, through

Paisley, a thriving town, celebrated for its manufacture of shawls and other woollen, cotton and silk fabrics; with a fine old Abbey Church (scarcely worth breaking journey to visit, however); and the Ellerslie Oak in sight at the left, under which Wallace is said to have hidden from the pursuing English.

In the little seaport town of Ayr, proper, the most interesting object is to be found in the two bridges, an old and a comparatively new one, immortalized by Burns in the poem of the "Twa Brigs." On what is called the Wallacetown side of the river, stands

The Wallace Tower, on the site of the dungeon where he was confined; with a statue of the hero in front and the clock and bells of the old dungeon at the top. A carriage should be taken, after the local surveys, to visit

The Burns Cottage, about two miles from Ayr— a very humble house, with two rooms and in bad repair, where the poet was born in 1759. Some two miles beyond is

Kirk Alloway, the haunted church made memorable in "Tam o' Shanter"; and in the immediate neighborhood runs

The Doon, a quiet little stream, sacred to poetry and song, from the "Banks and braes o' Bonny Doon," crossed by the single-arched stone bridge where Auld Clootie pulled off the tail of Tam o' Shanter's mare.

The Burns Monument, near the banks of the Doon, has been built about fifty years, is a handsome Corinthian-columned structure of 60 feet, with a cupola, and has many interesting reminders of the poet in a room on the ground floor—among other things, a portrait, the Bible which he gave to Highland Mary, a snuff-box from the wood of Alloway Kirk, etc. The scenery of the Doon is worthy of its poetic reputation; and as the return can be made to

Glasgow the same night (by rail from Ayr), the day is one not to be missed.

GLASGOW TO EDINBURGH, BY THE SHORTER ROUTE.

The shortest route from Glasgow to Edinburgh, with any glance at the Highlands, may be made in a single day, though two would be more satisfactory. Whether taken in one or two days, however, it is one of the most charming on earth, especially in fine weather, which cannot always be calculated upon.

Leave Glasgow by rail, down the Clyde, with nothing of special interest on the way, until passing, on the left and on the near or upper bank of the Clyde,

Dumbarton Castle, now a cluster of ruins on a round hill skirting the river, but famous in history and once held in high estimation as a fortress, as well as being the spot from which Mary Queen of Scots, when a child, sailed away to France. Not far beyond Dumbarton, the disembarkation is made from the cars, at the little station of

Balloch, at the south end of Loch Lomond, where steamer is taken up the Lake,—the Lake itself and the Scottish Highlands, with

Ben Lomond crowning the prospect, being in full view thenceforth and the real charm of the trip begun. Loch Lomond is strikingly beautiful, with many reminders of the American Lakes George and Winnepesaukee, especially at the lower end, studded with beautiful islands; while it has a double interest in Ben Dhu, Glen Luss, Ross Dhu, Bannochar, Glen Fruin, and other objects which will readily be pointed out, on the left, referred to in the rowers' song ("Hail to the Chief") of the "Lady of the Lake;" and Ben Lomond, on the right, continues to attract the closest attention by its crag-broken peaks of green.

Landings are made at Luss, on the left, and at Rowardrennan on the right; and at Tarbet, again on the left, those go ashore who take coach for Loch Long, Inverary, etc. But the tourist does not land until he catches sight of

Inversnaid—Fort and landing—the latter a trifle, and the former a mere apology for a fortification, built for defence against the McGregors (with Rob Roy at their head) in 1713. Inversnaid has another interest, in the fact that it formed the "lairdship" of Rob Roy, before he became an outlaw and a freebooter. His "Prison," a rocky fastness at the water's edge, in which he was said to confine his captives, is passed lower down, at the foot of Ben Lomond, while his "Cave" lies above Inversnaid, and is only seen by those who continue upward to the head of the lake.

At Inversnaid four-horsed carriages are taken, across the beautiful heather-bordered strath towards Loch Katrine, with splendid mountain scenery in every direction. Part of this ride lies beside the little river and Loch Arklett; and at a certain point the spot is shown where not many years ago yet remained the cottage of Helen McGregor. All this, between the two lakes, is especially the "Rob Roy" country, and alluded to in the novel of that name.

Loch Katrine, claimed to be one of the most

beautiful lakes in the world, and certainly lovely in its mountain scenery, is reached after a few miles, the carriages being left and another steamer taken, at

Stronaclachar (or Coalbarns), a little landing at the extreme head of the lake, from which a glorious view can be caught of almost its entire length and of the historical mountains that gird it.

The "Rob Roy country" has been changed for that of the "Lady of the Lake," on leaving the strath and reaching Loch Katrine; and passing down the lake on the steamer, the points named in that remarkable poem rapidly present themselves. Of these one of the first and most interesting is

Ellen's Isle, a very small wooded island at the left, where the meeting between Fitz James and Douglas is supposed to have taken place, and where the immortal little lady was seen with her boat and paddles. A little farther onward, to the right, shoots up the giant mountain

Ben Venu, ragged and craggy in outline, and with what has been designated as "the sunshine rippling down the green, between its fretwork of bulging crags." Ahead shows the sharp, pointed summit of

Ben A'an, marking the pass through the Trossachs, through which the Knight of Snowdoun made his way towards Stirling.

The landing is made, all too soon, at a little covered toy-wharf at the foot of the lake, where open carriages are again taken, for the ride through the Trossachs to Callandar. The scenery is now among the finest in Scotland, and so continues for miles—

wild, wooded, craggy, mountainous. A halt is usually made for lunch at the pleasantly-situated hotel of

Ardcheanocrochan, in the Trossachs (literally "bristling country"), under the brow of Ben A'an. Two or three miles away, across the valley and Loch in front of the hotel, lies

The Clachan of Aberfoil, so well remembered by all readers of "Rob Roy;" and those who lie over for a day at Ardcheanocrochan (as many do) should make the short excursion to the little Highland hamlet of Diana Vernon and Captain Galbraith.

From Ardcheanocrochan the tourist pushes on, still by carriage, through the pass, amid splendid mountain scenery, much of it reminding of that at the Franconia Notch of the White Mountains. Very soon after leaving, Loch Achray appears on the right; and then the Turk Water is crossed, by the

"*Brigg of Turk*," celebrated in the "Lady of the Lake" as the spot where

"When the Brigg of Turk was won,
The foremost horseman rode alone."

Some of the very finest of the Highland scenery is here, for to the left, shortly afterwards, are seen the tall pines of wild Glenfinlass, back of the heathery Craig More and the Glenfinlass hills; then comes Loch Vennochar, to the right, with beautiful

Lanrick Mead ("Glendrig") on its border, where the Clan Alpine always gathered, and where the summons went out to assemble, in the poem. Some very pleasant glimpses of Scottish rural life are to be caught on the way along Loch Vennochar; and near the southern or farther end, comes a pretty fall of water, made useful in supplying the Glasgow Water-Works, but celebrated as

Coilantogle Ford, where Fitz James and Roderick Dhu had their conflict.

Ben Ledi, another of the Highland giants, comes into view here, at the left; and shortly after the way lies over Callander Bridge, and the tourist is ready for dinner at

CALLANDAR, a little old town with a street about one mile long, and of no particular interest. Here the carriages are abandoned and the railway is taken for Stirling. Two places of marked poetical interest are passed on the way, as the road passes through the village of

Dunblane, made famous by the old song of "Jessie, the Flower of Dunblane," and shortly afterwards over the

Bridge of Allan, made equally famous by the sweet old ballad of "Allan Water."

Approaching Stirling, a fine view is caught, on the left, of the unfinished

Wallace Monument, on the Abbey Craig, a tower which will be very imposing if ever finished; and then come

STIRLING AND STIRLING CASTLE, the former a very old, uneven-streeted, picturesque town, well worth some hours of rambling, and the latter a very high rock-throned fortification of irregular character, said to be not less than eight or nine hundred years old, overlooking the river and valley of the Forth, the

Carse of Stirling and the Battle-field of Bannockburn, so famous throughout all Scottish history.

The view from Stirling Castle battlements is wonderfully fine, covering the Highlands at the west, the Ochill Hills to the north and east, and the Campsie Hills to the south, the town of Stirling, the ruins of Cambuskenneth Abbey, the Abbey Craig, Bridge and Water of Allan, the Carse, Valley of the Forth, etc.; and by many it is considered almost unequalled in Europe. The old apartments within the Castle are well worth examination, especially

The "Douglas Room," where James II. assassinated the powerful and turbulent Earl of Douglas, about 1440; and to the north of the Castle should be visited the

"Heading-Hill," where many of the executions of old used to take place, especially those of the Duke of Albany, Earl of Lennox, Walter and Alexder Stuart, etc., by James I., 1424.

Excursions may be made to the

Field of Bannockburn, two and a half miles south, where the Scottish Bruce defeated the English Edward II., 30,000 against 100,000, on the 24th June, 1314, establishing again the Scottish monarchy and giving ground for Burns's ever-popular "Scots wha hae wi' Wallace bled!" Many points of local interest, thereabouts, will be explained and shown by the guides—among others the Bore-Stone, the Bloody Folds and the Gillies' Hill, all connected with the battle. A profitable hour may also be spent, before leaving Stirling, in visiting the ruins of

Cambuskenneth Abbey, near the town; and, if time allows, also

Doune Castle, a very fine old remain, not far from the Bridge of Allan. It was among and around this scenery that Sir Walter Scott spent many of his early days, forming his taste for the historical and romantic.

There are also several buildings in Stirling proper, worthy of visit and notice by those who tarry yet longer; among others the Grey Friars' Church, near the Castle, built by James IV.; Argyle's Lodging; Mar's Work, etc.; but these are all secondary in positive importance, to those who have but a limited time for stay.

The run from Stirling to Edinburgh may be made in either of two ways: by rail, requiring a couple of hours, or by boat, occupying about three, and passing down the River Forth to the Firth, and landing at Leith (port of Edinburgh), with excellent views of the Firth and its islands, Inch Keith, etc., and of the coast, the fishing-town of Newhaven (scene of Charles Reade's "Christie Johnstone"), etc. In fine weather, the latter is by far preferable. From Leith, if proceeding by boat, two miles by carriage to Edinburgh.

GLASGOW TO EDINBURGH—THE LONGER ROUTE, BY OBAN AND INVERNESS.

Those who are pursuing any other than the briefest route marked out in the present volume, may profitably proceed from Glasgow to Edinburgh by a line consuming three to four days or even longer in the transit, instead of one or two. For this, the following conveys all necessary general information:

Take steamer at Glasgow, down the Clyde, by Greenock, down the Firth of Clyde, between the island of Bute and the main-land; then through the Kyles of Bute into Loch Fine and up Loch Fine to Loch Gilp (its northwestern extremity) and to Lochgilphead, the termination of first steamer's route. From Lochgilphead, by boat on the Crinan Canal (towed) across the isthmus (neck of the Mull of Cantire) to Crinan, at the end of the canal, on the eastern side of Jura Sound. At Crinan, steamboat again across Jura Sound northwestward, through the archipelago of islands formed by Luing, Scanna, Sera, etc., to

Oban, on the west shore of the main, opposite the island of Mull. Much of the scenery through all this route is charming, blending the marine and the mountainous as possibly they are blended in no other spot on the globe.

From Oban, which is nothing except from its surroundings, an excursion of one day should be made, by steamer, across the Sound, below and around the south coast of Mull, to

Iona (or Icolmkill), a beautiful little island lying a little northwest of the extreme southwest point of Mull, displaying some of the most lovely of the rugged coast-characteristics of the Western Islands, and

FINGAL'S CAVE (*Staffa*), a basaltic columned natural curiosity, of giant size, jutting into the sea and presenting many of the characteristics of the

Giant's Causeway (Ireland), but with peculiar features of overhanging roofs and arched caves, rendering it perhaps even more interesting than its rival. The return from Staffa and Iona will be made to Oban.

From Oban, those who have no longer time at command, can take the Scottish Grand Junction Railway, running directly east across the head of Loch Awe (the Campbell country) to Crianlarich, a few miles north of the head of Loch Lomond. Thence either by carriage or by rail to the head of Loch Lomond, and down it by steamer to Inversnaid, where the previously-marked-out route from Glasgow will be taken, leading by Loch Katrine, the Trossachs, Stirling, etc., to Edinburgh.

But those who can spare yet a day or two in addition, should take, at Oban, the steamer up Loch Linnhe, Loch Lochy, Loch Ness, etc., and the grand Caledonian Canal forming a connection between them, something over one hundred miles, through the most magnificent of Scottish lake and mountain scenery, including Ben Nevis, the Grampians, etc., with one of the noblest works of modern engineering (in the canal itself), to

INVERNESS, a handsome and thriving town, supplying the metropolis to that portion of North Britain, lying at the head of Murray Firth, on the eastern coast of Scotland, some three-fourths of its whole length northward.

From Inverness the return may be made by canal; but more variety is found by taking coach from that place, southward through the whole of the Highlands, over splendid roads and through and among the mountains that have been passed on going up, skirting some of the finest of the Perthshire scenery, to the head of Loch Lomond, where boat may be taken to Inversnaid, and the route pursued by Loch Katrine, the Trossachs, Stirling, etc., as before indicated. It is not too much to say that while either of the previous routes affords glimpses of some of the very best of Scottish scenery, those who would know Scotland even moderately well should endeavor to afford time and means for making the whole of the last.

AT AND ABOUT EDINBURGH.

Edinburgh, the capital city of Scotland, lying some two miles from the south side of the Firth of Forth (at Leith), will be found at once one of the most beautiful towns in Europe in location and buildings, and one of the most interesting in the historical, romantic and poetical associations with which it is studded. It has a population ranging between 150,000 and 175,000; is divided into two parts, the Old and New Town, by a deep ravine or gulch, once a deformity, but now spanned by beautiful bridges and overhung by charming gardens (the "Prince's Street"). It has three points of principal interest, all elevations, and lying nearly equidistant from each other, in a triangle: the first being the Calton Hill, the second Arthur's Seat, and the third the Castle; while in passing through and looking down a single street in the Old Town (the High Street, changing into the Canongate), and a single one in the New

Town (Prince's Street), the difference between modernism and antiquity will be wonderfully well shown.

The at-all-hurried traveller should " do " Edinburgh by cab—an open one if the weather is fine, and a close one in the opposite event; the driver, here as elsewhere in Europe (*not* always in America), being one of the most useful of guides.

Calton Hill may well be first visited, with its Nelson, National, and other monuments, Observatory, fine views over the Firth of Forth, etc.; and on the way down from it will be passed the

Burns Monument, a beautiful structure, pillared and Grecian, with winged griffins supporting an hour-glass, and a bust of the poet;

The Bridewell and Debtors' Prison, very handsome embattled buildings—too handsome for their use. It is worthy of particular note that on the spot where the prison now stands, stood the old " Kirk of Field," in which Darnley, Queen Mary's husband, was blown up and killed in 1567. Passing down the North Back of the Canongate, the visitor will be in a moment at the

PALACE OF HOLYROOD, a queer but handsome old French-looking chateau, with pointed pepper-box turrets, by far the most interesting building in Scotland, and unexcelled by any in Europe.

This Palace (or " Holyrood House," as it is oftener called) is said to have been founded by David the First, the Crusader (who figures in Scott's " Talisman "), about 1130 or 1140; and it has ever since held a prominent place in Scottish history, being generally the residence of the royal family while there was one to reign, and especially sacred to the fortunes and misfortunes of Mary Stuart.

The gateway of Holyrood is handsome, and noteworthy from its still bearing the arms of Queen Mary. Opposite to it is a very handsome fountain, erected by the late Prince Consort (Prince Albert); and across the Court-yard is an humble building, much observed, said to have been Queen Mary's Bath.

Within there are state apartments for the present royal family when visiting Holyrood, but they are of no consequence after (or before) seeing the corresponding apartments at Windsor Castle. The rooms especially commanding attention are

The Picture Gallery, a very long low-ceilinged chamber, filled with royal portraits (ugly enough, most of them) of all ages, but showing a much greater attraction in having once been the great Hall of Holyrood, and the spot where Charles Edward Stuart, the Pretender, when holding Edinburgh in 1745, held the "Hunters' Balls," one of which is made so notable in the pages of "Waverley." Among the portraits best worth observing here, however, are those of Robert Bruce (1306); David the First (1124); James the Fourth (killed at Flodden Field, 1513); James the Fifth (the "Fitz-James" of the "Lady of the Lake," and father of Queen Mary); Charles the First; Duncan (murdered by Shakspeare's Macbeth); Macbeth himself; and Malcolm (Malcolm Canmore) who succeeded the kingly murderer.

Lord Darnley's Rooms come next in order of showing, with pictures and tapestry; then

The Staircase is seen—that narrow staircase up which the assassins crept to murder David Rizzio. It is on the floor above that the two most interesting rooms in Holyrood are to be found:

Queen Mary's Audience-Room, where that unfortunate queen gave her audiences and was lectured by John Knox. On the magnificent canopied bed, with its rotting velvet, still standing here, Charles the First slept while at Holyrood; the Pretender, in 1745, and the Duke of Cumberland after Culloden. The next room is still more interesting and mournful—

Queen Mary's Chamber, where she slept; the room panelled in ceiling and with tapestried walls; and the bed still standing as she left it, rotting, now, canopy and covering; while several other remembrances of her—table, work-box with work, etc.—fill up the room, one of the most sadly attractive on earth. Close adjoining is

The Supper Room, where Rizzio was stabbed while clinging to the very skirts of the Queen; and just beyond is

The Ineffaceable Blood, the spot at the stair-head where Rizzio was dragged to die, and where a large dull red stain appears, which those who have " faith " enough may believe has lingered, spite of fading and scrubbing, for three hundred years! Adjoining Holyrood House are the ruins of

Holyrood Abbey, of which the roofless walls remain, with very handsome Gothic gateway and windows, old tombs in the pavement, and recollections of the altar where Queen Mary was married to Darnley.

Away from Holyrood the drive should be resumed, up the "Queen's Drive" and around

Arthur's Seat, the high hill overlooking Edinburgh, with a collar or ruff of rocks under the brow, called Salisbury Crags. Some fine views are caught in skirting the hill; and one of the noblest in Europe is attained on leaving the carriage and climbing to the rocky top, whence Edinburgh, the Lothians, the distant Highlands, the Frith, etc., are all spread before the eye. Coming round the hill toward the town, excellent views are caught of

Jeanie Deans's Cottage, the *Wall of Dumbiedikes*, and *Muschat's Cairn* (near Salisbury Crags), all immortalized in Scott's "Heart of Mid-Lothian."

Many interesting objects present themselves in driving from the foot of Arthur's Seat, up the Canongate, the High Street, the Lawn Market and Castle Hill, to the Castle. The very tall old houses (some of them twelve stories!); the narrow alleys, or "Wynds"; some of the churches (among others the Tron Church, in which may be seen the altar at which the real and actual Annie Laurie was married)—Dr. Guthrie's, St. Giles (with its splendid spire), the Assembly Hall, etc.); the old

House of John Knox; Argyle's Balcony; the Tolbooth (prison); the old Parliament House; and many other objects of interest stud the drive, until

EDINBURGH CASTLE is reached, rock-throned, commanding and picturesque, with a narrow and winding entrance, odd old chambers, the

Birth-Room, where Queen Mary bore James VI.; the

IN SCOTLAND. 115

Regalia-Room, where the regalia of Scotland is preserved and shown (by order obtained at the Council Chambers, High Street, every day between 12 and 3), with an antiquity dating back beyond record, while it has figured in nearly every phase and period of Scottish history. Principal among the incidents connected with it, meanwhile, will be remembered its capture from the English by the Earl of Moray (by escalade of the rock, as Quebec was taken by Wolfe) in 1313,—and its long defence for Queen Mary by Kircaldy of Grange, in 1573. Among the notable curiosities connected with the Castle, is

Mons Meg, an immense old cannon (till the days of our late war), founded in France, known to have been used at the siege of Norham Castle in 1514, and burst in firing a salute to James Duke of York (James II.) in 1682—perhaps as a warning of the blow-up that was coming to *him!*

Among the other objects which should certainly be seen at Edinburgh, is the

Scott Monument, on Prince's Street, a Gothic structure of more than two hundred feet in height, with a magnificent colossal statue of Sir Walter, by Steel, shrined within, many emblematic figures, an inscription by Jeffrey, and altogether one of the finest monumental works of the age.

George Heriot's Hospital (made memorable by Scott, in the "Fortunes of Nigel"); Scott's old residence; the Greyfriars' Church and Churchyard; the Antiquarian Museum; George's Square; Bruntsfield Links (meadows); the Edinburgh Cemetery; Leith, with its magnificent Granton Pier, and Leith

Walk leading down to it—these, and fifty other objects of interest, present themselves to longer tarriers in the fine old town, though hasty visitors will scarcely find time for them.

An evening may generally be spent very pleasantly at the Theatre Royal, which supplies the leading spectacular entertainment of the town; and Edinburgh is somewhat noted for its literary reunions and entertainments.

One excursion should certainly be made, on a Wednesday or a Saturday if possible, either by cab, or by the Peebles railway, to

Rosslyn, *Hawthornden*, and *Dalkeith Palace* (seat of the Duke of Buccleugh). Rosslyn Chapel, without and within, is a marvel of laborious beauty, besides showing an antiquity dating back to 1446. Some of the clustered and spiral columns in the interior are held to be matchless, especially the "Prentice's Pillar," of which the guide will very readily tell a tough legend. The ruins of Rosslyn Castle stand by the Esk side, and are very picturesque—believed to date back to 1100 or 1200, and certainly the old family seat of the St. Clairs, Earls of Caithness and Orkney.

Hawthornden is a fine old mansion, once the residence of the poet Drummond ("Drummond of Hawthornden"), with subterranean caverns beneath, exciting much interest.

Dalkeith Palace is a large square structure, surrounded with an extensive park, with great antiquity and an intimate connection with the fortunes of the Grahams and the Douglases, from the latter of whom it came to the family of Buccleugh. Anne, Duchess of Buccleugh and Monmouth, lived here after the execution of her husband for the "Monmouth Rebellion;" and long before, Froissart, the French chronicler, is said to have here visited the Earl of Douglas.

Other pleasant excursions may be made, if time allows, to Newbattle Abbey, Dalhousie Castle, Craigmillar Castle (ruins once occupied by James V. and Queen Mary), etc.; and yet a little additional time, will allow of taking the Edinburgh and Berwick railway, to Melrose station, whence may be visited

Abbotsford, on Tweed-side, the splendid baronial residence of Sir Walter Scott, with many interesting memorials remaining of that great poet and romancer. For this, carriage should be taken at the station, for the drive of three miles and return. Very near the station lies

Melrose Abbey, founded by David I., in the twelfth century, and considered one of the finest Gothic remains in Europe, while it is full of reminders of the numbers of the Scottish Kings, and the heart of Robert Bruce, buried here, as well as doubly immortalized by Scott in his exquisite

"If thou wouldst view fair Melrose aright,
 Visit it by the pale moonlight," etc.

Some three or four miles in the opposite direction lies

Dryburgh Abbey, only less beautiful as a ruin, and containing the tombs of Scott, his wife and eldest son, besides kingly memorials. Thence to Berwick and by Great Northern road to London.

X.

SHORT TRIPS IN ENGLAND.

The points of interest presented, in England, are so many and varied that only a few of them, though the most interesting, can be culled by the short-trip traveller, who yet wishes to see other countries and does not go beyond the extreme four months for all. The points of approach, too, will necessarily be varied, as before indicated, in trips of different length between the two extremes of one-and-three-quarters and four; and it is again necessary to refer to the second paper in the present volume, "Time of Trips," for the order in which it will be most convenient to visit them, as one or the other arrangement is adopted.

The shortest of the short trips contemplated gives us only, in England,

LIVERPOOL AND CHESTER, TO LONDON.

Liverpool, lying in South Lancashire, on the north side of the river Mersey, is the largest seaport on the globe, the trade of a whole world literally concentrating here; and it is as a seaport, with its magnificent docks and the variety of shipping passing in and out from them, that its predominating interest is to be found.

The city itself is large, populous, and many portions of it (especially in the suburbs) notably handsome. There are few public buildings worthy of note, however. St. George's Hall, standing at the apex of the hill on which the town rises from the Mersey, is one of the noblest buildings in Great Britain, and worthy of close attention, without and within. After this, the new Exchange, the Assize Courts, the Town Hall and Custom-House, are the most notable; though to commercial visitors the heavy and ponderous mercantile buildings on the lower streets near the river may be quite as interesting. There are a few monuments worth notice—especially the recently-erected equestrian statue of the Prince Consort, in front of St. George's Hall; that of Nelson, by the Exchange; that of George III., at London Road, etc. The principal cemetery is St. James's, very tasteful and with a handsome statue of Mr. Huskisson, the great commercial founder. But far beyond any mere buildings, at Liverpool, in interest, are the famous

Liverpool Docks, the most costly and extensive in the world, some six miles in extent, on the north or city side of the Mersey, and constructed at a cost of £17,000,000 to £20,000,000—equal to $85,000,000 to $100,000,000. They are, commencing at the west or seaward end of the line, the Canada, Huskisson, Sandon (graving docks), Bramley-Moor, Nelson, Prince's (at the centre of the city), St. George's, Salthouse, Queen's, King's and Brunswick; while across the river, at Birkenhead, there are some (including Laird's building-docks) of quite equal interest and magnificence.

The Sandon Docks are immense basins, like those in the Navy Yards at Brooklyn and Charlestown, arranged for the floating in of vessels for repair, closing of gates, and pumping out until the hulls are left dry for the workmen. The others, or commercial docks, are rendered necessary by the immense height and depth to which the tides rise and fall (eighteen to thirty feet, against our New York five to eight); and they act upon the exact reverse of the Sandon principle—upon exactly the same principle, in fact, as that of "locking" on our great canals.

These great commercial docks, constructed of Scotch granite and iron, are, indeed, purely and simply immense canal locks, with swing-gates, into which vessels are taken at high tide and the gates closed so as to retain the water within and keep them afloat and at the proper height for convenient receiving and discharging. The machinery for moving the gates is only less massive than the docks, partly hand and partly hydraulic power. Except at periods when repairs may be demanded, the water in the docks seems never to be allowed to run down; and to secure this end all entrances and departures of vessels are made somewhere within about two hours of high tide, the gates never being allowed to open otherwise than during that limited space at and near high water.

It is at and around the Liverpool docks, too, that the best idea can be formed of the immense extent of the commerce of the port, from the vessels of all nations lying in dock—of the paltriness of English river-boats, the meanness of English ferry-systems, etc., while in going to and from them some idea may be formed, along miles of "gin and spirit stores," how England guzzles, even worse, if possible, than America.

The Liverpool cab-system is very like that of London—cheap and excellent. With the use of these vehicles the sight-seeing may be quickly and cheaply dispatched; from the docks to the splendid railway-stations, there are really few public buildings worth internal view.

There are some highly interesting rides, a few miles into the suburbs, to be enjoyed by those who have abundance of time; but these are scarcely to be taken by the short-trip traveller, who can find their equivalent elsewhere and with less delay. There are now two excellent theatres, the Prince of Wales's and Royal Alexandra, at either of which an evening may be well spent, especially as almost always during summer they are occupied by London companies turning the metropolitan vacation to profit.

There is one excursion, from Liverpool, that must be made, even by the most hurried—that by rail, with half an hour's ride, across the beautiful rural scenery of Cheshire (southward of the Mersey) to

CHESTER, on the little river Dee, one of the oldest cities in England, and on some accounts among the most interesting. It has figured in history from and before the time of the Romans, some of whose mosaic pavements are yet existing; while the walls surrounding the town are known to be so old as to have been *repaired and extended* in A. D. 73! The fine Welsh mountains are in full view from it, and they supply a reminder that it was the fortified town so long held by the De Lacys, " Constables of Chester," who with its aid beat back the wild Welsh barbarians making incursions across the marches.

The Old Walls are first among the curiosities of Chester—with the walks they supply on the broad top and the towers that stud them at various points. The most interesting of these latter is King Charles's or the Phœnix Tower, on the top of which Charles the First stood to see his last army defeated on Rowton Moor. In this tower there is a small but very interesting museum of antiquities, including the Castellan.

The Cathedral comes next—a fine old Gothic structure of 700 or 800 years in age. It is interesting, throughout—the great Chapel, the Crypt and Chapter-house; and there is an especial interest in the latter, in two flags hung over the doors, carried by the Cheshire Regiment (22d) up Bunker Hill in our Revolution, and by Wolfe at the taking of Quebec.

The Old Houses of Chester follow close after the Cathedral in interest. Their arcaded first-stories give the streets a strange appearance, apart from the upper stories hanging out beyond the lower; and in two of them—known as the Old Derby Palace and God's Providence House—are to be found some of the finest timber-and-plaster work in Europe. There is an old Roman Bath on Bridge Street, well worth attention; and as much may be said of the four old Gates (arched gateways), giving admission within the walls. The Castle is better worth visiting on account of the old one which stood on its site, than for any historical interest that itself possesses. If time allows, a visit should be paid to

Eaton Hall, in the immediate neighborhood, the splendid seat of the Marquis of Westminster (the richest nobleman in England), and one of the handsomest residences in the kingdom.

For a day, or half-a-day, at Chester, a cab should be taken (easily found near the railway station); and the local guide-book should be bought (cost one shilling) there as elsewhere—more for after reading than use on the spot, where the driver-guide is usually worth twenty books.

The run from Chester to London may be made with or without returning to Liverpool. From Liverpool, the direct line of the London and Northwestern road is taken, across Cheshire, Staffordshire, Warwickshire, etc., and by Crewe, Stafford and Rugby; and from Chester a branch of the same road may be taken, joining the main line within a few miles, at Crewe (the great railway-repair-shop of England),—or the Shrewsbury and Hereford road may be taken so far as Shrewsbury, with a cross-cut thence to the main line at Stafford.

AT AND ABOUT LONDON.

LONDON is, to Americans, the most interesting of all the great cities of the Old World, from the triple fact that it is the largest city of the civilized globe —that in it, alone, of the capitals of Europe, the language is the same as our own, so that signs, directions, inscriptions, etc., can all be understood by the least-learned visitor—and that, as mainly descended from the same people inhabiting it, the historical memorials involved are to some extent our joint property. The same fact, in some degree, exists with regard to everything in England; but there is probably no other point, except possibly the neighborhood of Shakspeare's birth-place, where it asserts itself so strongly as at and around the great capital.

Scarcely any traveller but is advised that London lies on the Thames, at some fifty miles from the mouth of that river, and that it was a city when the Romans ruled in Britain; but some may need to be reminded that it occupies both sides of that river, nearly in equal proportions—the northern section being comprised in the County of Middlesex, and the southern in that of Surrey; and that it has as many divisions as Philadelphia (formerly) or Boston, under the different names of The City, Westminster, Marylebone, Finsbury, Lambeth, Tower Hamlets, Chelsea and Southwark. It may be also necessary to give another reminder—that the population of this immense human hive is now between 3,000,000 and 4,000,000; and that the city and suburbs (comprised within the above designations) cover a space of about twelve miles by ten, or one hundred and twenty square miles, so that a city of the size of New York could be cut away from one side of it without leaving any greater proportional mark than would be the cutting away of Yorkville and Harlem from the American commercial metropolis.

Of course no attempt at description could be here either necessary or possible : all that can be supplied for the benefit of the unaccustomed traveller, is á statement of the objects best worth visiting, and directions for reaching them most conveniently.

The cab-system of London (though the grumbling John Bulls are always faulting it) is the best in the world, or only rivalled by that of Paris. Hansom cabs (two-wheelers) and four-wheel cabs are to be found everywhere. Their fares vary from one shilling sterling to two and three shillings, for either one or two persons, according to distance; and they can be employed for two shillings per hour. Carriages, for larger parties, or those who wish to ride more luxuriously, can be obtained for about one-third what the same vehicles cost in New York: as, for instance, during the height of the season of 1867, three persons hired a faultlessly-appointed open carriage-and-four, with driver in full livery, from a fashionable coach-office, for the round of the Parks, involving some three hours, for ten shillings sterling, equivalent to $2.43 cents (gold) with a few pennies additional as the driver's fee !

But to return to the cabs. They are the *legs of London*, so to speak; and the hurried traveller should use them freely, thus not only saving time and fatigue, but having a guide always at hand in the driver. With their aid, the places named may be visited with great rapidity and yet with pleasure and satisfaction. A good local guide-book, with map (Routledge's can be bought for one shilling), will also be found convenient, though more for future reference than use on the spot—as may be said of all local guide-books.

Westminster Abbey is probably the first object of interest in London, from the number of great dead lying within its walls. It can be comfortably "done" in one day—the first half devoted to Poets' Corner, and the other "free" parts of the Abbey, where stands the long array of tombs and tablets to the British poets, artists and worthies, from Shakspeare's time to the present, with a few noble nobodies intermixed; and the latter half to an hour of listening to the very fine organ and choral service, with a ramble, at an expenditure of sixpence to the guides, through the royal chapels and the tombs of the Kings. The objects of most marked interest in the Abbey are the noble building itself, with its wonderful aisles, arches and forests of noble columns; the tombs of Shakspeare, Ben Jonson, Dryden and the other poets, in Poets' Corner; the splendid architecture of Henry the Seventh's Chapel, stalls and banners of the Knights of the Bath, there, and magnificent tombs of the founder, of Queen Elizabeth, Mary Queen of Scots, etc.; the golden-mosaicked old altar-tomb of Edward the Confessor, in the Chapel of the same name, with the tombs of Edward the First, Henry the Fifth and other warrior-kings, the weapons carried by some of them, and the coronation-chairs in which every sovereign of England since William the Conqueror has been crowned, with the old Scottish Scone-stone (coronation-stone) set in the bottom of one of them. The tombs of Mrs. Nightingale, Fox, Pitt, the Duke of Argyle, and hundreds of long-departed kings and nobles, will also command attention, so far as time may admit, from various causes certain to suggest themselves through the eyes, the memory, and the inevitable pamphlet-guide which every visitor must purchase at an outlay of sixpence.

The Houses of Parliament (Westminster Palace) may well supply the next object of interest, the splendid structure towering immediately over the Abbey. The Chambers of the Lords and Commons should both be seen, with the Queen's Throne in the former, and the paintings and fine bas-reliefs in some of the other rooms of the building—to all which, if unguided, direction can easily be procured from the attendants and policemen on duty. If Parliament is in session, the use of a small *douceur* to attendants, or the influence of the Legation, will almost always secure admission to the Commons: to the Lords the access is more difficult, though even that can generally be managed in the same way. Before quitting the building, a look should be taken through Westminster Hall, now an immense empty space, but in which so many of the great criminal trials, from Charles the First and Strafford to Warren Hastings, have taken place. Half a day is quite sufficient for the Parliament Houses and Hall, except when a parliamentary session is to be attended.

The Tower of London is the next object of interest, if it does not take precedence of the last-mentioned. It can be reached either by cab or one of the small steamers on the Thames; and half-a-day will well suffice to visit it. It stands at the Thames side, near London Bridge; and visitors are admitted by tickets purchased at a ticket-office without, and accompanied through (as well as watched) by one of the Queen's yeomen (called "beef-eaters," originally *beaufetiers*), in the costume of the time of Henry the Eighth. The leading attractions in this wonderful cluster of fortifications are to be found in the Traitors' Gate, seen on entering, through which the accused used to be taken in from boats on the river; the window of the Bloody Tower (seen from without), just within which the two princes are said to have been smothered by order of Richard the Third; the Horse Armory (in the White Tower), in which effigies of half the dead sovereigns ride on horseback in full armor; Queen Elizabeth's Armory, in the same tower, where Sir Walter Raleigh was so long confined, and where the fatal axe and block are yet to be seen, by and on which fell so many royal and noble heads; the Jewel Tower, where the regalia of England, crown, sceptre, sword, etc., are shown in an iron cage; the Beauchamp Tower, where so many noble captives languished away their lives; the tremendous collection of ancient and modern arms and armor, etc. The Tower represents more than eight hundred years of English history, and not even London has a more powerful attraction to the intelligent traveller.

St. Paul's Church, the *Royal Exchange*, *Mansion House*, *Bank of England*, and *Guildhall*, may all be included within a single half-day's visit, by cab, with propriety. St. Paul's is simply the noblest and grandest church-pile on earth, except St. Peter's at Rome.

It is a wonderful sight, to stand within the dome and look up four hundred feet to the angels that really seem to be flying in the blue sky. It has some fine monuments, and in the Crypt below are the resting-places of both Wellington and Nelson, and the funeral-car of the former. Guildhall is mainly interesting for the sake of the civic banqueting-hall which gives it name, at the end of which stand the famous giants, Gog and Magog, of London history. The other three buildings named need only be admired from without, except the traveller has special reasons and privileges for entering.

The British Museum demands a full day, from even the most hurried. It is a noble building, containing the most wonderful and varied collection, from books to statues, medals, relics and objects of natural history, from all ages and all countries, ever gathered in any one place upon earth; and no word in addition, here, could increase the force of such a statement or add to the knowledge of the visitor, who will be wise, however, to pay earliest attention to the great Reading-Room, the Layard stones from Assyria, the letters and autographs of eminent persons, the collection of seals, British antiquities, etc., if losing everything else for their sake.

The Crystal Palace, at Sydenham, demands a day, and is reached by rail from Victoria Station. It rivals the British Museum in the wonderful variety of its collection; and yet nothing within the building can compare with the wonderful size and beauty of the erection of glass and iron itself—an exaggeration, eight or ten times the size, of our lost New

York Palace. The grounds are only second to the building in beauty; and scarcely a day occurs, in summer, that some musical festival is not given in the afternoon, enabling the visitor to combine two enjoyments.

Windsor Castle and Park are reached by rail, taking an open cab or fly from the Windsor Station, and a fair idea of them may be caught in half-a-day, rail included. The Castle is shown, whenever the Queen is not resident there, as she generally is not in summer. The Castle is exquisitely tasteful in location and grand grouping of towers; and the view from the Terrace is wondrously beautiful. The most notable rooms, within, are St. George's Chapel, where all the Knights of the Garter are installed, and most royal ceremonials take place; St. George's Hall, devoted to the festivities of the order; the Waterloo Chamber, with portraits connected with the great battle, etc. It is almost needless to say that the acme of art and luxury is reached in these regal apartments, and that nowhere else can such glimpses be caught of the state surrounding an English sovereign. The Castle overhangs the quite old town of Windsor (Windsor of the "Merry Wives"); the Home Park, in which Herne's Oak, of that play, stood until 1864, immediately adjoins it; and a drive of matchless beauty, three miles long and bordered with the noblest elms in England, leads away to the Great Park and the beautiful Lake, Virginia Water, which should be driven to, and the latter walked around, after leaving the Castle.

Hampton Court, splendid old palace and park

(Bushy Park), once belonging to Cardinal Wolsey, and then to Henry the Eighth, with fine old pictured-galleries, beautiful gardens, and the celebrated Labyrinth of Fair Rosamond in the wooded grounds;

Kew Palace and Gardens (Royal), where the art of landscape-gardening, in England, is literally exhausted and the Palm House contains the finest collection of tropical trees in Europe; and

Richmond Hill, with its celebrated "Star and Garter" Hotel, unrivalled in its view over the Thames, and where people from all Europe go to eat festive dinners,—

All these may be reached and hastily enjoyed in a cab-ride of half to three-quarters of a day, the three lying on the same route, along the Upper Thames, in passing over which, in addition, Twickenham, Brentford and other rural villages will be skirted and a very pleasant acquaintance made with English semi-rural suburban scenery.

The London Parks that specially demand attention are Hyde Park, the Green Park, St. James's and Regent's. Hyde Park should be taken in the afternoon, after the hour of adjournment of Parliament (5 to 6), and ridden through in an open carriage, to meet the "notables." The others will be driven round in due course, a pause being made at the Regent's, to see the Zoological Gardens, with their fine collection of well-kept animals; and in the circuit of the Parks, any intelligent driver will point out and afford good views of

Buckingham Palace (the Queen's town residence),

St. James's, Carlton House, Marlborough House (the Prince of Wales's residence), etc., and many of the most interesting of

The monuments, of which London has very many notable ones, the most prominent being the Duke of York's Column, in Waterloo Place; the equestrian statue of Charles I., at Charing Cross; the Havelock and other monuments in Trafalgar Square, the "London Monument" on Fish Street Hill; the equestrian statue of Cœur de Lion, before the Parliament Houses; etc., etc.

A spare hour or two may well be spent at one of the most interesting old churches in London—the Old Temple Church, with its gardens, on Fleet Street, the church with many monuments of the Knights Templars, and the Temple buildings, redolent of *law.* Acquaintance will be made, at the same time, with the far-famed Temple Bar, which changes Fleet Street to the Strand.

The Bridges of London, of which there are now no less than ten, all elegant and substantial structures, should receive an hour or two of daylight attention —as well as the railway travel passing over them, the odd aspects of the boats lying at the wharves, the miserable little steamers passing up and down the Thames, etc.; and an hour at night, standing on any one of them and admiring the lines of lights crossing the dusky river on the others, would be by no means wasted.

The Railway Stations, of which London has now several of the finest in the world (Charing Cross, Victoria, King's Cross, Euston, Bishopsgate, etc.), will naturally be observed in arrivals and departures; and the railway system, as contrasted with our own, may be studied in the same connection with interest and advantage.

The *National Gallery* (occupying the north of Trafalgar Square), and the *South Kensington Museum*, both supply interesting collections of pictures, which should be seen by art-lovers if time permits, though neither comes within the range of the first curiosities of London.

The *Thames Tunnel*, crossing beneath the river from the Middlesex to the Surrey side, is a well-enough thing to " do," for those who " wish to say that they have been there," and who do not mind going down into unpleasant and doleful places to be able to make that boast—as Tom Sheridan begrimed himself by going down into the coal-pit. It is a costly humbug and failure, however.

The *Underground Railways* (" Metropolitan ") of London are features, and at least one ride should be taken on them by the visitor. To the thinking of the writer, one ride will be quite enough for each.

Greenwich Hospital and *Chelsea Hospital*, the former the naval asylum of Great Britain, and the latter the military, are interesting places to visit, to those who may happen to have a little more time than otherwise demanded, in and about London. Many mementoes of British heroes may be found in both (especially in Greenwich, where Nelson figures largely); and the old pensioners are themselves a study. Greenwich may be reached by rail, from Charing Cross, but even better by one of the boats plying down the Thames; while Chelsea lies at the southwest end of the city itself, and is within cab-distance.

Kensal Green is the only cemetery at or near London, presenting any peculiar attractions; and in its case they are found in the burial there of Thomas Hood, Sydney Smith, W. M. Thackeray, Allan Cunningham, the children of Sir Walter Scott, etc.

Spurgeon's Tabernacle, at the Elephant-and-Castle, is one of the "lions" of London, and may be reached on Sundays, in half-an-hour's ride by cab or omnibus, from any of the great city centres.

London Theatres are very numerous, and celebrated for the splendor of their entertainments, though scarcely one of them but is dark, dingy and uncomfortable to those familiar with the handsome entrances and fine lights of American houses. Two or three evenings' patronage of them must of course be governed by the current performances; but on the average the wisest selections will probably include the Haymarket, Adelphi or Olympic, and Princess's, at any one of which the time spent is not likely to be thrown away, especially with the opportunities which performances supply for studying the playgoing habits and manners of the Londoners.

Some of the most charming peeps into the ruralities of England, attainable anywhere, can be caught in brief rides out of London, by cab or rail—into Essex, Kent, Surrey, etc.; and half-a-day spent in running down to Waltham-Cross, in Essex, and Broxbourne and the Rye-House, a few miles beyond, will not only show the very fine old Cross, the ruins of the Abbey, and the scene of the "Rye-House Plot," but some of the very loveliest quiet rural scenery on earth, and many glimpses at the midland-English modes of farming, farm-laborers, agricultural utensils, etc.

It is not to be supposed, either, that nearly all the objects of interest of the great metropolis have been alluded to, or that every short-trip traveller can pay attention to all mentioned. But, taking them in the order of importance here observed, and using the remarkable facilities at hand for reaching them—certain it is that in the six to eight days allowed in either of the tours contemplated, a very respectable knowledge of the British capital may be obtained by the intelligent and quick-witted tourist, however unused to the details of travel.

TO AND AT THE CUMBERLAND LAKES.

The Windermere Lakes, or Cumberland Lakes, as they are oftener called, lie nearly on the extreme northwest of England, in the two counties of Cumberland and Westmoreland. The Lakes are several in number, within a limited space, ranging from Windermere, Ulswater, Wastwater, etc., of some miles each in length, to mere little ponds or "tarns," like Grasmere and Thirlmere, and yet smaller, like Loughrigg Tarn, Elter Water, etc. They lie embosomed among mountains of singular beauty, with Skiddaw, Helvellyn and Scawfell among the highest, and nearly of the altitude of our Cattskill highest peaks; and though it is not to be denied that, even more than those of Killarney, they look petty and bandbox-y to an American full of memories of Superior and Erie, or even of Winnepesaukie and Lake George, so that the droll Illinoian who was about to drink out of one of them hesitated for fear that he should drain it dry,—yet there are few spots on the earth, lovelier or more worthy of a little time spent in catching hurried glimpses.

There are two modes in which the Lakes are likely to be reached by American tourists, the point of approach in both instances being the village of Windermere, in Cumberland, and the first object Lake Windermere, by far the largest of the whole cluster.

Of these approaches, one is from Liverpool, by the London and Northwestern Railway, to Oxenholme, on the Lancaster and Carlisle branch of that road, and then by the Kendal and Windermere spur of the same road to Windermere. This route will be pursued, whether the visit is paid as merely an excursion from Liverpool, to return,—or the temporary break is made at Oxenholme from the main line from Liverpool to Carlisle and Edinburgh. The principal places passed through, thus running north, are Preston, Lancaster, Wigan and Kendal, all manufacturing in appearance; and the country passed through shows some of the loveliest rural scenery of the west of England, beginning soft and handsomely hedged in South Lancashire, roughening through North Lancashire, and becoming broken, hilly, and finally mountainous, a little after passing Lancaster and catching a view of Morecambe Bay, with Duddon Mouth and Sands, stretching away to the Irish Sea. The ride seems like a somewhat long and weary one, from Liverpool; but as the sun, in this latitude, at midsummer, seems never to go down and it is daylight till midnight, there is no fear of losing the appearance of the mountains as they finally rise on the sight.

The other ordinary route of reaching the Lakes is from the north, coming down from Edinburgh or Glasgow by Carlisle, making the change of trains at Oxenholme (which a facetious American lady spells: "Ho-hex-he-hen-haitch-ho-hel-hem-he"), as in going north, and the near approach being consequently made in the same manner.

WINDERMERE is a hamlet rather than a village, lying on the east side, nearly at the edge, and almost at the centre, lengthwise, of Lake Windermere, with the rival town of Bowness a few miles below. Once reached, it seems too pretty and rural, and too antique-looking (though really not very old) for the railway approach that has been made; and there and in the excursions from it which fill up the few hours that can be afforded by the hasty traveller, the most striking feature is found in the quiet grace of the rural scenery, the placid character of the waters, the beauty of the walled and hedged lanes, and the antique, peaceful loveliness of the whitewashed, thatched-roofed, lattice-windowed, ivy-grown and rose-climbed stone cottages.

The excursions from Windermere and Bowness, through the district, planned in Miss Martineau's entertaining "Guide to the Lakes" (which the traveller may well buy and bring away with him, but should avoid reading and thus becoming confused, while on the spot) — these excursions, echoed and enlarged by hotel placards and insisted upon by guides and drivers, are well-nigh numberless. But alas! human life is brief and hurried, and busy men cannot pass it all at Windermere.

In arranging these short trips, the shortest time allowed at and about Windermere, is one day; the longest, two; time for going and returning being otherwise allowed. With only one day of stay, what seems the most sensible plan is to be content with what the local excursion placards set down as "Excursion No. 1"—some twenty-two miles in extent, by carriage, and comfortably made during somewhat less than the long day of the latitude, with time for stop (and possibly dinner) at Grasmere.

On this excursion the very loveliest scenery of the district is passed, as follows: By the east side of Windermere Lake, in full view of it, past the little hamlet of Lowood, with the Dove's Nest in sight just beyond—a pleasant house in which Mrs. Hemans, the poetess, passed the last years of her life; the hills of Wansfell Pike showing finely to the right and ahead, and Wray Castle prominent to the left, on the opposite shore of the Lake; past Ambleside Water-Head; and then bearing to the left and westward, past Loughrigg Tarn and up the steep Red Bank, with splendid views up the craggy-peaked Vale of Langdale; over Red Bank, with a lovely view down over Grasmere Lake, Village and Valley, with Helvellyn and the other mountains behind; then down to

Grasmere Church, with opportunity to view that

church, said to have been commenced before the Conquest — the pew, font and monument of the poet Wordsworth within, and his grave and that of Hartley Coleridge without. Dinner, or at least a rest, at Grasmere; then round by Rydal Water and the Vale of Rydal, past

Rydal Mount, the old home of Wordsworth, and back through the handsome old village of Ambleside, past the residence of Miss Martineau, along the east side of the Lake again, back to Windermere.

The tourist who has but the one day at Windermere will yet find time, after returning from the ride already described, to walk through the grounds of the late Professor Wilson ("Christopher North"), remembered and loved about Windermere as few men can hope to be in any neighborhood,—and to make the slight ascent of Orrest Head, and thus catch one of the loveliest of all the views over the Lake and the old village. The return from Windermere, whether going north or south, will of course be made by the same route as the approach—taking the railway back to Oxenholme and there making the main-line connection.

With a second day at disposal, and the first spent as before advised, it will be policy to go down yet the same evening to Bowness, by boat or carriage, to be ready for the very different tour of the next morning, which has its proper commencement there.

The event of the second day will be a visit to Furness Abbey, one of the most interesting old ruins in the West, to make which the route will be to Newby Bridge (over the river Severn, at the extreme south end of Lake Windermere), — through scenery less wild than that of the previous day, and passing Burnside, Ferney Green and other pleasant rural hamlets before reaching the Bridge. From Newby Bridge, by carriage, eight miles to the pleasant little town of Ulverston; and from Ulverston either by rail or carriage, only half-a-dozen additional miles, to

Furness Abbey (originally "Furnesse," Norman French), said to have been founded in 1127, by King Stephen, and especially favored by that king and his queen, Maude, effigies of whose heads are to be seen near one of the western windows. The Abbots of Furness (Bernardins) are alleged to have ruled over something like a kingdom; and the massive character of the yet well-preserved ruins well attests the size, splendor and stability of the building in its days of religious occupancy. Some of the clustered columns, many of the fine Gothic windows and gateways yet remain, and the grounds (once embracing nearly seventy acres) have interesting remains of fish-ponds, granaries, and many of the other conveniences of the "lordly beggars" who once held it.

From Furness there is no occasion of returning to either Windermere or Bowness, to leave the Lake country. Returning to Ulverston, the rail may be taken for the main-line at Carnforth Station, whether for going north or south; and for going north alone, and with a fancy for much sea-view from carriage-windows, the rail may be taken at Furness, by the Furness and Whitehaven and Maryport and Carlisle roads, around the coast by Whitehaven, Maryport, etc., across to Carlisle on the Edinburgh or Glasgow route.

TO AND AT THE SHAKSPEARE NEIGHBORHOODS OF WARWICKSHIRE.

These favored and attractive districts lie nearly equidistant from Liverpool and London, and not more than three hours by rail from either. To reach them, from London, the London and Northwestern road should be taken to Rugby; then the branch line to Leamington; then carriage from Leamington to Stratford-on-Avon; then rail (or carriage) from Stratford to Warwick; then carriage (certainly) from Warwick to Kenilworth and Coventry; then rail from Coventry to Birmingham and the main-line for either a return to London or the routes northward to Sheffield, northwestward to Liverpool, or westward to Shrewsbury. Such a disposition of route and conveyance will give infinite variety and permit the favorable (even if hurried) seeing of one of the loveliest counties of England.

The larger proportion of Americans, however, who visit the Shakspeare neighborhoods at all, will be likely to do so on their way down from Liverpool to London; and it is from that point of view that the foregoing succession will be reversed and the principal points of interest hurriedly indicated of what is unquestionably one of the most fascinating and indispensable short routes on the globe.

The route by the London and Northwestern, from Liverpool to Birmingham, passes by Crewe and Stafford, as if on the way to London. Trains are changed at Stafford for Wolverhampton and Birmingham. The smooth scenery of Cheshire, changing to the rougher character of Staffordshire, affords infinite variety in landscape; and almost from the moment of entering Staffordshire the number of furnace-chimneys becomes so great that they stupefy wonder as well as excite it. In the neighborhood of Wolverhampton the heart of the iron-country is reached; and here the wilderness of chimneys, the pack of blazing and smoking furnaces, and the torn-up and mangled character of the ground, yet worse disfigured by the heaps of refuse ore, combine to produce an impression very little else than infernal. In the very midst of all this, embowered in extensive woods, on a hill, stand the noble ruins of Dudley Castle (burned some years since); and the view from the castle ruins at midnight, over mile upon mile of country apparently all belching flames, is said to be magnificent beyond description, and at the same time infernal without qualification.

Wolverhampton itself is chimneys, coal-smoke, iron-dust and grime—iron, and the manufacture of iron, everywhere. It offers no inducements for stoppage, to the ordinary traveller. Nor is there much of additional interest in the scenery, until reaching

BIRMINGHAM, the spot where iron, and brass, and all other metals are kept for sale, in a showy form of hardware, and the very name of which has been corrupted into "Brummagem" as a synonym for all that is plated, pinchbeck and bogus. It has very few attractions, as a town, outside of the shops and shop-windows, the Town Hall and Corn Exchange being really the only two handsome buildings. All the inhabitants ignore the sidewalks and walk in the middle of the street; and umbrellas are in demand, as it generally rains, whatever may be the state of the weather elsewhere.

The ride by rail is only a few miles, through lovely shaded Warwickshire scenery, from Birmingham to

COVENTRY, famous both in history and romance, and especially so in poetry; and rivalling if not surpassing even Chester in the beautiful antiquity of some of its buildings. The story of the Lady Godiva, said to have ridden naked on horseback through the town, many centuries ago, to induce her husband, Earl Leofric, to take the heavy taxes off from the inhabitants, has been for ages commemorated by processions embodying that alleged event; and both Leigh Hunt and Tennyson have embalmed the incident in poetry, that of the latter being most familiar to American readers.

The approach to Coventry by the railway is very beautiful. The "bridge" on which Tennyson describes himself to have been "hanging" (lounging) when he "watched the three tall spires" and devised the poem, is very near the railway station, over a mere gully; and from it the three spires, all looking nearly alike and very sharp, seem to be set almost in a triangle. All three of the churches are worth visiting, but especially

St. Michael's, by far the oldest, and interesting without and within, from the marks of extreme age exhibited; and

St. Mary's Hall, immediately adjoining, shows very finely the effect of many centuries on both wood and stone.

The Old Houses of Coventry, many of them of wood-and-plaster, the upper stories projecting over until they almost touch across the narrow and winding streets, are objects of great interest—among the finest in Europe; and everything about the old town is odd and picturesque, not forgetting its pretty girls.

Peeping Tom, one of the "lions" of Coventry, is a painted wooden figure of life-size, looking out of an open upper window not far from St. Michael's, in commemoration of the one villanous tailor who *would* look out to see Lady Godiva when she rode, and who was stricken blind for that meanness. The figure is said to be at least three or four hundred years old, and no one should leave Coventry without seeing it.

Some of the finest fruits and flowers in England are to be found at and about Coventry, and indeed all over Warwickshire, at midsummer.

A "fly" or carriage (open, if the weather is fine) should be taken at Coventry, for Kenilworth and Warwick, as no other mode of transit will show the lovely "Heart of Warwickshire" to such advantage. The road toward Kenilworth is wonderfully bordered and shaded with fine elms, passing through the property of Lord Leigh, fine farms and some charming very old cottages, clusters of cottages, and rural hamlets, until reaching

KENILWORTH CASTLE and village—the latter very quiet and antiquated-looking, with plentiful shade and cottages humble but picturesque; and the former one of the most interesting mediæval relics in England. It is said to have been founded by one of the Clintons, ancestors of the present Earls of Lincoln, in the time of Henry I. (about 1110), and was afterwards in the possession of Simon de Montfort, the great rebel Earl of Leicester, and of John of Gaunt. But it derives its chief celebrity from having been the property and residence of another Earl of Leicester, Robert Dudley, Queen Elizabeth's favorite of that name, and his having entertained the Virgin Queen there, with more than royal state—as commemorated in Sir Walter Scott's novel of "Kenilworth." Though entirely in ruins, the pile is still noble in both extent and marks of original architecture, some of the splendid foliated windows, the stairways and part of the arches of the banqueting-hall yet remaining,—while the all-covering ivy has made the desolation doubly beautiful; the gardens yet retain a wonderful variety of flowers, and the great lawn and tilt-yard can easily be traced by those who have any idea of the construction of ancient castles and their grounds.

Half-an-hour's ride from Kenilworth, still by carriage, an outer, and if desired an inner view, can be caught, by turning a little off from the road to the left, of

Guy's Cliff Mill, a very old stone structure standing beside the Avon, said to be as old as the Norman Conquest, and of

Guy's Cliff (*Castle*), celebrated as the residence, many centuries ago, of the famous and unfortunate champion, Guy of Warwick, whose cave in the solid rock, well also in the rock, bed hollowed from a log, and other relics, are still shown. No better opportunity can be found for surveying one of the country houses of the old nobility, than by going through Guy's Cliff, always open to visitors when the owner (Lord Charles Percy) is absent with his family. The Chapel (very old) and the caves in the rocks, once occupied by the monks, who founded the pile, may also be seen to advantage.

A few miles farther, still by carriage, and the end of the most beautiful of rides is reached, in

Warwick, a very old town, displaying many of the same characteristics as Coventry, with the bear-and-ragged-staff of the Warwick family conspicuous on the public houses, and the most prominent buildings are the very old one called "Leicester's Hospital," peculiarly interesting to Americans from the visit paid to it and charmingly described by Hawthorne, and the Church of St. Mary's with its many fine antique monuments.

Warwick Castle, standing on a rocky eminence overlooking the town and at the side of the Avon, is a massive pile of great beauty, yet in repair and resided in by the Earl of Warwick. The finest view, and one immortalized in many paintings, can be caught from the old bridge over the Avon, and it is one never to be forgotten. Access may be had to the Castle at certain hours (before 10 A. M., when the Earl is at home); and within may be seen the celebrated "Warwick Vase," splendid armor and relics in the Armory, etc.

At Warwick rail may be taken, for a very brief ride through lovely scenery, to

STRATFORD-ON-AVON, the home and burial-place of Shakspeare, and the pilgrimage of more of the worshippers of genius than possibly any other single spot on the globe. A quiet, lazy old town, with the Avon flowing gently through it, and the whole atmosphere seeming that of centuries ago. At Stratford, unlike other places, the first object of interest is found in a hotel,

The Red Horse, made famous to Americans by Washington Irving in his "Sketch Book," and almost as distinguished, now, as the old home of the poet. From the Red Horse it is but a few minutes, on foot, to

Shakspeare's Birth-Place, an humble old timber-and-plaster building, partially restored and well preserved, on Henley Street, so well known as to all its characteristics that nothing more need be said than that the birth-room is found on the second floor, front, with its window covered with inscriptions, like the walls; that there is a Shakspeare Museum attached, in the more modern part of the building; and that the house is courteously shown as well as carefully kept by Mrs. and Miss Ashwin, the latter deservedly complimented by Hawthorne in his "Old Home." The same walk may be easily extended to the

Church of the Holy Trinity, a handsome half-modern building standing amid fine elms at the Avon side, and within which Shakspeare's tomb and monument, and the tombs of his family, are shown in the chancel ; the record of his birth and death in a very old parchment-bound book, in the vestry ; the font in which he was baptized (if at all), in the nave, etc. The Grammar School, New Place, the bridges over the Avon, etc., should also be included in the walk, the whole not necessarily occupying more than two or three hours. One of the open carriages, or "flys," for which Stratford is not a little famous, may profitably be employed for a two or three miles ride across the edge of the lovely Vale of Evesham, coming round by

Anne Hathaway's Cottage, at the very old and tumble-down but attractive-looking little hamlet of Shottery, where the dramatist courted and married his wife, and where, apart from those associations, a charming antique cottage and many interesting relics are shown. The fly should be dismissed at Shottery, in fine weather, and the way made back to Stratford on foot, across the fields, by what has been known ever since his day as " Shakspeare's Courting-path."

Stratford should be left by carriage (fine weather again understood, and likely to be found in June, best month in England), for the twelve or fifteen miles to Leamington. The scenery is somewhat tame, but softly beautiful throughout. At three or four miles from Stratford will be skirted the grounds of

Charlecote Hall and Park, alleged to be the place of Shakspeare's early deer-stealing (in a different way from that at Shottery) and of his arraignment for the offence. The Park is magnificent, with its massive old oaks, fine sward, and herds of deer—

really among the finest belonging to less than royalty in the kingdom; and Charlecote Hall, imposing without, offers, within, to the few favored visitors (it is not commonly shown) even more of charm, in splendid rooms, fine pictures, many antiquities, and one set of ebony-and-ivory furniture, presented to the Earl of Leicester by Queen Elizabeth at Kenilworth, matchless in rarity and value.

Ten or a dozen miles beyond Charlecote, with a few pleasant little hamlets passed, presents the end of the brief but charming Warwickshire pilgrimage, in

Leamington, one of the Saratogas or Ballstons of England—handsomely situated on the little river Leam—clean and a little too dainty-looking, with fine grounds and walks and a weakness for "Parades" and "Villas." It is well worthy of an hour or two of stroll, and a little of the Spa-water should be drunk, to see if it is any worse than that of the American Spas, after which

Rail for the brief ride from Leamington to Rugby, one of the three great stations on the Liverpool and London road, where Dickens's "Mugby Junction" may be seen by peeping into the refreshment-rooms, and whence the way will be direct to the British capital if the tourist wishes to go southward.

MANCHESTER AND SHEFFIELD.

Neither of these towns, the one the head of cotton-manufacturing in Great Britain, and the other supplying the same place to steel and cutlery-work of perhaps the whole world—is reckoned as coming within the short-trips previously arranged. But those who may have even a day more of time on their hands at Liverpool, than originally contemplated, or who may choose to neglect something else for them, can see both, hurriedly, within that space.

MANCHESTER lies only about thirty miles east of Liverpool, and can be reached in an hour, by rail. It lies on the Irwell, a small branch of the Mersey, has nearly half-a-million of inhabitants (second or third in the kingdom); has some handsome bridges connecting it with Salford (opposite); the Cathedral Church of St. Mary's, old and with fine monuments; the Exchange, Town-Hall, etc., all worthy of notice; but of course the prime motive of visit is to see

The Cotton-Mills, wonderful in their number and extent, and the perfection of their machinery, and supplying more than half the cotton-goods used in the world. Permission to go through them is attainable through introduction to any of the managers, easily obtained at Liverpool by those who have any commercial, shipping or personal acquaintance there.

SHEFFIELD lies some fifty miles beyond Manchester, still eastward, and is reached by the M. and S. Railway from the latter place, in one-and-a-half hours. It has not much more than one-quarter the size and population of Manchester; the prevailing furnace-smoke makes it dingy and dusky; and there are few public buildings of prominence. The attraction nearly all lies in the immense

Steel and Cutlery Manufactories, models of their class and unequalled in size and costly machinery.

Admission liable to the same conditions before noted with reference to Manchester.

PROMINENT ENGLISH WATERING-PLACES.

The English watering-places are very numerous, and the short-trip tourist may manage to visit one or more of them, marine and inland. A brief note of several of the most prominent will be made, with directions for reaching, as off-shoots from other routes, and hints of their several characteristics.

CHELTENHAM, the most fashionable of the Spa-Springs, lies about thirty miles due south from Birmingham and may be most conveniently reached by rail from thence, except by those who are going farther south to Bristol or Plymouth, who will necessarily pass through it. Or, it may be taken on the way from Liverpool to London, by Birmingham; from Cheltenham to Bristol, and thence by Great Western Railway direct to London. Or from Cheltenham across to

OXFORD, the great seat of learning, with its wilderness of Colleges and fine grounds, and thence to London.

The attractions of Cheltenham are very like those of Saratoga, though with greater age and finish. Beautiful grounds and parades, costly hotels and innumerable boarding-houses, spring-houses and all the accompaniments of pleasure-seeking, make it singularly-pleasant and fashionably-popular.

BATH, formerly the superior of Cheltenham in Spa-visiting, but now only its rival, is a handsome old town lying on the Avon, ten miles from Bristol (on the G. W. Railway towards London); and has all the characteristics spoken of with reference to Cheltenham, with yet more pretentious buildings, some ridiculously-pleasant memories of the Prince Regent, Beau Nash, and other prominent fops, and a fine old Abbey Church, with monuments.

LEAMINGTON, the third of the Spas in importance, has already been spoken of and the mode of approach indicated, in the just-closed account of the Shakspeare neighborhoods of Warwickshire.

Of the sea-shore watering-places the most fashionable, at the present writing, is

SCARBOROUGH, on the northeast coast, about forty miles northeast from York, and reached by rail from that city. It has a fine bold coast, splendid bathing, fine hotels, and now attracts much of the best society. Next to it (formerly far before it), comes

BRIGHTON, for many years the sea-bathing-place *par excellence*, of the British Islands. It lies on the British Channel, about forty miles east from Southampton, or from the eastern point of the Isle of Wight —about fifty miles from London, whence it is reached in two hours by the London, Brighton and South-Coast Railway. It has a regular population of some 80,000, very often increased by visitors, in September and October, to 100,000. It has many fine buildings—among others the Royal Pavilion, built by George IV. when Prince Regent; and the Marine Wall, Chain Pier and promenade are all worthy of special notice, while probably at no place in Great Britain can the mixed-society and customs of a watering place be better observed. Steamer can be taken from Brighton to Dieppe (France) if desirable.

THE ISLE OF WIGHT and the coasts opposite form a collective summer resort for many thousands; while the Queen's residence on the island (Osborne House), the abode there of many other distinguished people, Carisbrooke Castle (in which Charles I. was confined), and the neighborhood of the Portsmouth and Gosport great navy-yards and naval depots—make this section a very interesting one to those possessed of more spare time than the supposed short-trip tourist. (Southampton, Portsmouth, the Isle of Wight, etc., are reached in some three hours by railway from London, from which they lie southwest.)

RHYL AND LLANDUDNO are two Welsh watering-places of prominence, both lying on the coast, not far from Liverpool and easily reached by boat thence. Both give fine views of the Welsh coast and mountains; Llandudno is now very fashionable; and Rhyl is famous for the donkey-rides which it supplies mountainward.

MARGATE, RAMSGATE and HASTINGS supply sea-bathing very extensively to Londoners, and especially to the middle classes at an earlier period of the summer than witnesses the filling up of the more fashionable resorts. Margate lies at the south lip of the Thames, some seventy miles from London, east, and just within the point known as the North Foreland; while Ramsgate lies a few miles southward, beyond the point and on the open channel. Both are reached by the Southeastern Railway from London, in some four hours; and both have certain curiosities in the way of piers, promenades, etc., deserving attention; while at Ramsgate particularly, and at Margate in only a less degree, the system of bathing by means of bathing-machines, or covered carts (rendered necessary by the great rise and fall of tide), can be studied to excellent advantage.

HASTINGS (one of the Cinque Ports) on the Channel, some twenty miles east of Brighton, is also a place of considerable resort, to be reached by either the Southeastern or the London, Brighton and South-Coast Railways.

There are a variety of other and minor watering-places, marine and inland, but the most notable have here been indicated; and the hurried tourist will easily be able to select any lying nearest to his intended route and involving the least extra-expenditure of time and money.

ENGLAND TO SCOTLAND.

There are three principal approaches to Scotland, for American tourists, and their routes are generally determined by those modes of approach.

The first is by steamer direct to Glasgow (as treated of in the chapter on "Look-outs and Land-makings"),—or by coast-steamer from Liverpool to Glasgow, on the west, or London to Edinburgh, on the east.

The two great remaining approaches are both by railway—from Liverpool to Glasgow, to go eastward through the Highlands to Edinburgh—and London to Edinburgh, to go westward through the Highlands to Glasgow.

Liverpool to Glasgow.

By the first, the London and Northwestern road is taken at Liverpool (as in going to the Cumberland Lakes), passing through Lancaster, Preston, Kendal, etc., as by that route, to

Carlisle, on the Border, situated on the bank of the river Eden, which runs into the near Solway Frith. It has some manufactories, but is much more interesting for its associations with border-warfare, and for the remains of the old Castle, said to have been built as a defence against the Scots, by William Rufus.

The head of the Solway Frith is crossed a few miles beyond Carlisle, and the course then continues northward and westward, through somewhat rugged and fine scenery, without passing through any towns of special importance, though here and there with a reminder of history—to Glasgow. Time from Liverpool to Glasgow, nine to ten hours.

London to Edinburgh.

Those who go up from Liverpool to Glasgow, can most properly return from Edinburgh to London, the eastern as well as the western part of the kingdom being thus traversed. For such as do so, the route following will only need to be precisely reversed in its details.

From London to Edinburgh, the Great Northern Railway is taken—actual running time about twelve to fifteen hours. The first stopping-place of the express-trains is at

Peterborough, a small old town, with no particular interest except the remains of a fine old Cathedral in which Catharine of Arragon (Queen of Henry VIII.) and Mary Queen of Scots (originally) were buried.

The next place of importance is

Newark (from which the New Jersey town took its name), a small town, with, again, little of interest except an old castle, now in ruins, said to have been occupied by King John at the time of his death. The next is

Doncaster, celebrated for its races, and not of the least importance except when they are in progress (during the early recess of Parliament—September). Then

YORK, a fine old city, on the Ouse, where Constantine the Great is alleged to have been born, some 1600 years ago, and famous in all English history. Even the most hurried should lie over one train, here, to see the magnificent

York Minster, or Cathedral, the second largest in England, and considered one of the finest in the world—begun in the seventh century, though principally built in the thirteenth and fourteenth. The old walls of the city are yet standing, and supply a charming promenade; while there are some public buildings well worthy of attention. A drive out of the town, about five miles westward, will supply an interesting view of

Marston Moor (Long Marston), where Charles I. suffered perhaps his worst defeat from the Parliamentary armies.

Beyond York, the ride is unbroken, until reaching

Newcastle-upon-Tyne, the celebrated centre of the English coal-trade, even a few minutes' pause at which shows that it is composed of coal, coal-dust, coal-vans, and other indications of the collieries. Shields, the great coal-port, lies a few miles eastward, at the mouth of the Tyne.

Beyond Newcastle the tourist crosses the historical Northumberland, the border-shire, celebrated in all the troubles with the Scots. If time does not press too closely, by changing from the express to a local train at Newcastle, a visit may be paid to

Alnwick Castle, lying only two or three miles westward from the main line, with a branch-road leading thither. Alnwick, the old home of the Percies, Earls and Dukes of Northumberland, is one of the finest ruins in Great Britain; and it is peculiarly interesting to Americans, from the celebrity given to it by Halleck in that most charming of poems bearing the same name.

Taking the main-line again at little Alnwick Station, the road runs thenceforth very near to the border of the German Ocean on the right, with frequent views of that historical ocean, over which the Danes came to subjugate Britain—all the way to

Berwick-on-Tweed, at which fine old town the Tweed is crossed by a bridge and the scenery seems to roughen and become more picturesque from the very moment of touching the Scottish soil.

From Berwick the run occupies some two hours, through the mountain and coast scenery made immortal by Scott in the "Bride of Lammermoor," over Haddingtonshire and the Lothians, with a brief stop at the fine old town of Dunbar,—till the Frith of Forth opens ahead and to the right, and the tourist is disembarked at Edinburgh.

# XL

CROSSING THE BRITISH CHANNEL.

NEARLY a dozen routes of transit present themselves, between England and France, and especially between the two great cities, London and Paris. But three special routes seem to possess advantages over all others, and to these the hurried tourist may well confine himself.

Those three are:

1st. Steamer between Dover, England, and Calais, France. Distance about twenty-four miles, and time one and a half to two hours. From London by Southeastern Railway.

2d. Steamer between Folkestone, England, and Boulogne-sur-Mer, France. Distance about twenty-eight miles, and time one and three-quarters to two and one-quarter hours. From London by Southeastern Railway.

3d. Steamer between Newhaven, England, and Dieppe, France. Distance sixty-five to seventy miles, and time six to eight hours. From London by London, Brighton and South-Coast Railway.

By all these routes the passage is more or less terrible, except in unusually calm weather; and there is really very little difference between them, except as to the time consumed and the lines with which they connect. The boats on all of them are staunch, safe and uncomfortable—meet with few accidents, but generally land their passengers more dead than alive, from sea-sickness.

For going to France, with at all decent weather, and for the first time, the line by Newhaven and Dieppe may well be chosen, as it is to be supposed that the man (or even the woman) who has endured ten days on the Atlantic can endure six to eight hours on the Channel,—and as by that route both Dieppe and Rouen, two of the handsomest old cities in France, can be hastily seen, while the way toward Paris will be taken by the French *Chemin de Fer de l' Ouest* (Western Railway), through a portion of Lower Normandy more exquisitely beautiful than almost any other strip of the same extent on the Continent.

For the return to England, if to be made at all from France (as usual) the *Chemin de Fer du Nord* (Northern Railway) should be taken from Paris, as by that route another portion of Normandy will be passed through, with the fine old city of Amiens; both Boulogne, on the French side, and Folkestone, on the English (termini of the other line) will be likewise passed through, though hastily; and the voyager will enjoy the opportunity of noticing the old walls and gates of Calais, so celebrated in the long wars of the Henrys and Edwards, between England and France, and of marking the appearance, from the Channel, of Dover Cliffs, made doubly notable by Shakspeare (in "King Lear"), Dover Castle, and the "White Cliffs of Albion," generally, as seen at their highest.

The route by Boulogne and Folkestone is meanwhile an excellent one, for either way, and the opportunity which it affords of spending even an hour in Boulogne, so well known as the paradise of runaway English debtors, is not to be despised. For the reasons given, however, the two others may be held preferable, in the order named for the going and return trips. It should be added that the run from Paris to Boulogne, so far as it goes, is the same as that to Calais—the French Northern Railway (*Chemin de Fer du Nord*), and that by that, also, Amiens is passed through, with its memories of a treaty in which the United States of America were once largely interested.

XII.

SHORT TRIPS IN FRANCE.

DIEPPE TO PARIS, BY ROUEN.

CROSSING the Channel from Newhaven, the first object of interest is to be found in the high piers, with narrow entrance and gaudily-gilded colossal crucifixes on them, of the very old French town of

DIEPPE, port at which the English kings were in the habit of landing in their wars with France, and to which Sir William Wallace, the hero of Scotland, is said to have brought the pirate Longueville after capturing him off the harbor. Some hours can be profitably spent here, in viewing the odd French houses; the old Chateau de Dieppe (Castle) on the hill to the west, said to have been founded by Charlemagne; the bathing-grounds, with their fine *Etablissement des Bains* (dancing and gambling house); the splendid hotels, with their handsome gardens and lawns; some of the narrow streets with very old houses; the confined dock-basins; the handsome old churches of St. Jacques and St. Remi, etc.

If time suffices, a ride of two or three miles, and return, will afford an excellent peep into mediæval history, in the

Castle of Arques, once owned and occupied by Henry V. of England, and near which he won the decisive battle of that name — now a splendid old ruin, with one of the grandest of the archways yet remaining.

Away from Dieppe, the railway, as has been already said, crosses one of the loveliest lines of Lower Normandy, with willowed water-courses, picturesque hills, valleys, chateaux and cottages, passing the chateau-dominated old town of Monville on the left, and striking the pleasant winding Seine but half-an-hour before stopping at

ROUEN, after Paris, unquestionably the most interesting city in France, from historical associations, architecture, and beauty of location. It lies on the north bank of the Seine, with rolling hills westward; has extensive cotton-manufactories stretching along the river; and historically recalls (principally) Henry V., who besieged it for nearly a year—Joan of Arc, who was burned here—and the Regent Duke of Bedford who burned her. In architecture and relics it is even richer; for the Cathedral and the Abbey Church of St. Ouen dispute with Notre Dame, at Paris, the claim of being the most magnificent of churches, while the great stained-glass windows of St. Ouen certainly excel either, and the monuments of the Cathedral include those of Rollo, first Duke of Normandy, Richard Cœur de Lion, Prince Henry, and many others; in the Place de la Pucelle is to be seen the spot where Joan of Arc was burned by the English; in the Church of St. Gervais is remarked the spot where William the Conqueror died ; and in the Museum of Antiquities are to be found the heart of Cœur de Lion (what little remains of it) in a glass casket, charters signed by William before Hastings, etc.

All these, and some of the finest old houses of Rouen, can be well enough seen in one day, though longer space could be well employed. So much "skims" the glory of the old city, at least, and the route to Paris may be resumed.

There is not much of additional interest between the capital of Normandy (Rouen) and that of France. The scenery is tamer, though very pleasing in portions; and only one town of importance is passed, after leaving Rouen,—Tourville, at only half-an-hour's distance. Nearly all interest, however, is concentrated on the pleasure in advance; and indeed it is not certain that some tourists do not commence to look for the spires and monuments of the great city, from the very moment of leaving Dieppe.

The run from Dieppe to Paris usually occupies about six hours; and the approach, as the course of the road would indicate, is from the northeast. The first object meeting the eye, coming near, is the Fort of Vallerien, one link of the immense and formidable chain of fortifications surrounding the city, by which it could be laid in ashes or put under contribution within two hours. This is seen to the right, before the city is fairly visible. Then come the handsome Heights of Montmartre, towering over the city on the left, with their pleasant shade and suggestions of luxurious residences. And then, as the next curve of the railway is rounded, the city itself heaves into view, with one colossal pile seeming to overtop it all, which the tourist scarcely needs to be told is the Arc d'Etoile, or Arch of Triumph of the Star, hereafter to be alluded to, and one of the mightiest and most imposing of all the monuments of Europe.

Thereafter comes the necessity (easily supplied) of cab-hiring for destination, and the whirl, glitter and confusion of the nearest of all approaches to the stereotyped phrase, "Modern Babylon." But with this arrival comes the necessity of another paper.

AT AND ABOUT PARIS.

More guide-books, works of description, and would-be aids to the traveller, have been written about Paris than any other city on the globe—more, even, than about London, which is saying much. Most of them confuse the hurried reader by attempting too much; nearly all of them bewilder the hurried traveller, by supposing that he has four times the length of days or hours really at his disposal, and setting him at the impracticable. This error will not be reached in the present instance: all that will be attempted will be merely to indicate, in the briefest manner, a few of the most notable of the notable things of the "world's capital" (as Frenchmen and Franco-phobians delight to call it), and some order of time and mode for seeing them to the best advantage.

For a long stay, of course lodgings would be desirable; for a few days, some hotel is by far preferable, and there is plenty of choice. If very deficient in French, unaccompanied, and able to meet the small additional expense—the tourist would do quite as well to take an English-and-French-speaking *valet de place* (obtainable at any hotel, by inquiring at the office) for the most important of his sight-seeings. With such a guide, cab-hire will be a little reduced, as different objects of interest may be visited with less expenditure of time and "leg-weariness," through the valet's knowledge of "cross-cuts," in the latter of which Paris even excels Boston.

The *valet de place* out of the question, however, the cab recurs. The cab-system of Paris is very nearly or quite as excellent as that of London; and a cab for one or two persons (sometimes for three) can be obtained at $1\frac{1}{2}$ to $2\frac{1}{2}$ francs the course (any distance inside the fortifications), or 2 to 4 francs the hour, when many stoppages are to be made. The cab should accordingly be used freely, and the expense will be nearly saved in boot-leather and quite in health and temper, especially as Paris is sultry in midsummer.

(FIRST DAY.)—Devote half the day on foot, if accompanied or guided (distances being short), to

The Seine (river) its *Quays* and *Bridges*. The first is very small, muddy, and historically interesting; the second are very high, massive, and worth study for the sake of their cost, the charming walks and drives along them, the arrangements for getting down to the docks below, the baths along their sides, etc.; and the third are very numerous, handsome and durable, spanning the river at all points in front of the city, as well as from the Ile de la Cité (City Island), and the Ile St. Louis, lying above it. The next half day, and in immediate connection, may well be devoted to

The Palace of the Tuileries (outside), the residence of the Emperor; the scene of many historical events, including two attacks and captures by the populace, at the dethroning of Louis XVI. in 1793 and Louis Philippe in 1848; and the exponent of more orders in architecture, and a better effect produced by an indiscriminate jumble, than any one, not a madman, could have believed. Also to the

Gardens of the Tuileries, extended and beautifullys-haded grounds lying immediately in front of the Palace, with statuary of rare merit, fountains, etc., supplying one of the favorite promenades to Parisians of all classes and ages, and especially to children with their nurses. Next to the

Place de la Concorde, connecting the gardens with the Champs Elysées. An open space, with splendid fountains and colossal statuary, and with the great red-granite Obelisk of Luxor in the midst, brought from Thebes in Egypt at immense expense, and standing on the very spot where during the early part of the Reign of Terror stood the guillotine on which perished Louis XVI., his sister, Marie Antoinette, and twenty-eight hundred others. Next into the

Champs Elysées (Elysian Fields), adjoining the Place de la Concorde on the west, the great home pleasure-ground of Paris, covering some forty acres, bordering on the Seine and extending to the Arc d'Etoile at the extreme western point. Magnificently shaded; laid out with walks; cut through its whole length by the Avenue des Champs Elysées, through which all the aristocratic carriages drive, every afternoon, going to or returning from the Bois de Boulogne; full of arrangements for out-of-door amusements, and studded at every turn with *cafés chantantes* (singing coffee-houses), cafés for refreshment, etc.; and with thousands of chairs, kept for cheap hire by the hour, in which the tourist can sit when tired and see the procession of fashion and oddity roll by. Before leaving the Champs, a glimpse should be caught of the Elysée Napoléon, an old palace, once the Elysée Bourbon, at the north side, where Napoleon signed his abdication, while the whole building has had an intimate connection with French history. Return towards the centre of the city, if boarding there, as supposed, by the

Column in the Place Vendôme, a splendid spirally-wreathed pillar, erected by Napoleon in honor of his victories, and covered with emblematic figures of his campaigns, as well as topped with a figure of the Emperor. The day may properly be finished by a visit to

The Madeleine, one of the handsomest churches in Paris or the world—pure Grecian, with surrounding of splendid columns, and statues in niches, outside; and with elaborate architecture, marvellously rich altars and altar-services, and some *chefs d'œuvres* in painting and sculpture, over the altars and employed as altar-pieces. At no other of the Parisian churches, either, can better views be caught of the uniformed and sworded vergers connected with the churches, who seem a cross between a police-officer and a major-general. The evening of this day may well be spent in catching a first glimpse by gaslight of some portions of

The Boulevards, very wide tree-bordered streets, commencing at the Madeleine on the west, and running, with different names, across and around the principal portions of Paris, to the Place de la Bastille at the east. They are lined, throughout, with shops, brilliant with articles for sale ; with open cafés for refreshments within or on the side-walk; and no spectacle in the world is more brilliant than that presented on the Boulevards Italiens, des Capucines, Montmartre, etc., every evening from dusk till midnight, all nations, dresses, languages, and characters mingling in splendid confusion and forming one of the most attractive features of Paris.

(SECOND DAY.)—This day a cab should be taken, by the hour, as the distances to be made are much greater. The first visit may well be paid to the outside and inside of

The Bourse, the great stock-exchange of Paris, France, and half Europe, a splendid colonnaded building, with a magnificent and very large galleried hall within, surrounded by the names of the chief cities of France, where stock operations are carried on. (If a spare hour should chance to allow, a second visit here, at noon or a little later, would be well repaid by hearing what Frenchmen on 'Change *can* do in the way of gabbling and gesticulating.) From the Bourse to the

Palais Royal, once a royal palace, as its name indicates, and still retaining the galleries and immense and beautiful gardens of that occupation, within its extensive quadrangle—but now the most extensive collection of shops and restaurants in the world (the latter including the celebrated "Trois Frères Provencaux," "Verys" and other well-known and costly habitats of luxury. Passing towards the Ile de la Cité, be sure to look out for and note, in passing, the

Tour St. Jacques (Tower of St. James), a splendid Gothic tower of great height and beauty; the very old and odd-looking

Church of St. Germain l'Auxerrois, from which tolled out, from the bell still hanging (as is said), the tocsin for the awful Massacre of St. Bartholomew; and to visit the

Church of St. Roch, on the still-standing steps of which took place one of the bloodiest fights of the Revolution (that of the 13th Vendémiaire); while the church has the distinction of giving the best music in Paris, of possessing much internal beauty and splendor, and of showing many fine pictures, among others a "St. Roch, Preaching," by Ary Scheffer, with the most wonderful of golden lights shed on it through the stained glass above.

The Church of St. Eustache, where a common courtesan was once enthroned in the place of God, should also be seen; and near it, the

Halles Centrales, or Central Market of Paris, with its extent and peculiarities. So much done, it is well to cross to the

Ile de la Cité, noticing, on going over the bridge, the round, pointed-capped towers, studding the water's edge at the right side of the island, of

The Conciergerie, the terrible prison in which Marie Antoinette was confined before her execution,

IN FRANCE. 171

and from which so many hundreds of victims went forth to the guillotine, during the Reign of Terror. The unfortunate Queen's room may still be seen, within, by those who have time to visit it; and also on the upper end of the same island, for those who have both time and inclination, are the

Palace of Justice, a fine old building, with many historical reminiscences, and

The Morgue, the celebrated dead-house in which the bodies of people "found drowned" are exhibited for identification. But the principal attraction to the Ile de la Cité is found in the magnificent

Notre Dame, one of the architectural glories of Paris and the world—with two immense square towers, wonderful architectural effects in the portals and whole elaborate front, and some of the finest Gothic arches in Europe in the vast interior. Notre Dame has, in addition, a wealth of stained-glass windows of rare size and excellence; some splendid side-chapels; a magnificent High Altar, at which Napoleon and Josephine were crowned; and the additional celebrity of being the spot round which (see the novel for explanations—published in English under the title of the "Hunchback of Notre Dame") Victor Hugo wove his great novel, "Notre Dame de Paris." It is, perhaps, the most impressive ecclesiastical object in Paris, and scarcely excelled in Europe in either grandeur or historical association. (At the door of Notre Dame is the place for making arrangements for carriage to Versailles—as there is a specialty of the master of those excursions always keeping in readiness for any day and having an agent there for that purpose. Inquire for Mons. Dulorin.)

Crossing back to the north side of the Seine, from the Ile de la Cité, a visit should at once be paid to the

Hôtel de Ville (City Hall), standing on the river bank, opposite the island, and very pleasing in its antique architecture, at the same time that it possesses the very highest historical interest. A visit should be paid to the inside of this great municipal building, as many of its interior appointments are quite equal to those of any palace on the globe—fine pictures, statuary, costly hangings, etc. Immediately in front of it is the

Place de la Hôtel de Ville, now merely an open space, but formerly the Place de Grève, where the great body of the executions by the guillotine took place during the Reign of Terror, and where it is estimated that not less than thirty thousand persons fell by that colossal "chopping-knife." It is almost impossible, even now, to look upon it without a shudder and a suspicion that the ground must still remain soaked with blood.

From the Hôtel de Ville the ride is a brief one, through the Faubourg St. Antoine—what is known as peculiarly the "dangerous quarter" of Paris, to the place where the Bastille stood and was destroyed. During this ride, a few moments may be well spent in stopping at some one of the numerous poor-looking wine-shops, for some excuse, to observe the places where the dangerous "Jacquerie" met at and before the Revolution—well described by Dickens in his

"Tale of Two Cities." This section of Paris is very old and squalid-looking, and is not the place for night-rambles, however efficient the police. This brings us, however, to the

Place de la Bastille, the spot where stood the great fortress of oppression, where it was torn down with such threatening demonstrations in 1789, and where now stands the

Column of July, a tall and very handsome fluted column, crowned with a figure of Mercury, and erected in honor of those who fell in the street-fights of the Revolution of 1830, when Charles X. was driven from the throne.

Beyond the Place de la Bastille, at no very great distance, the tourist passes between the two buildings of the great criminal prison of La Roquette, handsomely built, like fortresses, and in the court-yard of which most of the executions by the guillotine, of the past years, have taken place. Beyond, very soon, all appearances indicate the approach to a great cemetery, especially in the number of cheap and tawdry articles for the decoration of graves, kept for sale on either hand. Then comes the gateway of

Pere la Chaise, the great cemetery of Paris, and renowned throughout the world for the vast number of its distinguished dead. As a cemetery, and compared with American grounds of the same character, it is a humbug and a swindle, having little or nothing of the beauty of either Greenwood, Mount Auburn or Laurel Hill, and not to be mentioned beside Glasnevin Cemetery, at Dublin. Carriages are not allowed to enter; and half to three-quarters of an hour's walk is quite sufficient to observe its street-rows of square tombs, with streets between them; its occasional spots of well-shaded beauty; the miserable shabbiness of its poor-quarter (at the back), huddled together, with wooden crosses and cheap wreaths; its little chapel on the top of the eminence, with altar and religious statues within, and a fine view of Paris from in front of it; and the tombs of Marshal Ney and a few others, with the splendid chapel-tomb of Abelard and Héloise, one of the pilgrimages of the cemetery, lying not far from the lower right-hand corner, taking the point of view from the entrance.

This round, with the direct drive back to the place of lodging, may well have filled the day pretty closely; but there may still remain spirit and wish for an evening ride to the Champs Elysées, to see its night-beauty of lights and breadth of gayety, to sup at some one of its many cafés, and perhaps to spend an hour of the earlier evening at the

Alcazar d'Eté, one of the most noted of the open-air concert establishments, where good singing is a certainty, and a later hour, or two, at the

Jardin Mabille, an exquisitely-wooded and shrub-beried circle, flashing with lights and supplying dancing-music all the evening, lying on the Avenue Montaigne, at the Rond Point and in the immediate vicinity of the Avenue des Champs Elysées—where the gayer varieties of Parisian life may be witnessed by those so inclined, and where the *cancan* may be enjoyed in what the Parisians (and some of the Americans) consider its " purity."

IN FRANCE. 175

(THIRD DAY.)—Cab again, for only a short distance, to the

Hôtel Cluny, site of the old Roman Palais des Thermes, part of the walls of which yet remain, while the Hotel itself contains a very interesting collection of antiquities (among other things the celebrated *ivory-lock*, which "must be seen to be appreciated"), chapel where James IV. of Scotland was married, etc. Thence over the Seine, by any one of the numerous bridges, to the

Champ de Mars, for a long time the great parade-ground of Paris, full of historical recollections of the Revolution and the First Napoleon, with the splendid and extensive buildings of the Ecole Impérial Militaire bounding it at the end opposite to the river. In the centre of this, as many thousand Americans fortunately know from recollection, stood the Great Exposition Palace of 1867, while the whole Champ was turned into a magnificent park, filled with floral and arboricultural treasures and the buildings of all nations. Within sight of the Champ de Mars, to the left and behind, diagonally, comes the great point of interest of the day, the

Hôtel des Invalides, an immense structure for military hospital purposes, built by Louis XIV., afterward taken up by Napoleon, and still used for that noble end. The principal points of interest to be visited are the Officers' and Soldiers' Refectories, with their scarred veterans, odd arrangements, old pictures of Louis XIV.'s battles, etc.; the picture-galleries, with much trash, but some valuable kingly reminiscences; the Chapel, where the rotting battle-flags, from the Oriflamme of St. Louis to those taken at Sebastopol, hang and moulder; and the Domed Church, commonly spoken of as

"*The Dome of the Invalides,*" at the opposite extremity of the entrance, and entered separately from without, in a sunken space within the floor of which, in a green marble sarcophagus, surrounded by his mouldering battle-flags, and weeping figures in marble, lies the body of the First Napoleon. The Church is very beautiful within; and the High Altar and the light shed upon it are peculiarly fine; while handsome monuments to Joseph Bonaparte, Turenne, Vauban, etc., are to be seen, besides the veterans of the First Empire, who there keep guard against any impropriety of action on the part of the ever-pressing crowd.

While on this side of the Seine, should be visited, too,

The Panthéon, largest of the churches of Paris, and one of the finest, with magnificent side-chapels (especially that of St. Geneviève, with its gilded screen); burial of Voltaire, Rousseau, Mirabeau, Marshal Lannes, Bougainville and many others, in the vault below; and noble inscription over the front (in French): "To the Great Men Remembered by their Country." Then comes the

Church of St. Etienne du Mont, near the Pantheon, very beautiful within, and especially noted for its splendid spiral stairway, unique in architecture, and some of its exquisite side-chapels. Glimpses may also be caught of St. Sulpice and other churches; and a visit should be paid to the neighboring

Palace of the Luxembourg, one of the largest and finest of the royal reminders, with its splendid collection of pictures and antiquities; and on the return homeward, corresponding glimpses may be caught, on the Seine bank, of the

Corps Legislatif, or Congress Hall of France, and many other public buildings, certain to be called to attention by guide or driver.

A third evening has now been found for any theatre or opera-house that may be chosen.

(FOURTH DAY.)—Take open carriage (weather allowing, as generally in Paris at midsummer), for Versailles by Sèvres. (Twelve to twenty francs per person—two-and-a-half to four dollars gold—will easily supply an excellent conveyance for the day, with guide, coachman, and fees paid.) The drive will be through the Champs Elysées, by the Avenue, to the end at the extreme height, where stands the

Arc d'Etoile, a magnificent sculptured arch, the largest in Europe, erected by Napoleon to commemorate his victories of 1805, and the colossal sculptures having reference to him. The ascent to the top of the Arc, which commands the finest of views over Paris, is a matter of time, taste, and *legs*. It is a better thing to say one has done, than to do. Beyond the Arc, and driving down the Avenue de l'Impératrice, by the Porte Dauphine, is almost immediately entered

The Bois de Boulogne, a splendid wood, once and a quarter the size of the New York Central Park, with unlimited expense lavished on its walks and drives; with two beautiful lakes (Lac Supérieure and Lac Inférieure), for pleasure-boating; a cascade at the extremity, of peculiar artificial grace (the Cascade de Longchamps); the Emperor's race-course of Longchamps in full view at the farther extremity; and all the peculiarities going to make up the handsomest pleasure-ground in Europe—though nothing finer, nor so fine, in bridges or other erections, as the Central Park will be when it has age and tree-growth. (The return from Versailles is also to be made through the Bois, at that early hour in the evening when all the fashionable riders of Paris and half Europe roll along these splendid drives in their carriages, with horsemen in abundance, and an unlimited quantity of foot people and couples of strolling lovers, taking the shady walks or lounging under the trees, not warned to "keep off the grass," as in American pleasure-grounds.)

Not far beyond the Bois de Boulogne the Seine is crossed, with a view of

St. Cloud, another of the royal-imperial residences, palace and park; and not far beyond comes

Sèvres, a small town, of which the only attraction is the imperial manufactory of porcelains, where tourists are allowed to inspect some of the most splendid works of art, in that line, made in any country. A few miles farther bring

VERSAILLES, palace and park, considered one of the wonders of the world, even among royal residences. Built by Louis XIV., and ever since more or less constantly occupied as one of the favorite residences of the ruler. Among the curiosities to be seen here, are the

IN FRANCE. 179

Great Picture-Galleries of the palace, filled with rare and valuable works in painting, sculpture and antiquities (the rooms said to measure some eight miles in extent); the

Napoleon and Josephine Rooms, with the beds, chairs, tables, and many other memorials of both; the

Trianon, with sedan-chairs and other memorials of Madame de Maintenon; the

Fountain of Latona, and other fountains in immense profusion—considered among the finest in the world; the

Gardens and Flower-Walks, likewise considered unequalled; the

Park, of wondrous extent and breadth of shade, with its culmination in the "Tapis Vert," voted as the finest avenue of shade and sward in Europe, and with Louis XV.'s "Petit Trianon" hidden away at some distance from the palace and nearer grounds.

Dinner should be taken, this day, at the Hôtel du Reservoir, once the residence of Louis XV.'s *chère amie,* Madame de Pompadour, and a favorite resort of gourmands and fashionables; after which the drive back, through the Bois de Boulogne (before alluded to) should include a visit of a few moments to the

Pré Catelan, an inner beauty of the Bois, more glorious in flowers and foliage than any other portion, with an oddly-pretty little open-air summer theatre; and if time should serve, then or otherwise, an hour in the
16

Jardin d'Acclimatization, a sort of floral and zoological garden, also within the Bois, especially noted for its variety of rare birds, goats, and the more harmless animals.

(FIFTH DAY.)—All this day, if possible, should be spent in viewing thé outside and wandering through the galleries of

The Louvre, once a royal palace, but now the most extensive museum in the world (with perhaps the exception of the British), adjoining the Palace of the Tuileries on the east, and of course reached on foot. Among its notable features, apart from the extent and beauty of the building itself, will be found the

Great Picture-Galleries, of which the extent, filled with rare paintings, sculpture and curiosities, is said to be about ten miles, affording one of the costliest and most celebrated of collections. Chief among these is the

Grand Gallery, filled with works by the great painters of antiquity, scarcely a notable name unrepresented, and the whole rivalling the galleries of the Vatican at Rome and Escurial at Madrid. Next in importance, to the tourist, are two apartments in what is called the "Museum of Napoleon III."—first the

Royal Antiquity Chamber, where may be seen the sword and sceptre of Charlemagne, the armor worn by Henry IV. at Ivry, the armor and swords of many of the other kings, the prayer-books of Mary Queen of Scots and Marie de Medicis, etc.; and next and even more important, the

Napoleon Room, where are to be found the coronation robes of the First Emperor, his camp-chest, camp-bed, clothes worn at St. Helena, and a hundred other affecting memorials of the Great Corsican, attracting undivided attention and interest.

These comprise, of course, only a fraction of the attractions of the Louvre, but they may be all that the short-trip traveller can command. To those who have abundance of time, abundance of other objects will present themselves, without any necessity of present mention. The Apollo and Vernet Galleries, however, should not be passed without notice; and the same may be said of the Hall of the Seven Chimneys, where Henry IV. died after being stabbed by Ravaillac.

(SIXTH DAY.)—Visit, at some six miles from Paris (by cab), the

Cathedral Church of St. Denis, in the old town of the same name, where the French kings have been buried, ever since the time of Dagobert, and where many interesting monuments and memorials of them can be found, though the revolutionary mob tore open their coffins and threw the bones into ditches, in '93, to have them restored with difficulty (!) in 1816. The Cathedral is itself very fine in architecture, with some of the best stained glass in France; and the vaults may be visited by those ambitious of royal mould and damp.

The St. Denis excursion can easily be made in half a day; and this, with six days to remain, leaves half a day for " chores."

One fact, however, should be mentioned. Some of the buildings which most positively require to be entered, are only open on certain days; and the succession of days here marked out may sometimes require to be changed accordingly, though with proper arrangement the order of any one day will not need to be so changed. All the churches, except Notre Dame, are open every day: that, on Wednesdays, Fridays and Sundays, 11 to 4. The Tomb of Napoleon, at the Invalides, can only be seen on Mondays and Thursdays, 12 to 3. The Bourse is open every day. Hôtel Cluny, every day, 11 to 5. Palace of the Luxembourg, every day, 10 to 4. Louvre, every day except Monday, 12 to 4. Versailles, every day except Monday. St. Denis, and all the public gardens, grounds and monuments, every day.

Not many visitors to Paris need to be told that Sunday is the liveliest day of the week, with everything open to the gay; while the more serious can find service in all the churches, and splendid choral services in the principal ones.

For those who have longer time to spend at and about the capital, there are of course fifty additional points of interest not here named—among others, the Conservatory of Arts and Measures, the Mint (Hôtel des Monnaies), the Gobelin Tapestry Manufactory, the Jardin des Plantes (natural history), the School of Fine Arts, the Museum of Artillery, the Palace of Fine Arts, etc., etc.

As to theatre-going—for grand opera, the Grand Opera is to be visited; for light opera, the Opera Comique or the Varieties is preferable; for comedy, the Théâtre Français; for spectacle, the Porte St. Martin.

XIII.

PARIS TO GENEVA.

[Before briefly sketching this route and the short Swiss tour to follow, it may be well to say that there is an Englishman named Thomas Cook, who has agencies in London, Paris and some other cities, for arranging "Excursions" and selling through tickets for certain routes and return, at much less than the regular fares demanded (first or second class, optional); and that for those who leave Paris for Switzerland and Germany, to return there, he may be dealt with to advantage—one of the benefits of the "Cook's Tourist Tickets" being the saving of much inconvenience in purchasing route-tickets at the various line-intersections.]

LEAVE Paris for Geneva by the early morning train of the Lyons and Mediterranean Railway, breakfasting before starting. Never take the afternoon train, as by that means much fine scenery would inevitably be lost on one portion of the route or another; and never arrange to go the whole distance without stopping, for the same reason. Those who leave Paris in the morning and go directly through, travelling all night, lose the Valley of the Rhone, one of the finest in Europe; and those who leave in the afternoon lose the views of the vineyards and rural scenery of Southern France.

The train passes, a few miles from Paris, running southeastward, by the town of Melun, and

Fontainebleu, tower and old royal residence, palace and park, of which a mere glimpse is caught from the train. The scenery is flat and tame, but "French"

and interesting, during all the early part of this day. Many river-glimpses are caught—first of the Seine, and then of the quiet little Yvonne, the banks of which are very closely followed by the railway, all the way to

Tonnerre (English, "thunder"), a town of no particular mark, where the halt is made for dinner, and an exceedingly good one (*table d'hôte*) always provided. The second halt of consequence is made, two or three hours later, at

Dijon, a fine old city, with abundance of historical reminiscences but little time to note them and still catch a trifle of supper. At Dijon the course changes to almost due south, terminating, at nearly nightfall, at

Macon, on the river Saône, famous for its wines, and well worthy of the evening spent before retiring, and the next morning before train-time,—to see its little "Champs Elysées," where the people amuse themselves in the evening, *à la* Paris; its odd old streets, fountain and market; its odder people, handsome modern church, river with boats running down to Lyons, etc. Sleep at Macon, and leave next morning by train for Geneva.

Cars are changed at *Bourg*, and again at *Amberieux*, to catch the train up from Lyons; but some pleasant glimpses of the Saône and the distant mountains eastward compensate for this inflection. Very soon after leaving Amberieux commences the ascent of the

Valley of the Rhone, one of the wildest and most picturesque on either continent; the road passing over steep inclines and through narrow rock-bound passes, until reaching

Culoz, where the scenery becomes yet wilder and grander, with the Rhone spanned by bridges, tunnelled for miles, rolling hundreds of feet below (something like Niagara below the Falls, but much wilder), and presenting one of the most splendid bits of engineering in any land—the "Tunnel de Credo," $2\frac{1}{2}$ miles in length, and the "Valserine Viaduct," rival of the Starucea, being among the most notable features, and ever-memorable glimpses of the distant Swiss mountains are caught, in fine weather, from Culoz, onward; but it is only on reaching

Bellegarde, where the route changes from France to Switzerland, that in the clearest weather is caught the

First glimpse of Mont Blanc, eighty or one hundred miles to the right, with the Aiguillettes and other points of the great snow range of Savoy. (In order to have even the chance of catching this never-to-be-forgotten first glimpse, the right-hand side of the carriage is desirable.)

One to two hours after entering the Swiss territory, all the while running through the passes and plunging across the ravines of the Jura range of mountains, is reached the end of that special journey, and one of the most beautiful, beautifully-located and historic cities of Europe,

Geneva!

XIV.

SHORT TRIPS IN SWITZERLAND.

GENEVA AND CHILLON.

GENEVA, charmingly situated, as already indicated, lies at the extreme southwestern point of the Lake of Geneva, otherwise known as Lake Leman. It stands on both sides the lake-foot, and of the Rhone, which here debouches from it. The views from it are perhaps unequalled by those from any other city on the globe, the lake spreading away far to the north and east, the fine dark range of the Jura in full view to the north and west, and the nearer mountains of the southern side of the lake (called by Cooper, in the "Headsman," the "ramparts of Savoy") showing to the southeast, with Mt. Blanc and the other giants of the snow-range always visible in fine weather.

The city is very old, and has much historical interest, especially as connected with the wars of Savoy, and with John Calvin (who preached and resided here), and many of the events of the Reformation. It probably contains about 50,000 inhabitants, has many manufactures; and is celebrated, world-wide, for its construction of the popular Swiss watches. The most interesting of all its buildings is

The Cathedral (St. Pierre), built about 1050, a noble Gothic building, containing the tombs of Duke

Henry de Rohan and the Comte d'Aubigny, French Protestant leaders under Louis XIII. and Henry IV.; and (under the pavement) of Cardinal Jean de Brognier, President of the Council of Constance, and other ecclesiastical celebrities; and the canopy of the pulpit (not the pulpit itself, as sometimes alleged) once filled by Calvin. The arches and stained glass, and the old presbyters' stalls, are very fine; and the echo of music or the voice is peculiarly notable. Next in interest to the Cathedral, come the

Hôtel de Ville, and the *Arsenal*, in the latter of which the collection of arms is very fine. After these, the next are the

Musée Roth (a Museum), with a very fine collection of pictures and sculpture, and the

Musée Académique, with antiquities, geological collection and reading-room; and

Rousseau's House, near the latter. But quite as interesting as any of the buildings, after the Cathedral, are the

Bridges — the beautiful Pont des Bergues and Pont du Mont Blanc, spanning the river at the centre of the city, while from the former shoots out a little shaded island, of peculiar beauty, forming a favorite promenade, known as

Rousseau's Garden (Ile de J. J. Rousseau), so named from its having been a favorite resort of the author of "Abelard" and the "Confessions." The promenades along the quais, on both sides, are very delightful, with their views of the lake, the odd lateen-rigged schooners, the distant mountains, etc.; and especially delightful is the

Jardin Anglais (English Garden), overhanging the waters on the south side, where military concerts are given almost every evening during the summer. (It should be added, that nearly or quite all worth seeing in Geneva can be better seen on foot than with the cost of a cab or other conveyance.)

Whatever the other arrangements, one day should be spent (leaving Geneva at 8 A. M.), in taking steamer up the lake to Chillon, and return at early evening. This gives the most delightful of views of lake and mountains, passing, and stopping at many of them (all on the north side) — the charmingly situated shore-towns of Versoix, Coppet, Nyon, Rolle, St. Prex, Morges, Ouchy (with Lausanne at a little distance behind), Lutry, Cully, Vevey and Montreux, until the landing is made at Veytaux-Chillon, and a few minutes' ride or walk (the latter easiest attainable) brings the tourist to the

CASTLE OF CHILLON, a fine old turreted chateau, more than half fortress, with round and square towers of very unequal heights, standing at the edge of the lake, near the extreme eastern end, overhung by frowning mountains. This was once a residence of the Dukes of Savoy, afterwards a prison, but owes nearly all its celebrity to Byron's having made it the scene of his affecting poem, the "Prisoner of Chillon."

The points best worth notice in this fine old pile are

The Drawbridge and Moat, where something may be learned of the uses and mode of operating those appendages, in the far past; the

Dungeons (*oubliettes*), part of them lying beneath the surface of the lake, and fearfully dismal; the

Great Audience Chamber, where the Dukes of Savoy gave audience, now occupied with arms and flags of the Helvetian Republic; the

Chapel, where the prayers must have been peculiar; then, *en suite*, the

Chamber of the Condemned, where the doomed passed their last night on cold stones; followed by the

Execution-Room, with a trap-door ready to slide the beheaded bodies into the lake, and so save trouble; and that succeeded by the last and most interesting of all,

Bonnivard's Prison, the scene of Byron's master-work,—with its "seven columns," the third bearing the name of "Byron," said to have been cut there by his own hand, and the fifth yet holding the massive chain and ring to which Bonnivard was fettered—its high, narrow-slitted windows, looking out over the lake (if they could only be reached) and all the suggestions of an age of cruelty not yet quite ended.

The return to Geneva is made by boat; and during the return-voyage, as in going up, if the weather is fine, there are many chances of seeing, once and again if not continually, Mt. Blanc, the "monarch of mountains," and some of his brother snow-capped giants.

EXCURSION FROM GENEVA TO CHAMOUNI, AND RETURN.

Those who make only the briefest of the brief tours in Switzerland, must give up the hope of seeing the Valley of Chamounix, and Mont Blanc from that much nearer point of view—(one of the noblest of all the attractions presented by the "land of mountains"), trusting to the mountains of the Bernese Oberland to supply the omission and give the best possible idea of the sharp, rugged peaks, bald or snow-crowned, and many of them of needle sharpness; the glaciers, or rivers of ice, that sweep between them and around their feet; the long strips of snow lying all summer down the vertical ravines, half way from peak to foot; the innumerable cascades pouring and dashing down from the melted snows, sparkling, flashing and gleaming white on every hand; the marvellously-fertile narrow valleys, with the green "Alps" stretching mountainward from them; and the infinite variety of hanging-roofed and galleried chalets (houses) often curiously carved and ornamented in their timber-and-shingle enclosures, and always with rows of large stones seeming to be holding down the roofs—all this, which combines to fill up the peculiar odd charm of Swiss scenery and make it a recollection never to be forgotten. These, for the very-short-trip tourist, must be deferred: he (as hereafter to be explained) must push on direct from Geneva for Berne and through the Oberland.

The luckier tourist, however, who can add some

four days to this portion of his whole route (as in the ten or thirteen weeks' arrangement), and the additional expense involved, should make Chamounix a certainty, going to it by one route and returning by the other, as follows:

Connect the excursion with that from Geneva to Chillon, leaving out the return from the latter. Leave Geneva by boat for Chillon, as before designated, visit the Chateau, take the evening boat from Chillon to

Villeneuve, only a mile or two beyond, at the extreme eastern end of the Lake, where the Rhone empties into it. From Villeneuve (a town of some age but little consequence), by rail, to

Martigny, a very old town, dating back to the Roman times, and said then to have been the capital of a province; now principally of consequence as the place whence the Monks of St. Bernard draw their supplies for the Hospice, and the point whence the ascent of the Alps is commenced by the Simplon or Great St. Bernard Passes, besides dividing with Sallanches (on the other side) the travel to Chamounix. It lies at the bottom of the depression formed by the sloping down of the Great Alps (Mt. Blanc or "snow range") on the south, and the Bernese Alps on the north, and necessarily ends railway travel in that direction.

The route from Martigny may be made on foot, by good travellers, but much easier by mule, for those who ride better than they walk, or even as well. The leading points of interest (fully pointed out and explained by guides, whether the tourist is mounted or on foot) are Martigny-le-Bourg (where the little river Dranse is crossed), La Fontaine, Sarmieux, Chavans en Haut, to the

Col de la Forclaz, the summit of which may be ascended by those who wish a splendid view over the whole valley of the Rhone, but avoided by the leg-weary who need to husband their strength.

From the Col de la Forclaz the road descends, passing the small village of Orient, directly winding through the dark Forest of Magnin, reaching, after rising again by a tough climb, the

Col de Balme, boundary between Switzerland and Savoy, from two different stations, on the top of which, in fine weather, perhaps the finest mountain-side view is obtained, in the world—the whole chain of Mt. Blanc being visible, from crown to foot, looking southward, with the Valley of Chamounix and the great Glaciers; and looking back northward, the Jungfrau, Finsteraarhorn and other giants of the Bernese Oberland being visible.

From the top of the Col de Balme the descent commences, in view of the river Arve, and passing a noted landmark, the

Homme de Pierre (Man of Stone), to Tour, a small village, with the Glacier de Tour near and in sight. Near Tour the little river Buisme is crossed; and half an hour brings the tourist to

Argentière, a mountain tour of much beauty and some prominence, whence a carriage may be taken or the route finished on foot, to Chamounix.

(The ascent from Martigny to Chamounix may be made by a very different route—that known as the Tête Noire, the divergence being made not long before reaching the Col de la Forclaz, and some of the most startling passes in Switzerland accomplished, besides passing through the Roche Percée [Pierced Rock]; but by that route the view from the Col de Balme would be lost entirely, and the increased fatigue of the passage, in that direction, induces the much more frequent taking of the course just described, while those going *from Chamounix to Martigny* oftenest take the Tête Noire.)

Chamounix lies at the head of the Valley of the Arve, northward of Mt. Blanc and so near that the great mountain may be literally said to overshadow it—views of the monster and its chain being attainable from any quarter. It has nearly a dozen of hotels and some 2,500 inhabitants; and it supplies a marked attraction during all the "Alpine season," in the number of tourists and pleasure-seekers continually arriving, departing, setting out upon and returning from the many excursions to be made in the neighborhood.

It is from Chamounix that the ascents of Mt. Blanc are made; but this, of course, is out of the line of the short-trip tourist (as indeed of most *sensible people*), who will not be expected to spend about $200 (gold), peril life, and fatigue himself beyond a month's recovery, by any such climb. Looking *up* to a mountain, from the immediate foot, is generally preferable (after one knows both) to looking *down* from it; and Mt. Blanc and the Vale of Chamounix furnish no exception to the rule.

There are some excursions, however, which may

and should be made, even by those who linger but a single day, while those who have several days at command (and who are consequently out of our purview) may easily learn more from the guides about more extended excursions, than could find any appropriate place here. This one day at Chamounix should be spent in ascending the

Montanvert (Green Mountain), an eminence on the east side of the valley, with some two to three hours' climb (two to descend), from which the most magnificent of views can be obtained not only of the great mountains of the chain, but of the Glaciers which fill all the higher gorges, called the *Mer de Glace* above and the *Glacier du Bois* below, and altogether some twelve miles long by $1\frac{1}{2}$ to $4\frac{1}{2}$ in width —the lower portion reaching down to the valley of Chamounix. This ascent should be made in the morning (always with a guide for whatever is to be done during the day), because then the rugged and difficult path is in shade and less fatiguing.

From the Montanvert it is usual (now, even for ladies, though they should only attempt it if in fair health and sure-footed) to

Cross the Mer de Glace to the Chapeau on the opposite side—a difficult ice-climb of half to three-quarters of an hour, which will generally be found quite " enough of glacier " for the moderate. The

Mauvais Pas (difficult steps)—steps hewn in the rock, not far from the Chapeau, is the most " pokerish " point. The view from

The Chapeau, a limestone precipice on the northeast side of the Glacier, is considered nearly equal to that from the Montanvert. Many pause here, for return; but those who have yet some strength and courage unexpended, will try the much more difficult scramble over the Glacier du Taléfre to

The Jardin, whence the views, so to speak, into the icy bowels of Mont Blanc can be better caught than elsewhere without ascending it. Of course provisions, as well as guides, require to be taken for the day; and of course the day is no " child's play," except to practised mountaineers. The return to Chamounix occupies some six hours—quite all that will remain of the longest day, which may be set down, however, if successfully carried through, as the most glorious in all European touring.

The return from Chamounix to Geneva should be made by way of Servoz, Sallanches or St. Martin, Cluses and Bonneville. Light carriages may be taken to

Sallanches, from the bridge of which, over the Arve, splendid backward views of Mont Blanc and other mountains may be obtained. From Sallanches to Geneva by diligence; the whole route being made in nine to ten hours, and the most wonderful splendor and variety of mountain scenery being threaded throughout.

GENEVA TO BERNE AND INTERLAKEN.

From Geneva to Berne by rail, close along the northwestern side of the Lake of Geneva, to

Lausanne, a very beautiful town, famous as a residence and with some historical reminders—among others, of Gibbon and Voltaire; then shooting away northeastward, from the Lake, with last glimpses of the Mt. Blanc range (in fine weather) by

Romont, "a very old town climbing up a sidehill," and very queer in its many towers and Lombardy-poplars, to

Freybourg, an older and larger town, straddling the gorge of the Sarne, with a fine old many-pinnacled Cathedral and the celebrated organ, built by Aloys Moser without help or money (some of us would like to have his secret!), and considered one of the grandest in the world. Many lie over at Freybourg for a train, to see the Cathedral and the great suspension-bridges, and hear the organ (played every day, at 12 noon and 8 P. M.), and the time is certainly not wasted. From Freybourg but a short additional ride to

BERNE, capital of Switzerland, lying on the rapid river Aar, with a specialty of "Bears," some 30,000 to 40,000 inhabitants, and much general interest. Among its features, noticeable even in a few hours' stay, are its splendid whole streets of arcaded shops (the Grand Rue especially notable); the marvellous amount of wood carvings kept for sale; the many old fountains; the Old and New Bridges over the Aar (the former said to be five or six hundred years old), and the railroad bridge (trellis), one of the highest in the world; and then of yet more important specialties,

The Cathedral, old and fine, with remarkably beautiful entrance, and grand organ, on which playing may be heard nearly every night during the summer, splendid statue of Rudolph von Erlach in front, etc.; the

Terrasse de Cathedral, a beautiful promenade, hanging pokerishly over the Aar, with some interesting monuments; a tough story of a knight, who once leaped down into the Aar on horseback and was not killed; and the most splendid of views, especially at early evening, of the Jungfrau, the Monk, the Eiger, and the whole white-crowned range of the Bernese Oberland. Then come the

Federal Palace (Congress Hall of Switzerland), of no special interest, however, without or within; and the

Fosse del Ours (bear-pit), lying beside the Aar, at the foot of the Grand Rue, with some noble specimens of the tribe of Bruin, who occasionally eat up a drunken traveller when he falls into their embraces.

Berne has also a mechanical clock worthy of notice, with a crowing cock and moving figures.

From Berne to the Lake of Thun (at Scherlingen-Thun) by railway; thence by boat down the Aar and the Lake, with magnificent views of the Jungfrau, Monk, Eiger, Aarhorn, Finsteraarhorn, and other great peaks of the Oberland, to Newhaus, where the diligences of the General Post are taken, and a brief ride brings the tourist to

INTERLAKEN, " heart of the Bernese Oberland," as it has been called—a very handsome and very Swiss old town, lying on the Aar, with Unterseen, a small suburb, across the river, and the Jungfrau in full view from any one of the many fine hotels that stud the principal street. Interlaken is famed for its shops for the sale of wood-carvings and other curiosities, and far more as the favorite resort of tourists who wish to combine magnificent scenery with tasteful quiet; and it may perhaps be considered matchless, as a summer residence, in Switzerland. It has a Kursaal, used for dancing, music and reading; mountain views almost unequalled; and a multitude of fine walks, combined with the opportunity for excursions innumerable. Those which should certainly be made, at all hazards, are the following:

By three-horse carriage (for a party of four, five or six, easily made up), up the Valley of Grindelwald, to the

Glaciers of Grindelwald, running down to the valley between the Eiger and Middenthal—with a walk (well wrapped) into the ice-caverns underlying it, and an ascent of one of them if none of those near Mont Blanc have been " done." (If they have, these may as well be avoided, as secondary.) Thence around into the Valley of Lauterbrunnen, to the

Falls of Lauterbrunnen (Staubbach), a single thin sheet falling a sheer thousand feet; in the midst of perpendicular-cliff scenery of wonderful grandeur. This double excursion will occupy one day, and a highly interesting and memorable one; and let not the tourist forget to set some of the " Alpine horns " blowing along the road (for a small fee) and carry away the fine echoes among the mountains—or fail to listen when, late in the return, his attention is called by guide or driver to the ruined Castle of Unspunnen, where Byron is said to have laid the scene of his " Manfred."

[Those who have a little more time at command and do not object to a little more sharp climbing—may well take the Grindelwald excursion as enough for a single day, and blend with that to Lauterbrunnen the ascent of the

Wengern Alp, in the neighborhood but beyond, where the national wrestling-matches are held on a broad pasture at the top, on the first Sunday in August, and from which the best of all views of the whole range of the great Oberland Mountains, the Jungfrau, Monk, Breithorn, etc., and the whole valley of Lauterbrunnen, may be obtained.]

The second of the absolutely-necessary excursions from Interlaken consists in taking the steamer on the Lake of Brienz (half-mile walk, east), to the landing of Giessbach, and thence ascending the mountain to the handsome hotel and

Fall of Giessbach, making some thousand feet in four leaps from the top of the cliffs to the lake, amid trees and spanned by airy bridges, and without doubt one of the loveliest cataracts on the globe. A night spent at the hotel is said to supply a great added charm in the *lighting of the Fall* (done every clear night); and the trip down the lake and back is a lovely one in the mountain-girt lake-scenery—not excelled by either Geneva or Lucerne.

Among the walks around Interlaken, which should be taken if time allows, is that to the Jungfraublick, from which one of the finest of all views is caught (half-hour walk); the Heimwehfluh (three-quarter hour), another magnificent view; the Hohbuhl (half hour); the ruins of Unspunnen (three-quarter hour), etc. Of rides, the finest remaining is that to the Schining Platte, from which the valleys of Lauterbrunnen and Grindelwald can both be seen at once.

INTERLAKEN TO LUCERNE, THE RHIGI AND BALE.

For Lucerne, the boat on the Lake of Brienz is taken, as in going to Giessbach, affording another view of that beautiful lake, and this time for the whole length. The landing is made at the old town of

Brienz, not especially notable except for that fact; whence diligences are taken, the route ascending sharply, with fine views over the Aar and the Lake of Brienz, to the summit of the

Brunig Pass (at Brunig-kulm); thence down, with corresponding rapidity and still with fine views, by the Lakes of Lungern and Sarnen (passed at the left), the scenery for the time softening materially, but the splendid pine timber of all the ride winning the heart of the American,—to

Alpnach, village at the southwest end of the Lake of Alpnach, to the southeast and nearly under shadow of Mont Pilatus,—where steamer is taken for the length of that lake, to the entrance of Lake Lucerne ("Lake of the Four Cantons," and scene of Tell's exploits); thence across Lucerne, northward, with Pilatus in full view at the southwest and the Rhigi across the Lake at the northeast, to

Lucerne (Luzern), one of the oldest cities of Switzerland, lying at the northwest point of the Lake of the same name. It stands at the junction of the river Reuss with the Lake; is a Catholic city and capital of the Canton of the same name; has part of the old wall still surrounding it on the land side; and offers, as curiosities, the three bridges over the Reuss (all odd, and the Muhlenbrucke with the singular ornamentation of thirty-six pictures called the "Dance of Death")—the Arsenal, in which some interesting antiquities are preserved—among other things, flags taken at Lepanto under Don John of Austria—and the rare monument, called the "Lion of Lucerne," erected from Thorwaldsen's designs, in memory of the Swiss killed at Paris in defending Louis XVI., in 1792. Lucerne has also the charm of vieing with Geneva in loveliness of location.

The Rhigi may be ascended from Lucerne, in either of two directions—from Kussnacht on the north (reached by carriage from Lucerne), the return made by Weggis,—or from Weggis, on the south (reached by boat), the return made by Kussnacht. In either case, sleeping accommodations at the top should be telegraphed for from Lucerne, a day ahead if possible. Supposing the first of the two routes to be taken—carriage to

Kussnacht, alleged to be the scene of Tell's exploit with the apple, and where some memorials of the hero are said to exist. Thence horses or chairs (carried by two men) up the mountain: not foot-climbing, except for very healthy and athletic people, and never for ladies. About three hours, by horse, after a succession of views embracing nearly all the cities, lakes and mountains of Switzerland, to the

Rhigi-Stœffel, half a mile from the top, where horses are generally kept and lodging may (or may *not*) be procured. Thence to the

Rhigi-Kulm (top), from which, if reached in time, one of the most memorable of sunsets is likely to be enjoyed. But the Rhigi is especially ascended to see the

Sunrise, which demands getting up at call, and some shivering, but presents one of the noblest mountain-top sunrise-views on the globe, embracing all Switzerland and seeming to embrace half the rest of the world.

Down from the Rhigi, the same morning, on foot preferable, by

Kaltbad, charmingly located half-way up, with many fine views of Pilatus, the distant Oberland, over the Lake of the Canton Uri, etc., to

Weggis, whence steamer back to Lucerne, whence rail is taken to

Bâle (Basle, or Basel), on the Rhine, reached in about four to six hours. It has some forty thousand inhabitants, and a thriving trade; presents the oddest bridge in the world—one side of stone and the other of wood; has rope-and-current ferries that no one should miss; shows an old Cathedral with the ugliest sculptures on the habitable globe, but some other good buildings, and is worth seeing in default of anything better.

This ends, of necessity, all that can be accomplished by the short-trip tourist in Switzerland, and it will be found to embrace the best of Swiss scenery. Those who have abundant means and leisure, of course, should see the Lakes of Zurich, Constanz, Neufchâtel, etc., the Falls of Schaffhausen, and the Monte Rosa chain of mountains; but only those who have both at free command, can hope for much more than has been here hurriedly outlined, except in making one or the other of the great passes of the Alps into Italy, briefly to be alluded to in a following paper.

XV.

BALE TO STRASBOURG AND BADEN-BADEN.

THE most closely pressed of short-trip travellers, having reached so far as Bâle, should not return without touching Eastern France and Germany, at Strasbourg and Baden-Baden. For this

Rail from Bâle, through the Lower Rhine provinces, with scenery altogether tamed down from that of Switzerland, and only a few glimpses of the mountains that are being left behind—with the only important stoppage at Colmar—some eight hours to

STRASBOURG, on the extreme eastern border of France, the most important eastern city of the empire—called, indeed, the "Paris of Eastern France." It is pleasantly situated; contains some 80,000 inhabitants; is heavily fortified and garrisoned, as a guard against German encroachments; and presents one of the most attractive points of all European travel. The most notable of its many curiosities are: first,

The Cathedral, or Münster, with the tallest spire in the world (said to be 475 feet above the ground), the steeple of such delicate tracery that it seems to be lace-work, and the immense building, the very body of which is higher than the other steeples of the city, a wilderness of fine sculpture, statues, bas-reliefs, rich Gothic taste and interminable labor. It is said to have been commenced in 1277 and finished in 1601. Within, the massiveness and height of its columns and arches are well matched by the splendor of its organ, pulpit and side-chapels; while its

Great Astronomical Clock is well known as one of the world's wonders. That ingenious colossal structure winds only once in ninety-nine years; shows not only the apparent time but the astronomical, the eclipses and other celestial phenomena; and at 12 noon, every day, the Cathedral is visited by hundreds to see the mechanical cock which surmounts it clap his wings, and hear him crow—and to see the Twelve Apostles make their circuit around the figure of the Saviour. Next to the Cathedral, in interest, is the

Church of St. Thomas, very old, containing the sarcophagus of Bishop Adeloque, died in 836; the splendid tomb of Marshal Saxe—one of the finest in France; and the ghastly but instructive embalmed bodies, in glass-covered coffins, of Count Nassau-Salberg and his daughter, of the sixteenth century; besides many other antiquities and curiosities. Next to this comes the fine

Public Library, with many antiquities in the art of printing, and a splendid statue of Guttenberg without; but scarcely second to these are the

Old Houses, some of them among the finest and best-preserved in Europe, and one of them, especially, authenticated as between 800 and 900 years old, and a marvel of stone-work, especially in its matchless spiral stairway. Within this house, too, are the fragments of the old clock (cock included) and of portions of the Cathedral destroyed by the revolutionists in 1793, but since restored. One other feature of Strasbourg deserves note and must command it—

The Storks, apparently the protected "totem" of the city, visible everywhere, with nests covering nearly one-third of the chimneys in the older portions. To this incomplete summary should be added, that Strasbourg is the home and centre of the *pâtés des foies gras* (goose-liver pies) manufacture, to be found in such freshness and perfection nowhere else,—and that marching troops are always to be seen, and drums and bugles always to be heard, in its streets.

From Strasbourg, by rail, across the Rhine, a few miles distant, to

Kehl, where France changes to Germany and baggage is examined. The changes of cars are numerous, vexatious and unexplainable, and some three hours are consumed in going only forty miles, at the end of which the dark hills of the Black Forest rise around the traveller, and he is disembarked at

BADEN-BADEN, chief and most beautiful of the gambling resorts of Europe. It is charmingly located in a valley at the foot of and partially surrounded by the hills of the Black Forest; and every appliance that art and taste could suggest has been added to make it attractive. Its first attraction, of course, is

The Kursaal (Conversation-House), a noble structure, with splendid promenade-grounds in front, and the rooms furnished and decorated with regal luxury —where the gambling-tables are ever filled from early morning to the closing hour at 11 P. M., and where the wealth, ruin, crime and opportunities for melancholy study (and often for something worse) are unbounded. The playing, principally *rouge et noir* and *roulette*, is carried on in three principal rooms, all ages, conditions, and nearly as many women as men, being among the gamblers. There are also private rooms, where, hazard, ecarté, etc., are played by smaller parties. One end of the great building is a restaurant, and the other a ball-room and theatre, with either balls or performances two or three times a week during the "season." In front of the Kursaal is a music pavilion, where some of the finest bands in Germany play, during afternoons in summer, to immense concourses of promenaders from all lands—besides supplying music during the evenings. Next in importance to the Kursaal is

The Trinkhalle (Drinking-House), an elegant building with magnificent piazza frescoed with the history and legends of Baden, standing to the left and a little in front of the principal attraction, with the Spa water (warm) always on free draught, and warm baths ready for those who desire to test the medicinal properties of the springs.

The Theatre, standing almost in front of the Conversation-House, is one of the handsomest in Europe, and opera is given there unexceptionably, two or three evenings a week, alternating the performance at the Kursaal, during the "season." Additional attractions are found in the very handsome walks and promenades with which the town abounds, and in the fine and costly wares kept lavishly in the shops that line the streets and stud the eastern side of the promenade-grounds.

The principal excursions from Baden are to the

Cours de Bade, or race-course, four or five miles away westward—famous for its green turf track, the gatherings of notables and heavy betting which take place there every year, in September, while the ride to it supplies charming scenery; and to the

Black Forest, the dark hills and sombre woods (mostly firs) of which surround Baden on three sides, with splendid dusky drives through them, and the two castles,

The Alt Schloss and *Nieu Schloss*, which crown eminences in the vicinity, and not only afford a very favorable impression of the old knightly robber-holds of Germany, but show subterranean passages between the two of great length, and some of the instruments of torture and death once said to have been employed by the dreaded Vehmgericht, or "Secret Tribunal of Germany." The Nieu Schloss is the residence of the Grand Dukes of Baden; the Alt was that of their ancestors. The ruins of the Alt Schloss are very fine; the rides through the forest to them are notably handsome and memorable; and charming views are caught from the heights (especially near the Alt Schloss) over the distant Rhine and low country—with even finer (including the spire of Strasbourg Cathedral) from the top of the immense pile.

There are some interesting excursions from Baden-Baden, to the Yburg, New Eberstein etc. (castles), but they are scarcely likely to be taken by the short-trip tourist.

Of course, for the visits to the *Cours*, the old castles, etc., already noted, carriages are required, and they may be had at fair prices, at the hotels, even in the height of the season: everything else at Baden may and should be seen on foot, the distances being trifling.

XVI.

SHORT TRIPS IN GERMANY.

By right of natural division, of course, that portion of the preceding paper, relating to Baden-Baden, should have been included in this. But so many persons, travelling on "tourist-tickets," merely run over the border to Baden without setting foot in another German city, that the division already made will be held excusable.

From Baden-Baden, those who end their tour eastward at that point return to Strasbourg and take rail direct thence back to Paris, the run being made in twelve to fourteen hours, by Nancy, Bar-le-Duc, Châlons-sur-Marne, Epernay (dinner, if by the morning-train from Strasbourg), Thierry, and Neuilly.

But even those who have but limited time and are not prepared for much additional expense, when at Baden should endeavor to strain a point, before returning to Paris and the English ports, so far as to do

FROM BADEN-BADEN DOWN THE RHINE.

For this the route is taken from Baden by rail (same road as on arrival), connection being made with main line, going north, at Oos—sometimes without change. First place of importance, passed through within a few miles, is

Rastadt, an old town, of which the chief point worth hurried observation is to be found in the very heavy and formidable fortifications, about which France and Germany are generally quarrelling. An hour and a half later,

Carlsruhe ("Charles's Rest"), capital of the Grand Duchy of Baden, and one of the most tastefully-laid-out, well-shaded and beautiful little towns in Europe. Glimpses can be caught, from the railway, of the Duke's Palace, an imposing and handsome building, on elevated ground; and those who have time for lying over one train, will find the Academy worth visiting for the sake of its pictures and frescoes. The next important stoppage beyond Carlsruhe, is

Bruchsal, where the rail from Constance and northeastern Switzerland, by Stuttgart, intersects; and no other point of importance presents itself, until reaching

HEIDELBERG, still in Baden, on the south bank of the Neckar (a confluent of the Rhine, running into it from the east), considered one of the handsomest towns in Germany, besides holding an almost unequalled reputation for the erudition of its very old University, and having a world of historical recollections connected with the Electors Palatine (who used to make their seat there), and the battles and sieges that have raged around it. The principal curiosities in the town (where a day should be spent if time allows) are the University; the Castle, a massive half-ruined structure, said to have been built as an Electoral residence in the fourteenth century, and especially noted for its extensive cellars and the celebrated "Heidelberg Tun" located there; the Church of the Holy Ghost, which has the odd peculiarity of being partitioned in the centre, so that Catholics and Protestants can hold service at the same time; the Church of St. Peter, where Jerome of Prague, the reformer, nailed his defiance to the Papacy; the fine views over the valley of the Neckar, from the terrace of the Castle; the very long and handsome principal street on which nearly the whole city seems to be built, etc.

From Heidelberg by rail, direct, in two to three hours, and passing through no places of special interest, though much fine Rhenish scenery, vineyards, etc., to

FRANKFORT-ON-THE-MAINE, lying, as its name indicates, on the river Maine, another eastern confluent of the Rhine. Frankfort is one of the oldest and most interesting cities of Germany, alike for its fine old buildings, its rich historical associations, and its having been for so many centuries one of the great moneyed centres of Europe. It had been, since the twelfth century, a free city, and the capital of the Germanic Confederation, until absorbed by Prussia in 1866. The Emperor Charlemagne is said to have had a palace here, in the eighth century, and all the Emperors of Germany have been elected and crowned in the Cathedral. The Rothschild family had their beginning here, and their house is shown; while the residences of other bankers are many and most magnificent. The first object of interest is the Cathedral (or "Dom"), with unfinished tower, dating back to the thirteenth century, with some fine monuments, especially those of the Emperors Gunther and Rudolph of Sachsenhausen; next the Town Hall, with its immense banqueting-tower and picture-gallery of the Emperors, and the market-place opposite, where at the imperial festivities they roasted oxen whole and outdid Jack Cade by making the fountains run with wine; next the State Museum and Academy of Painting, with many fine works of art; then the house and statue of Goethe (born here); the fine bridge over the Maine to the suburb of Sachsenhausen, etc. From Frankfort by rail, a very brief ride, to

Wiesbaden, capital of the Grand Duchy of Nassau, of which the best idea may be given in saying that it is a miniature Baden-Baden; dividing with Homburg the credit of being next to it in gambling; less select and more crowded in society; lacking the Black Forest hills which make one of the great charms of Baden, but supplying the deficiency with a charming little lake which forms the favorite pleasure-resort, with fine gardens, orchards, and a beautiful situation generally. It has a Kursaal, of course, and all the gayeties of its greater rival, but is not worth so extended a study. From Wiesbaden the run should be made back by rail, as if returning to Frankfort, to the fine old town of

Mayence (German "Mainz"), lying on the bank of the Rhine, a commercial city of importance, and chief town of Hesse-Darmstadt. It is heavily fortified and garrisoned; was one of the chief ecclesiastical cities in the centuries following Charlemagne;

and was held during a long siege by the French under Napoleon. Its principal buildings of interest are the Cathedral, an immense pile of red sandstone (which would have delighted Hugh Miller), now somewhat damaged by time and war, but with a wonderful collection of Electoral and other monuments within. Quite of as much interest will be found the "bridge of boats," nearly 1800 feet in length, across the Rhine; the site of the house of Guttenberg, inventor of printing (born here), etc.

At Mayence the rail should be abandoned and one of the steamers taken (going two or three times a day, first, second and third class, and with meals on board)—

DOWN THE RHINE, as here the beauty and interest of that river really begin. In the limited space at command here, of course no attempt at describing the scenery of that world-celebrated river can be made: all that is either possible or needful is merely to name the principal places of interest, and whether on the right or left bank, descending; a little faculty of observation and the "comparing of notes" inevitable on a Rhine steamer (always half-freighted with English and Americans), and a good local guide-book, which no one should fail to purchase at Mayence or earlier, will supply enough additional knowledge for identification.

One additional remark is, however, necessary, before proceeding—that nearly all the Rhine, from Mayence to Cologne, is hilly and rocky-banked, something like the Hudson in its wilder passes, but dotted with cities, towns and castles, picturesque in effect,—and that vineyards are almost universal. Perhaps no better description was ever given within the same space, than that applied to the Rhine by Praed, in the "Bridal of Belmont," and pages of dry phrases would not convey half so much:

> "Where foams and flows the glorious Rhine,
>   Many a ruin wan and gray
> O'erlooks the cornfield and the vine,
>   Majestic in its dark decay.
> Among their dim clouds, long ago,
> They mocked the battles that raged below:
>   * * * * * * Homes of pride
> That frown on the breast of the peaceful tide."

The first points of special interest, after leaving Mayence, are found, successively, in

Beiberich, on the right, celebrated for the quality of its wines; then

Johannisberg, castle and town, also on the right, yet more celebrated for the production of the celebrated "Johannisberger" wine—the vineyard once in the possession of Napoleon, and given by him (as he gave away crowns) to General Kellermann, the dragoon. Then

Rudesheim, also on the right, little less celebrated than Johannisberg, for a corresponding reason.

Very shortly after passing Rudesheim, the interest changes entirely to the left bank, in view of the pleasant little town of

Bingen (not "Binjen," as many call it—but "Bing-en"), lying at the mouth of the river Nahe, famous for its wine-trade, but much more for Mrs. Norton's touching poem, "Bingen on the Rhine."

On the opposite side of the mouth of the Nahe stands the

Castle of Ehrenfels, a picturesque robber-hold of the middle ages; and near the river mouth, on a low flat, a small square tower, the

Mouse Tower, immortalized by the story of Bishop Hatto, who kept his corn and starved the poor, then burned them in his barn—the revenge coming in the shape of all the mice in Germany (Southey blunders into calling them "rats") attacking the tower and eating up the Bishop with everything else!

Bacharach is passed at the left, not long after leaving Bingen; then

St. Goar, one of the old monkish holds, and very picturesque; then at

Lahnstein, on the left, the debarkation is made for Ems, another and smaller watering-and-gambling-place; while at the right, opposite, is the fine and well-preserved

Castle of Stotzenfels, belonging to the King of Prussia, and where he entertained Queen Victoria and Prince Albert in 1845, while the interior decorations of the Castle are magnificent, and it contains many curiosities in the armory—among others, swords of Napoleon, Wellington and Blucher. The next point of special interest is the large town of

Coblentz, on the left, at the intersection of the Moselle and the Rhine, heavily fortified, and with another bridge of boats; and opposite it the tremendous rocky fortress of

Ehrenbreitstein (the "bright stone of honor"),

nearly 400 feet above the level of the river, and believed to be impregnable, so that the tourist (and reader) may be spared the figures of its guns, cost and garrison. A short distance below Coblentz and Ehrenbreitstein, is passed, on the left, the

White Tower, where the French revolutionary army, under General Hoche, crossed in the face of the Austrians in 1797. Next are passed, on the right,

Neuwied, town, with a palace belonging to the King of Prussia; on the left,

Andernach, with heavy fortifications and a fine watch-tower near the river; on the right the

Castle of Hammerstein (fine ruins—800 years old); on the left the

Castle of Rheineck (ruins), with modern residence attached, and Brohl (village) near; then on the right, with heavy fortifications,

Linz (town); and near it, also on the right, the

Castle of Ochenfels (ruins, black and sombre). Just below, and among what is considered the very finest portion of the Rhine scenery, stands, on the left, the

Castle of Rolandseck, said to have been built by the celebrated paladin, Roland, that he might overlook the place of abode of his promised bride, who had believed him slain at Roncesvalles and taken the veil in the convent of

Nonnenwerden (St. Ursula—" silence "), of which the ruins are to be seen on a little island opposite. Nearly opposite Rolandseck, on the right, is the rocky

Drachenfels ("castled crag of Drachenfels,"

Byron), crowned with the ruins of an old castle, and around it the peaks of the bold group of hills called the " Seven Mountains," all 900 to 1,200 feet in height.

It is only a short time after leaving the Drachenfels, when at the left is seen

Bonn, with one of the largest and most excellent Universities in the world ; a Cathedral, or Minster, showing the oddity of five towers, and alleged to have been built by the Empress Helena ; and suburbs of singular shaded beauty. But all eyes are now necessarily turned ahead, to the termination of the Rhine trip, which is shortly after reached (for the short-trip tourist) at

COLOGNE, on the left bank of the Rhine, containing some 120,000 inhabitants ; and lying along the river-curve in a crescent bending outward. It is very old (said to have been founded by Agrippina, daughter of the Roman Emperor Germanicus) ; very picturesque in its old houses and river-frontage ; very dirty (as are, however, most German towns) ; and very celebrated as having given name to the " Cologne water," not one millionth part of which ever saw it. Of course people go to Cologne principally to see

The Cathedral, one of the most stupendous specimens of Gothic architecture in the world, and perfectly dizzying to the thought in the extent of its size and details. It is said to have been commenced in 1248, to be finished probably in 2048, when the two towers, as yet "no-horned," though even now wonderful in height, are each to reach 500 feet—the extreme length of the building. Within, it is quite as magnificent as without, with the Chapel of the "Three Kings of Cologne" (the three wise men of the East who came to worship the infant Christ) behind the high altar, and the wealth of an empire lavished on the case containing their bones, and on similar objects. The whole cathedral is full of relics and objects of devotion, besides some fine paintings; and no brief time will suffice to study it thoroughly within and without. But perhaps scarcely second even to the Cathedral, in special interest, is the

Church of St. Ursula, containing exposed the bones of the Eleven Thousand Virgins who accompanied St. Ursula on a pilgrimage to Rome, and were murdered by the Huns on their return, for refusing to break their vow of chastity. The whole church is full of bones and skulls piled on shelves and heaped miscellaneously; and the spectacle is edifying—more or less, according as one believes or disbelieves the story, or wishes or does not wish to see womankind reduced to "first principles." After St. Ursula, those of the many remaining churches of Cologne, best worth visiting, are, that of St. Peter, containing the font in which the painter Rubens (native of Cologne) was baptized, and his masterpiece of the "Crucifixion" supplying the after-piece; that of St. Mary, alleged to be nearly 1,200 years old, with some interesting effigies and pictures, that of St. Pantaleon, etc.

FROM COLOGNE WESTWARD TO PARIS OR THE CHANNEL.

(*Route I.*)

Return may be made from Cologne direct to Paris, by the Rhenish Railway, to

AIX-LA-CHAPELLE, a fine old town of Rhenish Prussia, boasting the residence of Charlemagne and the sepulture of that great monarch and many of his successors. Its first point of interest is the Cathedral, which is one of the oldest in Europe, and holds, besides the tomb of Charlemagne, the greatest collection of sacred relics, gathered from every land, to be found in any one spot on the globe. Among the chief of them (about the authenticity of which each may decide for himself), are a piece of the Cross, a locket of the hair of the Virgin Mary, the leathern girdle of Christ, the bones of St. Stephen, a piece of Aaron's rod, the Saviour's swaddling-clothes, the scarf He wore at the Crucifixion, the robe worn by the Virgin at the Nativity, the cloth on which John the Baptist's head was laid, etc. Aix has many historical reminiscences—(among others, several Peace-Congresses); a splendid bronze statue of Charlemagne in the market-place; has warm medicinal springs and a *Kurhaus;* and manufactures extensively.

From Aix-la-Chapelle, still by rail, to

LIEGE, in Belgium, handsomely situated on the river Meuse, with the most extensive cannon, firearms and iron manufactories, on the continent. It has a fine old Cathedral (said to date back to the tenth century), with some good paintings and the best carved pulpit (of oak) in Europe; a church of St. Jacques, with stained glass of rare perfection; a Palace of Justice, once the abode of the mighty Bishops of Liege, and famous as the scene of a large part of Scott's novel of "Quentin Durward." A little time can be excellently spent in Liege, examining the manufactories—especially those of firearms. From Liege, on by rail to

Namur, also on the Meuse, at its intersection with the Sambre—principally notable for its extensive manufactures of iron and steel, and its connection with the old wars of Flanders. From Namur, by rail to

Charleroi, heavily fortified, as affording one of the strongest defences of Belgium against France—and with coal-fields, iron-foundries, nail-factories, etc., seeming to blend English Birmingham and Wolverhampton.

Shortly after leaving Charleroi, France is entered (at Jeumont), where baggage is examined. Thence the route is pursued by Cambrai, noted for giving name to "cambric," first manufactured here, and for the treaty of peace between Charles V. and Francis I., some time after the battle of Pavia; by St. Quentin, memorable for its storming by the Spaniards and English, from the French, in the time of the English Queen Mary; by Noyon, with a fine old cathedral, and noted as the birth-place of Calvin; and by Compeigne, with the imperial palace and magnificent forest used in the hunting-season by Napoleon III.; to Paris.

(*Route II.*)

The tourist who has finished with Paris before going to Switzerland and the Rhine, should pursue the route already indicated, from Cologne by Aix-la-Chapelle and Liege to Namur, but there branch off by rail, directly northwestward, to

BRUSSELS, the capital of Belgium, beautifully situated on rising ground beside the river Senne, a southern branch of the Scheldt—considered one of the best-shaded cities and handsomest residences in Europe. It has many attractions, in the Palace and Park of the King of Belgium; the Parliament Houses; the Hôtel de Ville, very old and fine, with an enormous pyramidal tower nearly four hundred feet in height; the Old Palace, with its great variety of Rubens's and other pictures; the fine old churches of St. Gudule (Cathedral), La Chapelle, Bon Secours, etc.; some excellent characteristic fountains, the great carpet and lace manufactories, etc. Several days may be profitably spent in Brussels; but the short-trip tourist, with a good cab and intelligent driver, can " do " it very fairly in a single day, setting aside a second day for the indispensable carriage or stage ride to the

Battle-field of Waterloo, about twelve miles from the city, where the destiny of Europe is believed to have been decided in the final defeat of Napoleon by Wellington and Blucher on the memorable 18th June, 1815. Plenty of guides and local guide-books can be found both at Brussels and in the neighborhood of the battle-field; and there is not the least difficulty in purchasing, in either place, any desired quantity of relics of the battle—authentic or not, according as the tourist is of a robust faith. [N. B.— Those who do not wish to be excessively bored, should " check off " the guide at his first attempt to relate the events of the battle; though he may be allowed, with all propriety, to conduct the visitor up the great mound in the centre of the field, crowned with the bronze lion (arms of Belgium), and marking the spot where the Prince of Orange fell—as well as to show the site of the old Château of Hougomont, the Farmhouse of La Haye Sainte, and the Sunken Road from Wavres, points at and around which the battle was really decided.]

From Brussels, by rail, by Malines (one of the most celebrated of the lace-manufacturing towns), to

ANTWERP, on the river Scheldt, about half the size of Brussels, and second town of Belgium in importance—formerly the first. It has some shipping and foreign trade, and many buildings of great cost and beauty, while some of its streets, and especially the Great Place de Mère, may vie with any in Europe for beauty. Its chief attractions are to be found in the immense Cathedral, of magnificent architecture, and one of its two towers among the highest and most delicately-finished in the world; in the iron canopy, at the foot of the Cathedral tower, the work of Quentin Matsys, the blacksmith-painter; in Rubens's " Descent from the Cross " (his greatest work), found within the Cathedral, with other noted works by the same master; in the Museum, with one of the finest collections of pictures in Europe—especially rich in the works of Rubens, Vandyke, and other Flemish artists; in the churches of St. Augustine, St. Paul, St. Anthony, etc.; and the house where Rubens lived and died.

From Antwerp rail may be taken to the fine old walled town of

Ghent, scene of many of the most interesting historical occurrences of Belgium, and especially of the memorable episode of the patriot Philip van Artevelde. Among its leading curiosities will be found the very old Gateway, once belonging to the castle of the English John of Gaunt, Duke of Lancaster, built more than a thousand years ago; the Cathedral of St. Bavon, with a striking marble interior and Chapter Arms of the Spanish Order of the Golden Fleece, which once had its place of authority here; the Belfry Tower, near the Cathedral, from which the warning bell rang to announce the (frequent) approach of invaders—its summit dragon-crowned and its base a prison; the Church of St. Michael, containing Vandyke's "Crucifixion"; its many picturesque bridges; and the immense number of factories, for making everything, from laces and silks to dyes and whiskeys.

If the Channel is to be crossed from Ostend, the tourist proceeds by rail from Ghent to

Bruges, another fine old Flemish town, with even more bridges than Ghent, and almost as great a historical interest. It has a splendid old Cathedral (Notre Dame) with a tower of wondrous height, and within it may be seen the gorgeous gilded tombs of Charles the Bold (Duke of Burgundy) and his daughter Mary, Empress of Austria, as well as many fine pictures. There is also attraction to be found in the Hospital of St. John, with its many relics; in the Cathedral of Saint Sauveur, Church of Jerusalem, etc.; but, to Americans especially, one of the most notable features will be found in the Belfry, in the Market Square, very lofty and of splendid Gothic architecture, with a chime of forty-eight bells, some of them fabulously large, and almost constantly ringing — while Longfellow has doubly immortalized it in his fine poem of the "Belfry of Bruges," commencing

"In the market-place of Bruges stands a belfry old and brown,
Thrice consumed and thrice rebuilded, still it towers o'er the town."

From Bruges only an hour by rail to

Ostend, a fine old Belgian port on the Channel, with no feature, however, demanding stay. From Ostend steamers leave every evening for Dover, in England,—the time occupied being from five to eight hours, according to weather.

If, from Ghent, the traveller prefers less Channel-passage with more riding by railway, that end can be secured by running southward by rail, past Courtrai and Mouscron, to

Lille, another very old Flemish town, with nearly the same features of industry, manufacture and antiquity, observed from Aix to Bruges; thence by the Northern of France Railway to

Calais, with steamer passage to Dover in one-and-a-half to two hours.

HINT FOR LONGER TOUR — LAKE CONSTANCE BY INNSPRUCK, MUNICH, DRESDEN, BERLIN, ETC.

In the preceding has been given all that the short-trip tourist can hope to see of Germany during any one season; but a hint may be of advantage to those who have leisure for something longer, or to the same persons when chancing to be a second time nearly within the same districts.

One of the most splendid routes in the world, and certainly one of the most varied in scenery and the character of the inhabitants, may be pursued as follows, supposing the tourist to be a second time in Switzerland, or supposing him to prefer this to all or a great part of the German succession already given:

The Swiss Lake Constance (easternmost of the whole group, and not before mentioned in the short trips in Switzerland) may be reached by rail from either Berne or Bâle; then the lake is descended by boat to

Bregenz, at the extreme eastern end. From Bregenz, by eilwagen (mail-diligence), across the lesser mountains separating Switzerland and the Tyrol (Austrian), by Feldkirch, Stuben, St. Anton, Landeck, Imst, Silz, etc., through grand wild scenery and with excellent opportunity for studying the picturesque Tyrolese costumes, to

INNSPRUCK, capital of the Tyrol, splendidly situated on the river Inn, and almost completely hemmed in by mountains of great height. It has a wonderful variety of monuments in the Hofkirche, among the rest that of Maximilian I., one of the finest in Europe, that of the patriot Hofer, etc. The Imperial Palace, Museum, etc., and the old Castle of Ambras, are all worth visiting,—as also the scenes in the neighborhood where the Tyrolese won such bloody victories during the Napoleonic wars. From Innspruck, by rail, to

MUNICH, capital of the Kingdom of Bavaria, lying on the river Aar, and challenging all the other capitals of Europe for beauty, especially since the thousand costly improvements made by the late King Louis I. (friend of Lola Montez, who literally reigned here for a short period). It is almost equally matchless in buildings, public grounds, and disputes with Paris, Rome and Madrid the palm as a repository of art. The leading attractions are found in the Residenz, or Royal Palace, a part very old and a second part new and yet more elegant—with courts, fountains, statuary and antiquities, magnificent halls, etc.; the Pincothek, or Picture-Gallery, with some thirteen hundred of the best paintings of all schools (open every day except Saturday); the Glypothek, or Sculpture-Gallery (open Mondays, Wednesdays and Saturdays), only second to the picture collection; the Schwanthaler Museum; the Royal Brewery, where the celebrated Bavarian beer has its fountainhead; the Public Library, second in size in the world (nearly a million volumes); and many splendid churches and monuments, only to be intelligently seen with a guide or *valet de place*. From Munich, by rail, to

Augsburg, a pleasant old town on the river Lech, with many historical recollections, and the Bishop's Palace still standing in which the noted Augsburg Confession of Faith was framed, and where Luther held his interview with the Cardinal Gacta, before proceeding to the reformation extremities; the old

Fugger House, commemorating the Austrian Rothschild; the Fountain of Augustus; the wilderness of watchmakers' shops, etc. From Augsburg by rail to

NUREMBERG, on the river Pegnitz—once one of the richest cities in Europe, now principally famous for its monopoly of the making of toys, and to Americans as the scene of another of Longfellow's finest poems, "Nuremberg," in which

"In the valley of the Pegnitz, where across broad meadow-lands,
Rise the blue Franconian Mountains, Nuremberg, the ancient, stands."

It is famous in the world of art as the birth-place of Albert Dürer, the painter and engraver, and for the many fine sculptures in the Churches of St. Lawrence, St. Sebald (which contains the tomb of Dürer); and additional attractions are found in the rock-throned Castle, dating back to the eleventh century, the Churchyard of St. John, with many interesting monuments, etc. From Nuremberg, by rail, by Bamberg, Lichtenfels and Chemnitz, to

DRESDEN, the capital of Saxony, on the river Elbe, with an old and a new town (something like Edinburgh) on the two sides of the river, and a splendid bridge of 1,400 feet in length connecting. Dresden is so complete in situation, shade, walks and laying out, as to hold the name of the "Northern Florence"; and it is considered by many the equal of any other capital in Europe, while in works of art, and especially in antique jewelry and fine sculptures, it is certainly unequalled. Its leading attraction is

IN GERMANY.

the celebrated "Dresden Gallery," with world-wide reputation, and full of the best works of the old Italian and German masters. The Zwinger (buildings and promenade-grounds) contains a fine armory, with many military and historical curiosities—and a rich Museum of Natural History; and the Japanese Palace, with its collection, the Frauenkirche, etc., are well worth visiting.

From Dresden, by rail, to

BERLIN, the capital of Prussia, one of the largest, handsomest, and now one of the most powerful, of all the capitals of Europe. It contains nearly three quarters of a million inhabitants; is some twelve miles in circumference; holds in garrison from 20,000 to 50,000 soldiers; supplies one street, "Unter den Linden," lined with palaces and almost matchless in fragrant shade; has many handsome monuments, among which the colossal equestrian one of Frederick the Great stands without superior in Europe; has a Museum especially rich in works of art (ranking perhaps second in Europe); and supplies a world of other attractions, as well as temptations to residence, in its Royal Palace, Opera-House, Arsenal, and splendid walks and drives, when "done" as it should be, under intelligent guidance.

From Berlin, by rail, direct to

HAMBURG, on the Elbe, one of the leading free-cities of Germany, with a world of industry and manufactures and a heavy shipping-trade; while the city has a perfect circumvallation of gardens, and is tasteful and handsome. Its most attractive buildings are the Exchange and the Churches of St. Peter and

St. Michael—the latter with a tower of 460 feet and one of the finest organs in Germany.

From Hamburg, steamer may be taken to an English port, or to America if the tour is ended; or rail may be taken southward and westward, from Harburg, on the opposite side of the Elbe, across Hanover and Belgium, intersecting the railway from Cologne at Aix-la-Chapelle, and the route to the Channel pursued by Brussels and Ghent to Ostend or Calais, as before noted.

Or, this may be shortened a little by leaving out Hamburg, and taking rail direct from Berlin by Aix-la-Chapelle, to Brussels, etc.

XVII.

ACROSS THE ALPS TO ITALY.

THERE are three principal routes by which the passage of the Alps, southward to Italy, is effected. The first, or most westerly, is from St. Michel, France, to Susa, in Italy, and is known as the "Mt. Cenis" route. The second, next westerly, takes its departure from Martigny, near the eastern end of the Lake of Geneva (Switzerland), ends at Aosta, and is known as the passage of the "Great St. Bernard." The third, and most easterly, may be said to commence at Andermatt, after that point is reached from Lucerne by way of the Lake of the Canton Uri, Fluellen and Altorf,—is known as the "St. Gotthard," crossing the range of that name to Bellinzona, near the head of Lake Maggiore. There is yet a fourth, called the "Simplon," reached by going up the Valley of the Rhone from Martigny (first route), crossing by the mighty work of engineering performed by Napoleon, the "Simplon Road," passing near Domo d'Ossola, and also ending on Lake Maggiore, though near the centre of the Lake and much farther southwestward than the end of the St. Gotthard.

These passes are all picturesque, beyond comparison with any other European scenery; all more or less fatiguing, and often exciting to the timid or nervous; but none of them has any absolute danger, except when pursued too early in the summer or too late in the autumn, and ladies make them habitually.

THE MT. CENIS ROUTE.

By this route the amount of necessary fatigue is much less than by either of the others, while the travel is certainly much less picturesque. Up to 1867 the conveyance was from St. Michel, in the Maurienne Valley (reached by rail from either Paris, Lyons or Geneva, by Amberieux [junction—see "Paris to Geneva"], Aix and Chambery) by diligence over that fine mountain-range, with magnificent views of Mont Blanc and the whole range of the White Alps, caught northward at many points, in fine weather. By this route the road, after leaving St. Michel, sweeps a considerable distance northward and eastward, before entering the mountains—by St. Andre, Modane, Villeraudin, Termignon and Lans le Bourg; then sheering southward, the actual ascent is commenced at or near Tavernette, the crossing being thence made diagonally southeastward, on the eastern side of Mt. Cenis, to Molaret, where the sharpest line of descent ends, and thence to Susa.

In 1867, however, a new and marked triumph in engineering was inaugurated, in the completion of a temporary railway of peculiar character over the mountain, a third or middle rail, with extra horizontal or gripping wheels, enabling trains to be drawn up the whole northern steep with a slow, steady, and apparently safe motion, and to be lowered on the southern side at corresponding rate and safety. Henceforth, of course, the mission of the diligences ended, as this link completes the great railway line from France and all Central Europe to Italy and all Southern. Even this is but temporary, however, for the great Mt. Cenis Tunnel is slowly but steadily progressing through the bowels of the mountain, and by 1870 or 1871 it is expected that trains will be able to pass through it, on the ordinary level,—the result being that special lovers of their ease will all adopt the Mt. Cenis route and ride into Italy as elsewhere on the "dead level," while others who have more regard for the picturesque than the practical, will be driven away to some one of the other routes. This link, however, will also perfect a mightier chain than that of tourist-travel, by making complete the railway communication from Calais on the British Channel to Brindisi on the Adriatic (near the extreme end of the Italian "boot-heel" peninsula), whence the steamers leave for the shortest of all routes from Western Europe to India.

The disembarkation, by railway as formerly by diligence, will be made at

Susa (said to be the site of the old Roman Segusium), with fine mountain scenery, and two artificial objects commanding attention: the Roman Arch, erected B. C. 8, and once forming the entrance to the town from the Roman road to Gaul over Mont Genèvre; and the Cathedral of St. Justus, bearing date of the eleventh century, with some antique curiosities in the inner chapels. From Susa by rail to *Tu-*

rin, etc., as will be seen by the following paper, "Short Trips in Italy."

THE GREAT ST. BERNARD PASS AND ROUTE.

As already indicated, the commencement of the Great St. Bernard route is reached at Martigny, by steamer or rail from Geneva to Villeneuve and the termination of railway travel at Martigny—the route, thus far, being precisely the same taken on the way to Chamounix.

The time consumed on this route, between Martigny (Switzerland), and Aosta (Italy), should be from 18 to 22 hours. It may be made on foot by the very robust, in a somewhat longer time, and by spending one night at the Hospice. The better plan, however, is to take carriage from Martigny to the Cantine de Proz, only 7½ miles from the Hospice, with led mules attached, to be ridden thence to the Hospice, and either the same or other mules to St. Remy, five or six miles beyond. From St. Remy to Aosta, carriage again. Or, for those who prefer more saddle-exercise and less carriage-confinement, carriage may merely be taken from Martigny to Liddes, about half-way to the Hospice—then mules to the Hospice and on to St. Remy, then carriages down to Aosta, as before.

The principal points of interest on this route (by many thought to be very interesting) are the passage up from Martigny through the Valley of the Dranse, to Bovernier; then to Sembranchier, with the ruins of a fine old castle, said to have been once of great size and power, accommodating the Emperor

Sigismund, who stopped there, with 800 nobles to wait on him; then Orsières, with very fine view, especially of the snow peak of Mt. Velan; then Liddes (station), with entrance into the wild Forest of St. Pierre; then St. Pierre Mont Joux, with some fine waterfalls and terrible gorges just beyond, rendered memorable by the fact that from here to the summit was found the most disheartening difficulty by Napoleon and the French troops, dragging up their dismounted guns, with the carriages packed on mules, in that wonderful "Passage of the Alps," from Geneva by Martigny, in May, 1800.

Then *Cantine de Proz* (station—positive end of the carriage-road and commencement of the bridle-path), with still finer views of Mt. Velan, only a few miles southeastward. Thence the bridle-path traverses the pastures of the Plan de Proz, ascends the very wild Defilé de Marengo; not long afterwards passes two stone huts of interest, the one being a place of refuge for both people and cattle, and the other the old Morgue for preserving the bodies of those perished in the snow (see Cooper's "Headsman of Berne," Chaps. XXIII. and XXIV.); then the Dranse is crossed by the Bridge of Nudri, the Vallée des Morts (Valley of the Dead) is crossed, bringing the tourist to

THE HOSPICE OF ST. BERNARD, a monastery consisting of two large massive stone buildings, partitioned into many rooms for the care and resuscitation of travellers—one of the highest places of dwelling in Europe, as it is one of the purest of benevolences and most celebrated of landmarks. The buildings have stood for some three hundred years, being erected solely for the succor of those crossing the Alps; and the monks have their first duty (with the wonderful and somewhat fierce dogs kept here) in rescuing those who would otherwise perish in storms, and in attending on those who arrive for shelter. Most of the supplies for the Hospice are brought up from Aosta, but a few from Martigny; the fund for its support is derived jointly from the French and Italian Governments (some 50,000 to 60,000 francs per year), besides what is contributed by travellers, who are, however, neither charged anything nor begged from. Some 18,000 to 20,000 travellers are accommodated; but it is said that many, even of the wealthy, after eating and being served, *leave no remembrance behind them*, and that the institution is lately a little crippled in consequence. Several hours may be profitably devoted to inspecting the plain but perfect arrangements for the comfort of visitors, and the large collection of pictures, gifts from travellers, relics and other curiosities, as well as the monument to Dessaix, erected by Napoleon in the Chapel. Besides the benevolent-looking monks themselves, and their mighty dogs, the Morgue (or dead-house, where the perished are sometimes kept undecayed for years) is well worth visiting; and no one should quit the Hospice without remembering that Napoleon and his officers found shelter here, when they had at last surmounted the' pass, and that the whole French army was feasted (at the First Consul's expense) on the plateau in front of the buildings.

A little lake of some 500 feet long is passed soon

after leaving the Hospice, and at the end of it a pillar marking the division between France and Italy. Beyond it lies the green pasture of the Hospice cattle, called La Vacherie. St. Remy (station), the first Italian village, is reached in 1 to 1½ hours from the Hospice, whether by mule or on foot,—and has one peculiarity of entirely filling the gorge where it stands, as if it had been literally poured into a trough! From St. Remy the carriage-road recommences, while the valley is cultivated and all the character of the near scenery softened. The small villages passed are St. Oyen; Etroubles; Gignod (in a strong defile, and with the ruins of a defensive tower). Then the Val de Pellina opens, with a path over the glacier-pass of the Col de Colon. Then Signaye, at which the views of the splendid vineyards of Aosta begin; while in fine weather, looking back northeastward and northwestward, a view almost unparalleled in the whole world may be caught—Monte Rosa at the right or eastward, Mont Blanc at the left or westward! Below, at the traveller's feet, lies the termination of the Alpine passage, in the handsome Italian town of

Aosta (English "Augusta"), built and named after himself by Augustus, before the birth of Christ—magnificent heavy fortifications and walls remaining, and with a Triumphal Arch, Double Gate, Town Hall, Cathedral (with frescoes) Church of St. Ours, etc., worth what passing notice can be withdrawn from the natural aspects surrounding it. From Aosta by vetturino (diligence) to Ivrea; thence by rail ot TURIN, etc. (See "Short Trips in Italy.")

PASS AND ROUTE OF THE ST. GOTTHARD.

By many who have traversed it and the others, the pass of the St. Gotthard is considered the most picturesque of all the routes from Switzerland to Italy; and with those who do not care especially to guard against fatigue, it may probably be considered the most popular of the three.

As already indicated in the opening of this paper, this third route is commenced, ordinarily, from Lucerne, taking boat on the Lake to Fluellen at the extreme south end (called the "Lake of the Canton Uri"), then by carriage, two or three miles, to

Altorf, capital of the Canton Uri, a pleasant little town of about 3,000 inhabitants, with particular interest as the scene where Gesler is believed to have commanded and Tell shot the apple from the head of his son (though that distinction is disputed by Kussnacht, at the other or upper end of Lucerne, near the Rhigi). The most interesting objects it contains, are a splendid modern colossal Statue of Tell, with an inscription from Schiller; the Fountain, where the target-tree is alleged to have stood; the old Tower, with Tell frescoes; the very old Capucin Monastery, with the Bannwald or Sacred Grove (of Schiller) behind it, etc.

At Altdorf diligence is taken for the entire ride over the St. Gotthard to Bellinzona, occupying twenty-two-and-a-half to twenty-five hours; and as the ride is to be a long one and through some of the most magnificent scenery in the world, care should be taken to avoid the *inside middle seats*, from which little or nothing can be seen.

Some five or six hours, southward, through the magnificently wild Valley of the Reuss, by Botzlingen, Klus, Silinen, Amstag, Iatschi, Wasen; the "Devil's Bridge," with wildly-magnificent pass and fine fall), the Urner Loch Tunnel and the beautiful rock-hemmed Valley of Uri, brings

Andermatt, the principal town of the Valley and section, with a very old church (the charnel-house adjoining corniced with skulls), some fine views, and a splendid collection of minerals on sale, for those who can afford to buy them. Andermatt is also the travelling-centre of the section, from which tourists draw their supplies and make their forays in every direction.

From Andermatt to Hospenthal, with very fine view on the way of the Glacier of St. Anna, very high in air and singularly beautiful, and a remarkable old Lombard tower standing on a hill near the village. At Hospenthal the sharp ascent of the St. Gotthard (not single mountain, but range) may be said to commence, through a very wild valley on the left bank of the Reuss; and a somewhat weary ride, though with continual splendid views, is encountered before reaching the

Pass of St. Gotthard (top), surrounded by several small lakes, and with an alberge or post-station very near, as also a lately-erected Hospice, with beds for poor travellers, and fine dogs kept for sale. At and near the summit snow lies on both sides of the road, generally nearly all summer; and snow-storms and avalanches are not entire rarities.

Shortly after commencing the descent from the

Hospice, the road crosses the Ticino (German "Tessin"); and very near, an immense mass of rock and an inscription commemorate the victory of the Russian Suwarrow over the French, in 1799. Very soon the road enters the Val Tremola (Valley of Terror), a dismal valley into which many avalanches fall, and which is provided with several heavy timber "houses of refuge" against such chances. This is followed by the Valley of Airolo, and soon by the village of Airolo; after which the Canaria Valley opens with its wondrous geological specimens, and the Defile of Stalvedro, which was held by 600 French against 3,000 Russians for half a day, in 1799. The route now follows, with slight descent, along the Ticino; by Piotto, Dazio Grande, Faido, etc.; through the beautiful Valley of Leventina, the scenery alternately rugged and soft, with chestnuts, vines and mulberries (trees) beginning to appear, to Giornico, with a fine old tower and very ancient church, and the waterfall of Cremusina just beyond; by Bodio and Pollegio, where the Brenno joins the Ticino, and the hillsides become literally covered with vineyards; to Osogna, at the foot of a singular peak; then by several small and unimportant villages, to

Bellinzona, capital of the Canton of Tessin, with lofty walls and turrets and a most picturesque appearance on approach, and with three remarkable Castles ("Il Grande," "Il Mezzo," and "Il Corbé") worthy of examination, and a fine bridge over the Ticino.

From Bellinzona to Como (Lake of Como), by

diligence; thence by rail to MILAN, etc. (See "Short Trips in Italy.")

BY THE SIMPLON ROAD AND PASS.

The comparatively small number crossing between Switzerland and Italy, who wish to see Napoleon's great work and take the Simplon pass for that object,—proceed to Martigny, as if on the way to Chamounix or over the Great St. Bernard; then proceed eastward up the Valley of the Rhone, by railway, to

Sion, a town of some 5,000 inhabitants, capital of the Canton Valais, on the Sionne; crowned by two castles and with some fine ruins in the neighborhood; also with a handsome Cathedral and church of St. Theodule, and environs of peculiar beauty. At Sion diligence is taken for

Brieg, at the immediate foot of the mountains (celebrated by Dickens and Wilkie Collins in "No Thoroughfare"). At Brieg (or if preferred, at Sion) diligence is taken for the whole route to Arona, on Lake Maggiore, Italy. At Brieg, also, the ascent commences, the valley of the Rhone being abandoned and the course taken at first almost due southward. Nearly the whole road, from Brieg to Domo d'Ossola, is one continued reminder of the engineering determination of Napoleon, who commenced it in 1800–1, and finished it six years later at a cost of 15,000,000 francs, so that he could take cannon over the Alps with a little less trouble than by the Great St. Bernard.

The road is very picturesque, and the views of

peaks and glaciers are often excellent, though not to be compared with those by the St. Gotthard. Like the St. Gotthard, however, it has many avalanches, and the "houses of refuge" from them are frequent. The point of greatest interest is to be found at the

Simplon Culm and Hospice (the latter something like that of the Gt. St. Bernard, with entertainment), where "a broad open valley resembling a dried-up lake," bounded by snow-capped heights and glaciers, as it has been well described, forms the highest point of the Pass. Many curiosities of scenery exist in the neighborhood, for those who have time and spirit to examine them. But the diligence pushes on, thence, downward, through the beautiful Val d'Ossola, to Domo d'Ossola, a handsome little Italian town ; by Vogogna and Ornavasso, to Fariolo, surrounded by luxuriant olive-groves, vineyards and all the evidences of great fruitfulness. It is near Fariolo, too, that are caught the first glimpses of the beautiful Lake Maggiore, with Isola Madre and some others of its islands. Thence the shore of the Lake is skirted, by a road-of solid masonry, by Baveno, to

Arona, of no particular charm to the tourist, except for its location on the Lake. From Arona by railway to Milan, Genoa, Turin, etc. (See "Short Trips in Italy.")

XVIII.

SHORT TRIPS IN ITALY.

It is of course very difficult, in a single and brief paper devoted to the interests of the short-trip tourist in Italy, to be even as explicit as in some of the other countries, as to points of peculiar interest —nearly every step, in that land of natural beauty, and artistic and historic interest, being more or less a pilgrimage. All that can be attempted, in, this brief space, will be such an arrangement of short tours as seems most politic, with mention of a few of the objects of first interest in the leading cities visited. Local guide-books and valet-service are quite as useful in Italy as elsewhere, and no difficulty will be found in procuring either. One hint, before proceeding, as to time. The summer months are of course the best period for crossing the Alps, but July and August are neither comfortable nor healthy months for travel in Italy, unhealthy miasma being very common, and mosquitoes and other troublesome insects almost universal.

RESUMÉ OF POINTS OF ARRIVAL IN ITALY.

It will be remembered that by the Mt. Cenis route (No. 1) the tourist reaches Italy at Susa, near Turin; that by the St. Bernard (No. 2) he reaches it at Aosta, above Ivrea, and still not far from Turin;

that by the St. Gotthard (No. 3) he is disembarked at Bellinzona, at the eastern end of Lake Maggiore, with nearest communication to Milan; and that by the Simplon (No. 4) he finds himself at Arona, on the western side of the same lake, yet nearer to Milan. All these routes, however, end so nearly together, in comparison to the extent of Italy and distance between the leading cities, that with a little care they may be all made to converge so as to allow the main features of the hurried but comprehensive route about to be traced, to be preserved. In order to do this, one of two objective points needs to be kept in view as the first visited, and indeed the two must be made to work together—Turin and Milan.

TO AND AT TURIN, MILAN AND THE LAKES.

The Mt. Cenis passenger has but an hour's ride by rail, from Susa,—and the St. Bernard one only a little longer by diligence to Ivrea, and then on by rail, to

TURIN, in Piedmont, long the capital of Sardinia, and until the removal to Florence, that of the lately-erected Kingdom of Italy. It has so great an antiquity as to have been *destroyed* by the Emperor Constantine (about A. D. 330) for assisting Maxentius, when it had already an age of several centuries. It has since filled a notable place in history, being the seat of the Dukes of Savoy before and since they became Kings of Sardinia, and standing two sieges by the French, in 1649 and 1706.

Turin lies on the river Po, has a population of nearly a quarter million, and (for Italy) much growing prosperity. Its principal public buildings of interest are the Royal Palace, modern and of no great splendor, but with some royal apartments, statuary and paintings worthy of hasty notice; the Royal Armory, with an extensive collection of European and Oriental weapons and armor; the Pinacotheca, or Royal Gallery, with many paintings of interest and some of great merit, and a Museum of Antiquities in the same building; the Palaces Carignano (formerly the Chamber of Deputies of Sardinia), Alfieri, Sonnaz and San Giorgio; the Duomo, or Cathedral of St. John the Baptist, with no special architectural merit, but handsome interior decorations, in chapels, altars, monuments (to members of the House of Savoy) and pictures; the Churches of La Consolato, Corpus Domini, San Filippo, etc., all with a certain interest in monuments and pictures within; and the Basilica and Church of La Superga, in the suburbs, some four miles from the city centre, with interesting monuments of the Savoy family, and a magnificent view of the Alps and the surrounding country, from the roof. Turin has also at least a dozen public squares ("Piazzas"), nearly all with statues or monuments; a Cemetery with the resting-places of some distinguished persons; and three or four bridges over the Po and its little tributary the Dora. This is among the least interesting of the great cities of Italy, and may be even hurriedly visited without serious loss, but should by no means be altogether omitted, even by those who do not necessarily pass through it.

From Turin the tourist should take rail to

Novara, a town with a Cathedral or Duomo of some architectural and artistic interest, but principally noted as the spot near which (two miles southward) King Charles Albert of Sardinia was fatally defeated by the Austrian, Radetsky, in 1849. From Novara by rail due northward to

Arona (or Allesandria), for a view of

LAKE MAGGIORE ("Mah-zjo-ree"), the second-largest and by some thought the most beautiful of the lakes of Italy—some forty-five miles in length by an average of three in width; the north banks mountainous and wooded, the south sloping and well cultivated; the water having the peculiarity of being green at the north end of the lake and deep blue at the south; and the group of four known as the Borromean Islands (Isola Bella, Isola Superiore, Isola Madre and Isola San Giovanni), presenting what is considered the acme of shaded, villa-studded and graceful beauty, in that line of scenery.

Steamers run northward on the lake, several times a day, to

Magadino, near the northern extremity; and the most beautiful of extended views, with a landing at Isola Bella (considered the loveliest of the group, and holding the magnificent palace and grounds of Count Borromeo), may be enjoyed by taking one of the boats for the run to Arona and return. From Arona return by rail to Novara, thence direct by rail for the very brief ride to

MILAN, in Lombardy,—a walled town of ten gates, of great antiquity, having been at one time only second to Rome, in the Roman empire, in importance and population. It was afterwards the capital of a Lombard republic, then of a duchy in the hands of the powerful and ambitious Visconti and Sforzas. It was held by Spain after the battle of Pavia (defeat of Francis I. of France by the Emperor Charles V.); ceded by Spain to Austria in 1714; taken by the French republicans in 1796, and again by Napoleon after Marengo, in 1800. From 1805 to 1814 (fall of Napoleon) it was the capital of the Bonapartan Kingdom of Italy; falling again under Austrian control till the cession of the Lombardo-Venetian provinces to the new Kingdom of Italy.

Milan has many beauties, but one unapproachably far beyond the rest stands

The Duomo (Cathedral), commenced in 1387, and scarcely yet finished; built of white marble, of immense size; with a central tower, spire, and a perfect "forest of pinnacles" which give it an indescribably light and airy effect, in spite of its gigantic bulk. It has some thousands of statues in its outward ornamentation, and is considered the finest specimen of the Gothic in Italy and one of the grandest structures in the world—second to St. Peter's, if not indeed equal to it. The view from its roof, which can be ascended by 160 steps, is wonderfully fine as well as extensive; though those most familiar with the clear Italian sky advise that it should always be taken at sunrise or near sunset. Within, the Duomo is only less magnificent than without, the Gothic columns and arches having immense height and rare purity, and great wealth having been lavished through century after century upon its ornamentation. It has a magnificent high altar; much fine sculpture; a colored mosaic pavement eliciting universal admiration; many gorgeous side-chapels, with tombs, monuments, pictures and relics, demanding many hours for even the most cursory examination, and impossible to be even enumerated otherwise than in the easily-attainable local guide-books; some magnificent stained-glass windows; and in fine all the splendid features of one of the most stupendous churches and rarest artificial sights in the world.

Great Churches (other than the Duomo) also abound in Milan. Chief among these are San Ambrogio, singular as well as singularly old, having been built in the ninth century, with a very rare altar-front of gold-and-silver, some antique relics, paintings, etc.; San Carlo, with one of the largest domes in Europe; San Eustorgio, with a very beautiful bell-tower, some interesting works of art, monuments and relics; San Fedele, elaborately decorated; San Lorenzo, with the Colonne di San Lorenzo near (said to have been once part of a Temple of Hercules); Santa Maria la Madonna, considered next after the Duomo in imposing effect, without and within; Santa Maria della Grazie; Santa Maria della Passione; San Maurizio Maggiore; San Nazaro; San Pietro, etc.

Palaces also abound in Milan, some of them well worth a visit—the Royal Palace, modern, accessible to visitors, and with some fine paintings; the Archbishop's Palace, with the same features; the Palazzo della Citta (City Hall—now an Exchange); Loggia

IN ITALY. 249

degl' Ossi; Palazzo Borromeo; Pal. Litta (with some fine pictures); Pal. Marino (now the residence of the city authorities), etc.

Besides these, if time allows, may well be visited the Brera Museum (pictures and sculpture) and Library; the Pinacoteca, with many rare specimens of the old masters; the Biblioteca Ambrosiana, with pictures, library and many relics; the Museum of Natural History, etc.

La Scala, the great opera-house and theatre, one of the largest in Europe and celebrated in the history of song, should be visited if any performances are given there during the visit; and Milan has half-a-dozen other leading theatres and places of amusement.

Besides these, the principal objects of interest are to be found in the handsome Public Gardens; the immense Arena, of modern erection but on the plan of the ancient Amphitheatres, said to be capable of accommodating 30,000 spectators, where races, balloon-ascents and other diversions are frequent; the fine triumphal Arco della Pace, etc.

From Milan by rail to

Como, with some architectural charms and a lovely situation, at the Lake-side, for a view of the beautiful

LAKE OF COMO, third of the Italian lakes in size, but by many thought the first in beauty,—surrounded by bold hills and its shores dotted with luxurious villas and rich with olive-groves and vineyards, while it is the very paradise of pleasure-seekers in rowing and sailing. Lake Como has been best commemorated by Rogers in his poem of "Italy," when he

―"Turned prow and followed, landing soon
Where steps of purest marble met the wave ;
Where, through the trellises and corridors,
Soft music came as from Armida's palace "―

though the description given by Bulwer, in the "Lady of Lyons," in the passage commencing: "In a deep vale shut out by Alpine hills from the rude world," etc., is much more familiar. At all events, to see the Lake of Como and sail or row upon it, is one of the first necessities of travel in Italy.

From Como return to Milan by rail, for the route eastward and southward.

[This visit first to Turin and afterwards to Milan, it will be remembered, has been arranged for thôse crossing to Italy by the Mt. Cenis or St. Bernard routes ; for those who arrive by the St. Gotthard or the Simplon, a different succession will be advisable, as follows:

For the St. Gotthard passenger, disembarked at Bellinzona, the best route will be by diligence to

Magadino, at the head of Lake Maggiore ; thence by steamboat (three times a day in summer) down the Lake to Arona; thence by rail to Novara, whence the detour must be made westward by rail to Turin, if that city is to be visited, with return to Novara and on to Milan. Or, on to Milan at once from Novara, leaving out Turin, if time and expense are imperative. From Milan by rail to Como, and return to Milan, as in the case of passengers by the other routes.

For the tourist by the Simplon road, precisely the same course as that last named, except the run

IN ITALY. 251

from Bellinzona to Arona, he having disembarked from the route over the Alps at the latter place.]

The passengers by all the four crossings will thus have accomplished the most desirable objects in the northwest, and be ready for the second stage:

FROM MILAN BY LAKE GARDA, TO AND AT VENICE.

From Milan by rail, by Cassano, Treviglio, Bergamo (station, on the last verge of the Alps, with a notable church of Santa Maria Maggiore and some pleasant excursions in the neighborhood); Grumello, Seriaté, Palazzuola,

Brescia (second city in Lombardy,—the ancient Brixia, with a Cathedral and some public buildings and palaces of note), Ponte San Marco, Lonato, Sermione (with the battle-field of Solferino very near it and easily reached by carriage), to

Peschiera, on the river Mincio, at its exit from Lake Garda, one of the great fortified towns of what used to be the celebrated "Austrian Quadrilateral," and the southern port of the steamers on the Lake. Excursions may easily be made from it, by carriage, to the First Napoleon's great battle-field of Rivoli, and to

LAKE GARDA, the largest of the Italian lakes, considered less beautiful than either Maggiore or Como, sometimes rough and dangerous for boats, but a perfect highway of steamers. The northern end of it is narrow and shut in by the Alps, but the southern shores are fertile, and the soft climate is considered especially favorable for pulmonary invalids.

From Peschiera, by rail, on by Castelnuovo and Somme Campagna, to

VERONA, on the river Adige, second of the Quadrilateral cities, and heavily fortified, like Peschiera, and with many antiquities and other curiosities, but most interesting to English readers as the site of Shakspeare's "Romeo and Juliet," and "Two Gentlemen of Verona," as well as of many other plays and romances. It is known to be very old, and has had a most varied history — among other events, Marius having fought his great battle with the Cimbri here, and Theodoric the Goth defeated Odoacer. It was at one time the capital of the Kingdom of Italy, again the seat of a republic, and then governed by petty dukes or princes. During the last days of the Austrian supremacy, it was the centre of the military power of that nation in Italy.

It has very many objects demanding attention, but first among them all, of course, will come

Juliet's Tomb, in the Garden of the Orfanotrofio —not of much artistic merit, but notable as being possibly the real resting-place of the lady so immortalized, first by Da Porta, in the novel, and afterwards and so unapproachably by Shakspeare. Next comes

The Amphitheatre, another of the old Roman remains, and said to have held more than 20,000 spectators, originally, though much fewer when in modern times used as a place for holiday shows. There are also several palaces, particularly that of Del Consiglio, in front of which are statues of celebrated natives of Verona — Pliny the Younger, Cornelius Nepos, Macer, Catullus, and others; that of Delle Urbe, with the Exchange near it, etc. Of

Churches, the leading one is the Cathedral of Santa Maria Matricolare, said to have been originally built in the time of Charlemagne, the architecture pleasing, and the statues and monuments interesting; and there are also that of Santa Maria l'Antica, with tombs of the Scaligers; that of Santa Anastasia, very beautiful, without and within; that of San Zenone, very old (1138), with curious architecture and many odd interior ornamentations, historical and mythological bas relievos, etc.; those of San Fermo Maggiore, Santa Maria, etc. There is also a Pinacoteca, or Picture-Gallery, with many fine paintings of the Veronese school; the Campo Santo (Cemetery—near the Vittoria Gate) has some good monuments; and the Roman Gates, Dei Borsari, Dei Leoni, etc., should not be passed without notice. Taken all in all, Verona will be found one of the most interesting cities in Italy, and, if possible, some days should be spent at and around it.

A brief side-excursion may be made by rail from Verona southward to

Mantua, on the Mincio (in point of fact, in one of its "elbows"), and surrounded by a group of small lakes. It is said to be the oldest city in Italy—older than Rome, and has a Duomo and some other handsome churches (St. Andrea the handsomest), and an Imperial Palace of five hundred rooms, now deserted but still showing wonderful frescoes, floor-mosaics and other features of past elegance. It is another of the cities of the Austrian Quadrilateral, and heavily fortified, like the others already named, and has additional celebrity in Shakspeare's locating there part of the " Two Gentlemen of Verona," one act of " Romeo and Juliet," and the whole of the " Taming of the Shrew," of which the heroine, Katharine, is still said to live in the spirit of the Mantuan women. [Return to Verona by rail.]

From Verona on by rail to

Vicenza, at the foot of Monti Berici, and with many fine palaces, a Cathedral, Churches, a Museum, etc. Thence by rail to

Padua (by carriage, the short distance from the railway-station to the town), chiefly remarkable for its celebrated University (one of the oldest, largest and best in Europe), its Cathedral, Palaces, Churches, etc., and the fact that here, too, Shakspeare and others have located plays and romantic legends.

From Padua by rail direct to one of the chiefest of all the Italian pilgrimages—the " Bride of the Sea,"

VENICE, on the Adriatic, once the mistress of the commerce and half the power of Europe; one of the grandest of figures in history; and one of the oddest in geography, from the fact that its streets are canals, its conveyances are gondolas (boats), and that there is not a horse within its bounds. Of course its " cabs " are also the gondolas, and the only means of extended locomotion is by them, there not being even much opportunity for walking!

Venice is literally crammed with objects of interest, principally historical but many artistic; and only the briefest of resumés can be made of the more interesting. First in importance comes the

Piazza de San Marco (Place of St. Marc), an oblong square in the centre of the city, with colonnades all around it. At the east end stands the great

Church of St. Marc, a magnificent edifice of Saracenic character, commenced in 977 and finished in 1111, with the celebrated bronze horses of Constantinople over the grand entrance, the pavement of tesselated marble (pictorial) and the whole interior crowded with objects of beauty and interest, with the tomb of the Doge Andrea Dandolo (" blind old Dandolo ") one of the principal. Near it stands the

Clock Tower, with the Lion of St. Marc and a statue of the Virgin; and on the opposite side of the square the great

Libreria (Library); and close beside that the

Campanile (Bell-tower) dating back to 902 and offering a wonderful view from the summit. Between the Libreria and the landing-place stand the

Two Columns, of granite, so often seen in pictures, the one surmounted by the Winged Lion of St. Marc and the other by a statue of St. Theodorus. Almost beside the church of St. Marc stands the

Doges' Palace, one of the most perfect Moorish buildings in Europe, after the Alhambra at Grenada (open from 9 to 4, daily, except Sundays), its halls a wilderness of splendor in themselves, with magnificent staircases, portraits of the Doges, statuary, pictures (many of them historical) by some of the ablest pencils of the Venetian school—the whole demanding days in examination, with local hand-books or intelligent guides, and supplying one of the finest feasts of all European travel.

Only separated from the Palace by an arm of the Canal, are the

Carceri (Prisons), capable of holding 400 prisoners, and graphically described, with many other objects of great interest at Venice, by Cooper in his novel of "The Bravo." Connecting them with the Palace is the covered

Bridge of Sighs, so celebrated in history, and made doubly famous by Byron's lines in "Childe Harold":

> "I stood in Venice, on the Bridge of Sighs,
> A palace and a prison on each hand," etc.

The Rialto (bridge), so celebrated through Shakspeare's "Merchant of Venice," lies at some distance back of the Piazza of St. Marc, crossing the Grand Canal between the islands of San Marco and Riva Alto, and has streets and shops on it, as London Bridge used to have.

The Palaces and houses of note, at Venice, are legion; but first among them in interest, with many, is the

Palazzo Moro, where Cristoforo Moro, the *Othello* of Shakspeare, is said to have resided. Not many of them, or of the numberless churches, can be visited by the short-trip tourist, who should not fail, however, to visit the wonderful

Pinacoteca (picture-gallery—open from 12 to 3) with 600 fine paintings, most of them of the Venetian schools, distributed through twenty rooms. A visit should also be paid to

The Arsenal (open daily, 10 to 4), in which may be seen the standard of the Turkish Admiral, taken by Don John of Austria at Lepanto; a model of the Bucentoro or Doge's galley, in which he wedded the Adriatic; many magnificent suits of armor, etc.

It should be noted, before passing, that there are some thirty-five churches in Venice, besides San Marc—of interest to those whose time will allow visiting them.

The Gondolas will naturally be tried by the tourist, in the course of his visits; and a very good idea of the appearance of the Lagoon and the openings into the Adriatic may be found by taking ferry-boat or gondola to

Murano or *Torcello*, large islands in the Lagoon.

VENICE TO FLORENCE AND ROME, BY FERRARA, BOLOGNA, PISA AND LEGHORN.

From Venice by rail, by Rovigo (where one of the First Napoleon's important early battles was fought) to

Ferrara, a very old Roman town, famous for the sword-blades that used to bear the name of the great maker, "Andrew of Ferrara," with a Cathedral and Castle, both of some pretension; thence over a flat and highly-cultivated country, with no features of the picturesque, to

Bologna, famous for its University and its sausages, as also for having been the nurse of a school of painting producing Guido, Domenichino, the Caraccis, etc. It is handsomely situated, and literally crowded with palaces, worthy of attention from any one with abundant leisure, especially for the sake of the fine paintings abounding everywhere; but the short-trip tourist will necessarily push on to

Pistoja, where the rail intersects that from Leghorn,—thence to

FLORENCE, on the river Arno, and in the midst of the beautiful valley to which the river gives name—the Val d'Arno. It is divided by the Arno, something like London and Paris, and the communication is made by four handsome bridges within the city limits and two in the suburbs. There are walls entirely surrounding it—ancient, but rebuilt, with eight gates and two fortresses (Da Basso, north, and Di Belvedere, south), breaking the line. One of the finest promenades on the globe, the quay called

The Lung' Arno, extends along the north bank of the river, the houses on the south side literally overhanging the water; and the whole city is so embowered in trees and so enchanting in every detail of the quietly picturesque, that the tourist will have little difficulty in agreeing with the dictum which assigns it the place of the *handsomest city in Europe*.

Since 1866, as is well known, Florence has been the capital of the Kingdom of Italy (removed from Turin); previous to the late revolutions it held the place of capital of the Grand Duchy of Tuscany.

Remarking a few of the most notable curiosities of the favored city, the first in order will come the

Pitti Palace, the residence of the King of Italy—commenced in the fifteenth century, and with many beauties of architecture added to great extent, but especially famous for the wonderful collection of works of art in the great Picture-Gallery,—more than 500 in number, and, as alleged by experts, not one daub among them, while many of the very finest works of Titian, Raphael, Salvata Rosa, Rubens, Albert Dürer, Guercino, Andrea del Sarto, Leonardo da Vinci, Vandyke, Perugino, Carlo Dolci, etc., literally dazzle and confuse the unaccustomed beholder, and statuary from the most celebrated chisels, ancient and modern, serves to fill up the measure of wonder. (Open daily from 9 to 3, except on Sundays from 10 to 3 and on Mondays 12 to 3.)

Next to the collection at the Pitti Palace comes that of the

Galleria Uffizi ("official," formerly "Royal" Gallery), above the Italian Senate Chamber, containing another magnificent collection of paintings, sculpture, bronzes, etc. (Open at the same hours as the Pitti, except that on Tuesdays, here, instead of Mondays, there, the admissions are from 12 to 3— complete catalogues at the door.) This building was erected by Duke Cosmo I. (De Medicis), and has many charms of architecture. In the "Tribune" of this palace are collected the rarest of the rare in different walks of art—among others, the original "Venus de' Medicis," Raphael's "Fornarina"; Titian's "Recumbent Venuses"; Volterra's "Massacre of the Innocents"; Perugino's "Holy Family"; Correggio's "Adoration of the Virgin"; Michael Angelo's "Virgin and St. Joseph"; Vandyke's "Charles V.", etc.

There are some twenty or thirty other Palaces, Museums and Galleries, but the short-trip tourist will scarcely find time for more than the two mentioned; turning then to the Churches, and first to the gigantic

Santa Croce ("Holy Cross"), in handsome Gothic-Italian, with a bad steeple. The principal charm, however, lies within, in the splendid columns and roof; the tomb of Michael Angelo (buried here); monuments to Dante and Alfieri, respectively by Ricci and Canova; frescoed walls and gorgeous side-chapels; and so much of fine painting and sculpture that the church-character of the edifice is well-nigh forgotten in that of the picture-gallery. In some respects Santa Croce must yield to

The Duomo (Cathedral of Santa Maria del Fiore), commenced in the fifteenth century and not nearly completed. It has (as alleged) the largest dome in the world, and a rare peculiarity in the coating of the whole exterior with a mosaic of various-colored marbles; and within there is much of interest, in architecture and works of art—the most notable feature in the former being the Baptistery, with granite columns and mosaic floor, and in the latter a marble group of the "Deposition of Christ," left unfinished by Michael Angelo at his death. Adjoining the Duomo,

The Campanile, or bell-tower, is of four stories, in delicate Gothic-Italian, nearly 300 feet in height, and considered the finest structure of its class in the world.

The other most notable churches in Florence are San Ambrogio, Santa Annunziata, SS. Apostoli, La Badia, Il Carmine, Santa Felicita, San Lorenzo, San Marco, Santa Maria Novella, San Michele, Santa Spirito, Santa Trinita, etc.

The public-grounds and suburbs of Florence are very delightful, and while the former should be visited and enjoyed, especially the Piazzas Dell' Annunziata, Santa Croce, Del Gran' Duca, etc.—the latter should receive attention, if possible, in excursions to

Fiesolé (by carriage or on foot), to catch the fine view over the city, see the old Etruscan ruins and the very old Cathedral there;—and to

Vallombrosa (of the "thick leaves"), occupying a day by going to Pontassieve by rail, and thence to the Shady Vale of the Hills, and the Convent, by carriage to Pelago and light carriage or on foot for the remaining distance. The views caught in this latter excursion will be found wonderfully fine; and the eating of a fresh fish-dinner with the Monks is a pleasure to be remembered.

From Florence by rail, by Prato, Pistoja and Pescia, to

Lucca, principally notable for its Baths, which lie about fifteen miles distant and need about one day to make the excursion (by carriage) and return; thence by rail to

Pisa, of which the principal curiosities are the Duomo, or Cathedral; the celebrated Leaning Tower, or Campanile; and the Campo Santo, or Holy Field, a covered colonnaded space of considerable extent, the ground formed of earth brought from Mount

Calvary by fifty-three Pisan vessels, after the taking of Palestine from the Christians by Saladin—and the whole filled with the monuments of those buried there, through all the ages until it was full, from an Emperor to a mere successful surgeon. Of the Leaning Tower it may be said that it would be no attraction whatever but for the fact of its leaning, and that consequently the half-crazy builder has achieved what he attempted—a sensation.

From Pisa, by rail, direct to

Leghorn (Italian "Livorno"), an old seaport on the Gulf of Genoa, with very little other attraction than the fact that the ships and flags of all nations may generally be seen in the antiquated old port and roads.

From Leghorn, either by rail to La Annunziatella, and thence by diligence—or by steamer down the Gulf of Genoa, with views of the Italian coast, island of Elba (Napoleon's prison), and possibly Corsica (the place of his birth), to

Civita Vecchia (port of Rome), another seaport of much smaller size and no consequence at all except in connection with the historical arrivals and departures for and from the Holy City, which it has witnessed. From Civita Vecchia by rail, by Santa Severa, Ponte Galera and La Magliana, to

ROME IN A HURRY.

ROME, on the little river Tiber, something less than twenty miles from its mouth; with the Seven Hills underlying it, the Papal residence within it, a population of about 200,000, and so vast and varied a history, from the time when Romulus, its founder, was (or was not) suckled by a wolf, and that time, not long after, when its male population, very wife-hungry, carried off the Sabine women to fill that office—that the brain reels in the very attempt to recount rather what it has not seen than what it has! Once the Pagan capital of the world, then the Christian—the besieged and taken, the triumphant, the abhorred, the idolized, the knelt-to by Kings and the defied by men with no power—the city which has alternately enlightened and enslaved mankind, in letters, art and religion — it is scarcely wonderful that pilgrims from all climes flock to it to-day, as they have flocked for nearly two thousand years, and that it is reckoned the end and goal of European travel, as Jerusalem is considered that of journeys in the East.

It has already been said that scarcely a foot of Italian soil is other than a pilgrimage; but the remark applies with tenfold force to Rome, where the traveller is surrounded by so many relics of antiquity and glories of art that each one almost takes away from the importance of the other. In no place in Europe, meanwhile, is intelligent guidance (whether of friends or valet) more necessary to the hurried traveller, than at and around the Eternal City; but local guide-books, in English as well as Italian, are numerous and easily procured, and another advantage is to be found in the fact that of late years the English and Americans have partially taken possession of Rome, as they have almost entirely taken possession of Paris. Within the scope of the present volume, it is neither possible nor desirable to do more than mention a few of the more preëminent objects of interest, leaving all details to the local authorities.

First among these curiosities, of course, comes

St. Peter's, the largest church in the world, built on the site where once stood a temple of Jupiter (whence the jest of Rev. Sidney Smith, of the building and a celebrated statue within, that "there had only been a change in spelling—'Jupiter' having merely given way to 'Jew-Peter'"). The first structure on the spot is said to have been an oratory built within the first century on the burial-place of St. Peter, and the first church-erection one by Constantine the Great — of course after his miraculous conversion. The present building was commenced under Pope Julius II., in the sixteenth century; but the wonderful dome is ascribed at a much later period to Michael Angelo; the immense colonnades which sweep round on either side from the piazza (enclosing a space of nearly eight hundred feet) were designed by Bernini; and the front is credited to Carlo Maderno, who "improved" upon the plans of Michael Angelo after a not-very-rare system of altering at whatever cost.

Some faint idea may be formed of its immense size by a few figures, from which it appears that the façade (or front) is 379 feet long and $148\frac{1}{2}$ high— that the full length of the interior is 613 feet (a little more than three blocks of a New York street); the length of the transepts (cross) $446\frac{1}{2}$; the height of the naves, $152\frac{1}{2}$; the interior diameter of the great dome which crowns it, 139; and the exterior, 195½; the height from the pavement to the base of the lantern, 405; and to the top of the cross, 468. The curious calculation was made, some years ago, that a dozen churches of the size of the New York Trinity could be set within it, the fronts and steeples grouped around in a close circle, and there would be abundant room, while the top of the cluster of spires would not reach within an hundred feet of the inside of the dome!

The sensation created by the great church, from without, is really indescribable, as it towers over the city on approach, at an incalculable distance; but it is doubtful whether the impression, standing within, under the mighty dome and in the midst of its splendors in ornamentation, wealth of bronze, colored marbles, altar-decorations and monuments, is not even more overwhelming than in viewing it without. Those who ascend the dome (as all may do, entering before 11 A. M., by obtaining an order through the Minister or Consul of their particular nation, but all do *not* do!) say that the view from the top is magnificent beyond comparison, Rome, the Tiber, the Appian Way, the Campagna, the distant sea, all seeming at the very feet, and humanity in the street looking like so many little crawling insects!

Of course the crowning charm of St. Peter's is found in the religious services and the rare music which forms so large a part of them. The best of these, however, are only attainable at a few periods in the year, and most of them in the winter and early spring (favorite time for being at Rome). The most noted of these are the Grand Masses on Christmas and New-Year Day, and the ceremonies which follow throughout the month and extend into February. Yet more impressive than these are the round of exercises of Holy Week, commencing on Palm Sunday, and with a separate musical and scenic splendor for Ash Wednesday and Holy Thursday, culminating on Good Friday and Easter Sunday. The only summer festival is on June 28th and 29th, when the procession of Corpus Domini and grand masses take place. These are the only occasions on which the full splendors of the body of the Church or of the celebrated Sistine Chapel (properly Sixtine) can be witnessed, and then only by ladies in black, with black veils, and gentlemen in full evening dress. Vespers are sung every evening, from 3 to $4\frac{1}{2}$, in one of the side-chapels, and this must content those who miss the great festivals.

Next after St. Peter's (of churches) comes

The Lateran, where the popes are always crowned, alleged to have been begun by Constantine in the fourth century, and formerly ranking even before St. Peter's. Its colonnaded front is magnificent, and the interior is a mass of chapels, splendor, monuments and relics—among the latter of which may be mentioned a cedar table on which the Last Supper is alleged to have been eaten, while there is a staircase shown, without, claimed to have been that of Pilate's house, up which Christ was led to be judged! The principal religious ceremonies at the Lateran occur on the Saturday before Easter, on Ascension Day, and on the festival of St. John the Baptist.

The number of other churches in and about Rome is literally legion. They cannot all be visited, except by those who tarry long; and ignoring them, in the present connection, it will be necessary to turn to

The Vatican, Capitol of Rome and palace of the Popes, lying to the right of St. Peter's and entered by the right colonnade of that edifice. The number of chambers in its three stories and adjoining buildings are variously estimated at 5,000 to 13,000; and the cluster certainly covers a space of some 1,200 feet in length by 1,000 in breadth. Within the Vatican is found the

Sistine Chapel, where a part of the exercises of Holy Week take place,—rich in every detail of decoration, and especially in the great frescoes of Michael Angelo and others, the "Last Judgment" of that master, and one of the world's wonders, being the most notable feature. But it is to the

Galleries of the Vatican that the tourist's visit is principally paid, after all, for in these almost endless rooms are gathered the grandest works of art of a world. Raphael's greatest works are here, in fresco and in oil,—headed by his "Transfiguration"—so many that for even their names the local guide-book and catalogue must be referred to. Then, many of the masterpieces of Giulio Romano, Perugino, Murillo ("Marriage of Saint Catharine," among others), Domenichino ("Communion of St. Jerome," etc.), Titian ("Madonna and Child," etc.), Guido, Paul Veronese, Correggio, and in fact all the giants of ancient art, making the collection unparalleled in extent, interest and value. Then follow ancient and modern sculpture in almost equal profusion, with the celebrated group of the "Laocoon" (sung by Byron), the "Apollo Belvidere" (ditto), the "Cupid" of Praxiteles, the "Amazon," the "Ariadne," etc., to lead the sense of admiration.

But long before traversing and inspecting all these, the tourist will have turned to the special and mighty antiquities of Rome, to the

Walls, a part of them so very old, so many times destroyed and rebuilt, and with their odd old fortifications; to the

Bridges, of which something more than half-a-dozen cross the Tiber, nearly all ancient—tracing out particularly the remains of the Sublicius, where

——" Horatius kept the bridge,
In the brave days of old! "

to the

Seven Hills, now more than half uninhabited, though he will find no difficulty, history assisting, in tracing out the Aventine, the Palatine, the Cælian, the Esquiline, the Viminal, the Quirinal and the Capitoline, the two latter being really the only ones that can be said to be dwelt upon. He will have visited

The Forum, and seen the wonderful grouping of antiquities all around it, the very names of which, in one cluster, would fill pages here, as they have done in history. He will have climbed to

The Capitol, remembered the victors and the vanquished who went up there, wished that they would let him ascend the Tower (as they will not) for the best view over Rome,—then stood beside the "Dying Gladiator" in the hall of that name, and wondered whether that marvellous statue or Byron's description, is best; then wound away from the Capitol to the

Tarpeian Rock, from which they threw the condemned, and doubted whether the fall would always be fatal; and then—culmination of all—stood within

The Coliseum ("Colosseum"), by daylight and if possible by moonlight, beholding at once the re-remains of the mightiest structure ever raised by the hand of man—the Pyramids alone excepted — and the record of a historical cruelty unparalleled even in thought. The Coliseum is known to have been built in honor of Titus, conqueror of Jerusalem, and tradition says that 60,000 captive Jews were engaged for ten years upon it, while, at its inauguration, A. D. 71, 5,000 animals and 10,000 of those less valuable animals, captives, were slain. It is alleged to have given seats to 87,000 spectators; and even that may be possible, when it is remembered that the circumference is 1,641 feet and the height of the outer wall 157, the whole covering six acres. Before going to the Coliseum, however, unless the passage is "by heart," no one should fail to read over again that wonderful description of Byron:

"On such a night
I stood within the Coliseum's wall,
'Mid the chief relics of almighty Rome.
The trees which grew along the broken arches
Waved dark in the blue midnight," etc.

There are a thousand other objects of interest, in and around Rome, but when the tourist has seen these, and the gigantic

Castle of St. Angelo (once Hadrian's Tomb); the *Pantheon*, in wonderful preservation, though built by Agrippa, about A. D. 30 or 40, as the monument of old Roman genius, but now doubly sacred as containing the Tomb of Raphael; the

Arch of Titus, and the Baths of the same Emperor, with a few hundred ruined temples, etc., and driven out on the

Appian Way to Albano and its Lake, with interesting remains studding the whole Campagna,— and visited a few of the sculptors' studios,—he may be said to have "done" Rome quite as well as can be expected of the short-trip traveller.

(Before leaving Rome it should be said that May and June are the pleasantest months there, and that possibly August and September are the least so; while, in spite of a heavy atmosphere not favorable to the lungs, a "winter at Rome" is held to be "not a bad thing to do.")

ROME TO NAPLES AND NORTHWARD.

From Rome direct, by Albano, Capua, Frascati, Caserta, etc., in nine to ten hours, to

NAPLES, on the Bay of the same name, now the largest city in Italy (with nearly half a million inhabitants), and for a long period one of the most popular of resorts for tourists and invalids. It was, until the late formation of the Kingdom of Italy, the capital of the Kingdom of Naples, ruled by Bourbon princes except during the brief period of the occupation of the throne by Napoleon's proxy, Joachim Murat. It is also the very paradise of beggars—bad enough throughout Italy, but here unendurable; and to be either penniless or deaf and blind is rather a blessing than otherwise to the traveller, just here. Much curiosity, to those fond of such things, is to be found in the port, with extended break-water piers, or "moles," and in the fortifications near, that have once been formidable but are now dismantled or used for barracks, etc.

The buildings of most importance are the

Royal Palace, some three hundred years old, of which some of the rooms are shown, with a few good pictures; the

Castle of St. Elmo, standing on the hill directly back of the central port and fortifications, once very formidable and feared by the inhabitants as a "continual threat," but now used for barracks, like those at the water-side; the

Museo Nazionale, with its great collection of antiquities from Pompeii and Herculaneum, and the Farnese collection from Rome (open, except on Monday, from 9 to 3, and Sundays from 9 to 1), forming one of the most interesting gatherings of the antique, in all Europe; the

Cathedral, dating from 1272 to 1420, with considerable pretensions in architecture, some statues worth noting, at the entrance, and some frescoes, paintings and historical tombs within; the

Church of Santa Chiara, interesting as being the burial-place of the Neapolitan Bourbons and having many of their monuments; that of

San Domenico, considered the handsomest in Naples, antique, but restored, with some good monuments and pictures, etc. (The other 300 churches of the city are mostly very uninteresting, and many of them shockingly out of repair.)

Very much of the interest of sojourn at Naples, however, will be found entirely removed from the city itself—in the lovely

Bay of Naples, considered one of the finest, in every point of view, in the world, with its great

Isle of Ischia and some other and smaller, lying at the north lip of the Bay, and the more diminutive but more beautiful

Isle of Capri, holding a similar position across the Bay from the city, at the south lip; in the aspects of

Mount Vesuvius, lying a few miles east and south of the city, in full view, and easily reached, by those who wish to make the excursion and ascent, by the short railway to Resina (where guides can be procured), thence on horseback up the mountain-side to the Hermitage, thence to the top on foot—the whole excursion and return occupying a laborious but most interesting day. The volcano may or may not happen to be in a state of eruption; but at all events, the débris, or "hash," of what it has already done, may prove to be quite sufficient, even if a stream of flowing lava should not chance to be met coming down as the tourist is going up!

(It is to be presumed that no born American, making this excursion, will need to be advised to obey the guides, keep at the windward side of the crater, and avoid tumbling into the same—in the which tumble he would be likely to illustrate Latinity on its own ground and discover the meaning of "*facilis descensus Averni,*" without consulting the books! Any undue exposures in this direction, as in climbing Swiss glaciers, should be left to madmen, members of the English "Alpine Club," and people who have their lives heavily insured without any proviso against suicide.)

The next excursion, also occupying one day, will be that to

Pompeii and *Herculaneum*, the two cities buried by an eruption of the before-named (and visited) Vesuvius, in A. D. 79 if the history of the affair is to be credited. The visit may be made either by railway, to Herculaneum first, leaving at an early hour in the morning and laying over one train there before proceeding on to Pompeii,—or by private carriage, at very nearly the same cost if a party of three or four are to make it together. The theatre, really an "amphitheatre," is the only monument enough dug out to be recognizable, at Herculaneum; but at Pompeii there are very many curiosities, enough to occupy hours in examination—among which perhaps the most interesting will be found the House of Diomed (see Bulwer's "Last Days of Pompeii"), the Street of the Tombs, the City Gate (with the sentry-box where the soldier was found dead on duty), the City Walls, the Street of Abundance, Forum, Amphitheatre, etc. An excellent local map may be bought on the spot, with the streets and houses named, and it will be found indispensable. (A single word of warning: the propensity to carry off relics from Pompeii is very general, and visitors are very closely watched—it is not policy to make the attempt: better buy them—genuine or counterfeit—at Naples.)

Other charming excursions may be made, if time allows, to Castellamare (very short, by railway); to Sorrento (ten miles by carriage from Castellamare); to Capri (island, very beautiful and famous resort for invalids) by boat from Sorrento; to the ruins of Pæstum (by railway from Naples to Vietri and thence by carriage—whole day for this alone, if attempted).

From Naples, take steamer of the French Messageries Imperiales (with calls at Civita Vecchia and Leghorn and distant view of Corsica and Elba) to

GENOA, on the gulf of the same name—almost as well known, throughout the world, as "Genoa la Superba" and the "City of Palaces." Though very many of the houses of the old nobility have now been turned into places of trade and common residence, yet the name has not been forfeited, for whole streets are yet lined with buildings that are palaces indeed and still retaining their aristocratic inhabitants. Of these

Palaces, the most interesting are the Palazzo Brignole Sale (or Rossi), with many fine pictures; the Doria Tursi, with interesting reminders of Columbus ("native of Genoa"); the Doria and Balbi, both with pictures; the Ducale, once the residence of the Doges or Dukes of Genoa; the Reale and Pallavicini, both with fine pictures; the Spinola, Università, etc. Of

Churches, the most interesting is the Cathedral

of St. Laurence, erected in the eleventh century, in alternate layers of white and black marble, and with a very fine interior and many relics and curiosities, among which by far the most striking is the green glass dish said to have contained the Paschal Lamb at the Last Supper!

There is interest, also, in the fine fortifications surrounding the city; in some of the promenades—particularly the Acquasola, an esplanade on the old fortifications, with view over the gulf; and in the Monument to Columbus, an elaborate allegorical group, in the Piazza d'Acquaverde.

From Genoa by diligence (vetturina) occupying two days and spending the night at Oneglia—by the

Corniche Road, one of the most beautiful in the world, literally overhanging the Gulf of Genoa, throughout almost all the route, and supplying the loveliest of sea and shore views,—to

Nice, on the Gulf of Genoa, formerly belonging to Sardinia but now to France, with some interesting antiquities, much beauty in location, and a peculiarly soft climate making it the paradise of invalids. Thence by rail to

MARSEILLES, on the Gulf of Lyons—the Paris of Southern France as Strasbourg is that of Eastern—one of the oldest cities of the Mediterranean, founded by the Phenicians 600 years before Christ. It has a population of a quarter million, and a harbor said to be able to contain 1,200 vessels; its fortifications, including the works of the islands Pomegue, Ratoneau and the Chateau d'If (the latter immortalized by Dumas, in the "Count of Monte Cristo") are very formidable; its *Canabiere*, or great promenade, can show more different nations in a cluster than even Constantinople; and it is, in point of fact, the oddest, most thriving, dirtiest half-oriental old town on the European continent, besides having given birth to that tocsin of revolution, the "Marseillaise."

From Marseilles, either with or without the run of a few miles, by rail, to

Toulon, the great naval arsenal of France in the Mediterranean, the place of Napoleon's early exploit, and the depot of the criminal "galleys,"—if to Toulon, then with return to Marseilles, and thence by rail northward to Paris and the French or English ports.

Or, if intending to return to Switzerland and pursue any of the Swiss or German routes—then by rail from Marseilles to

LYONS, at the junction of the Rhone and the Saone —another very old city, now of some 200,000 inhabitants, and principally noted as the most extensive silk manufactory in the world. It has splendid quays along the rivers, is a thriving and important city, and will be specially dear to every spectator (which means *everybody*) of the "Lady of Lyons." It has some Roman antiquities; some buildings of historical importance (particularly the Hotel de Ville, where the revolutionists, after the siege of the city, planned their horrible atrocities, during the Reign of Terror); a Museum, with some fine pictures; and an out-look, from the tower on the Heights of

Fourvières, from which Mt. Blanc, one hundred miles distant, can easily be seen in clear weather.

From Lyons by rail, by Amberieux to Geneva and the Swiss and German routes,

Or, by rail to Paris, etc., from Lyons,

Or, by rail westward to Orleans, Tours, etc., for southwestern France, and the entrance into Spain.

XIX.

SHORT TRIPS IN SPAIN.

THE most convenient way of entering Spain, from France, is from Bayonne, one of the most strongly-fortified cities in France, famous for having given birth to that deadly instrument of warfare, the "bayonet," and reached by railway from Paris by Orleans, Tours (both fine old cities, with Cathedrals and much historical interest), Bordeaux (on the Garonne, the head of the Southern French wine-trade, with beautiful quays and much commercial prosperity, a handsome Cathedral, some Roman remains, a Triumphal Arch, etc., all worth notice).

From Bayonne, by rail, to

Biarritz, within a few years made famous by its becoming the favorite sea-side resort of the Emperor and Empress of France, who have a villa (the "Villa Eugénie") here.

By rail from Biarritz, for a very brief ride to the Spanish frontier-town of

Irun, where the division between the two countries is crossed and change of trains is made from the French *Chemin de Fer du Midi* (French Central Railway) to the *Ferro Carril del Norte* (Northern Spanish). From Irun, passing at the edge of the Pyrenees, the tourist will be principally occupied with going through tunnels (of which there are some fifty before reaching Madrid), and in noticing that everybody smokes, incessantly, besides enjoying something like the same description of scenery, in crossings at great elevation, and peepings down into awful ravines, while going up the Valley of the Urumea to Tolosa,—that has been enjoyed in riding up the Valley of the Rhone from Culoz to Geneva. By Miranda (junction with the Bilbao railway); after which the first stop of any importance (which should be for at least one day) is made at

Burgos, one of the finest of old Spanish cities, though very damp, cold and windy—for a long time the capital of Spain, scene of many of the exploits and the " Wedding " of the Cid Campeador, as well as of the tragedy of " Count Alarcos." Burgos lies on the side of a hill, beside the river Arlanzon; has a handsome Calle Espolon (main street) facing the river; a

Cathedral, commenced in the thirteenth century, built in the most elaborate Gothic "renaissance," with two pointed towers at the west front and one pinnacled at the east, bearing the reputation of being almost equal, in both grandeur and elaborate architecture, to that of Strasbourg—while within there are many splendid side-chapels, handsome monuments, the old "Coffin of the Cid," chained up against a wall, and constantly thronging men and women who show the dark eyes and picturesque costumes of Spain; several other handsome churches; and the bones of the Cid, kept in a walnut urn in the chapel of the Town Hall.

From Burgos by rail to

Valladolid, very handsomely situated on the left bank of the river Pisuerga, at its confluence with the Esqueva. Formerly another of the capitals of Spain; and seat of a University of eminence, which still remains; and notable as having been the death-place of Columbus. Its principal present attraction is the Museum, with some good pictures and sculptures; and it has also the old Royal Palace (decayed) and a Cathedral worth visiting. From Valladolid by rail to

MADRID, the capital of Spain, standing in the middle of a plain nearly twenty-five hundred feet above the level of the sea (boasting to be the "highest capital in Europe"), with a population approaching 300,000, a climate which requires warm wrapping up for nine months and constant fanning for three (French *mot* with reference to this: "*La Madrid a neuf mois d'hiver et trois mois d'enfer!*"— literally, "nine months winter and three hot enough for the infernal regions"), a painful absence of shade, and a history of much interest, especially in the earlier centuries, before Philip II., when it had not yet become the exclusive capital of Spain, to the disadvantage of the half-dozen former capitals of provinces—Toledo, Cordova, Seville, Granada, Burgos, etc.

The fashionable promenade and drive of Madrid is

The Prado, considered among the finest, as it is among the largest, public-grounds and afternoon-drives, in Europe, nearly two miles long and thickly studded with elm-trees; and the centre of the city and place where Madrid life of all sorts may best be seen, is the

Puerto del Sol, or Central Square, where the most infinite variety of characters and costumes may be observed, nearly every province having its representatives and no two provinces dressing alike. An early visit, of course, is always paid to the

Royal Palace, an immense and imposing pile, built by Philip V., covering a space of 470 feet in each direction by one hundred feet in height, and considered one of the most magnificent royal residences in the world. The interior is said to be especially rich in statues and marbles, and in the gorgeousness of the throne-room; but owing to the vandalism of some of the visitors, a few years ago, no admissions are now granted. A fine statue of Philip IV. stands in the gardens adjoining. At the southern end of the Palace is the

Royal Armory (admission on any day by presenting passports), containing probably the finest single collection of old armor, weapons and warlike curiosities, on the globe—among the most notable, armor worn by Charles V., Philip II., Francis I. (of France), Christopher Columbus, Queen Isabella (at the siege of Granada), etc.; with a very rich collection of guns and other weapons, a crowned and robed effigy of St. Ferdinand, etc. The Naval Museum, near, has also many notable curiosities. But the greatest of all attractions, at Madrid, is the

Royal Picture-Gallery, containing undoubtedly one of the finest as well as most extensive collections in the world—the only collection of works of the great Spanish painter Velasquez, in point of fact, being found here, as well as the "Immaculate Conception" and many of the best other works of Murillo, and hosts of those of Spagnoletto, of Rubens, of Titian, of Vandyke, of Claude Lorraine, of Raphael, Correggio, and all the group of great masters, demanding days to give them even reasonable attention. (Complete catalogues can be found at the doors, and admission can be procured every day.) The

Churches of Madrid are many and mean, as compared with several other Continental cities. The most interesting is the Convent of Atocha, with its miracle-working Virgin, and the handsomest that of San Francisco. The

Palacio del Congreso (Congress Hall of Spain), Hôtel de Ville and other public buildings, are also worth a visit.

A day should be devoted to an excursion, by rail, to

The Escorial, church-palace-tomb of the Spanish monarchs, built by Philip II. in fulfilment of a vow, and probably the largest specimen of architectural bulk on earth, after the Egyptian pyramids. It is 700 feet long by 564 wide; massively ugly without and massively-gorgeous within; while the royal vault chamber, under the high altar, where all the kings are buried, in marble sarcophagi with names in gilt letters, in niches in the deep walls—may well vie with any other attainable spot in its mixed and painful lesson. The Sacrista should also be noted, for its fine frescoes; the Dome should be ascended (for those strong of leg) to obtain the fine view therefrom; and many other objects of interest will be found—among others the room where Philip II. died in torture, and the Casa del Principe, a perfect toy-house, with furniture and pictures, built for Charles IV. when in his boyhood.

A Bull-Fight may be witnessed within almost any three days of stay in Madrid, in the Plaza de Toros, an amphitheatre in the outskirts—by any who are desirous of feasting themselves with a little extra-brutality. But it is pleasant to say that the laws of Spain do not make it obligatory upon the traveller that he *shall* do so before leaving the capital!

From Madrid by rail (changing trains at Alcazar), and by Ciudad Real, with perhaps a dash of *diligencia* (stage-coach) for a portion of the route, as the finishing and running of Spanish railways is always a little problematical—to

CORDOVA, on the Guadalquivir, once the capital of the Moors in Spain, and where the celebrated "Cordova leather" used to be manufactured, but now in decay and tumble-down, with only a few leading curiosities remaining, in the Great Mosque with its "Moorish battlements and Catholic dome" and its "Court of Oranges"; the Bishop's Palace, also in a state of decay; the ruins of the Palace of the Moorish Kings, etc.

From Cordova by rail to

SEVILLE, also on the Guadalquivir, famous for its oranges, its picturesquely-dirty people (gipsies included—from whom Murillo was said to have drawn many of his models),—for the

Giralda, splendid square Moorish tower, of 350 feet in height, and one of the most picturesque of the works of that race, remaining; the

Cathedral, with its massive Gothic architecture, its " Court of Oranges," too, its magnificent stained-glass windows and many fine pictures, with some of Murillo's master-works among others; the

Museo, where the wealth of pictures by Murillo (native of Seville) is to be seen; the

Alcazar, part of an old Moorish palace, now rebuilt; and the Casa de Pilato, said to be an exact imitation of Pontius Pilate's house at Jerusalem.

From Seville by rail, across the beautiful wine-producing districts of Andalusia, to

CADIZ, on the Bay of Cadiz, the great seaport of southwestern Spain, its commercial interest oddly mingled with the reputation of possessing the most beautiful women in Spain—the "dark-eyed girls of Cadiz," sung by Byron, Moore, Hans Christian Anderssen, and others. It has two fine promenades— on the Alameda, and on the fortifications near the port, where the sea-view is especially beautiful at evening and the crowd of loungers very picturesque.

Cadiz (wonderful relief!) happens to have no old Cathedrals, Museums or ruins, worth the visiting, so that it forms the pleasantest of places for a little lounging and sea-coast life, those feminine people with the dark eyes, long lashes and passionate temperaments being kept duly in view!

From Cadiz by steamer, through the straits of Gibraltar, with views of the wonderful natural and artificial fortification of Gibraltar, and also of Tangier, on the Barbary coast, opposite—to

MALAGA, famous for its wine and raisin, lemon and orange export-trade, and one of the most important commercial cities of Spain. It has a handsome modern Cathedral, a pleasant Alameda for promenading, and the loveliest of climates for pulmonary invalids; and like Cadiz, it offers no bother of art or antiquity, except the ruins of the walls built by its Carthaginian founders.

From Malaga by diligence, by Loja (about fifteen hours), to

GRANADA, the old Moorish capital, on the Darro, lying on a beautiful plain some 2,000 feet above the level of the sea, and at the base of the Sierra Nevada Mountains. It is very oriental of aspect, especially from the minarets which yet remain from the Moorish days; and its climate vies with that of Malaga for temperature and healthiness. But of course the visit to Granada is principally paid, by travellers from all parts of the world, and yet more by Americans, familiar with Washington Irving's "Alhambra" and Prescott's "Ferdinand and Isabella"—to see

The Alhambra (guide or *valet de place* necessary), the old palace of the Moorish kings, and by far the finest Saracenic remain in Europe. All the features of this "wonder in the earth" will be shown by guide and local guide-book, and any attempted enumeration of them, here, would be idle. From approaching the entrance, where stands the unfinished palace of Charles V., the front split by an earthquake and the work stopped in consequence—from the Alberca, or Fish-Pond (Bathing-room of the Sultanas), through the Repose-room, the Bath-rooms of the King and Princes, the Saloon of La Barca, the Saloon of the Two Sisters, the Hall of the Ambassadors, the Saloon of the Abencerrages, the great Court of the Lions—through all these, and others, and everywhere, the airy lightness of Oriental work in marble, the effect of mingled color, the adaptation of natural forms (as flowers, snow-wreaths, leaves, etc.) to the purposes of art, form a combination of beauty and grandeur to which only the one word can be applied—bewildering. Hours must be spent in wandering through the Alhambra and remembering the power, crimes, virtues and sorrows of the race who built it; but days would be better adapted to that end.

Granada has yet other attractions, in the

Cathedral, a massive structure, of the sixteenth century, with some statues and pictures within; the

Genoralife, another fine Moorish remain, opposite the Alhambra and across the deep ravine beside it—now belonging to a Genoese nobleman, who has never even taken the trouble to visit it; the Torre de la Vela, near the Alhambra, commanding a fine view of the architectural wonders; the Gold-Washings in the Darro, where the ladies go on St. John's Eve to wash their faces and derive good complexions for the year; the Carthusian Convent (a mile from the town), with some good marbles; etc., etc.

From Granada, return to Malaga by diligence,

or if preferred, on horseback in somewhat longer time, by Albana.

From Malaga, steamer to Marseilles for return northward.

XX.

HINTS FOR A SHORT ROUTE IN THE EAST

STRICTLY speaking, the short-trip tourist does not make any run to what is called "the East:" if he does, he is in danger of moulting his title in the very act, and becoming the "long-trip" traveller—just as the Frenchman's little dog, all the value of which consisted in his remaining little, would insist upon growing to a big dog, and thus spoiled himself. It may be, however, that some of those who begin with the intention of only making short trips in Europe, may change their intention or find themselves differently circumstanced from what they had supposed; and it is especially for their benefit that the following mere hints and outlines for seeing the most interesting portion of the Orient in economic connection (time and money, both), is here inserted.

The most convenient point, generally, at which the routes before marked out can be departed from, is to be found at Venice. From that Italian city, by rail to

TRIESTE, the most important commercial town of Austria, and the successor of Venice to the great trade of all that portion of the Mediterranean—lying at the head (northeast) of the Adriatic Sea. Its principal interest lies in its harbor, where a system of canals (devised principally by the Empress Maria

Theresa) supplies the want of natural advantages. It has, however, two interesting public squares, the Piazza Grande and Borsenplatz; a Cathedral (Byzantine) of the fourth century; and what is called the Piazzetta (little-place) de Ricardo, where Richard Cœur de Lion is alleged to have been confined by the Duke of Austria on his return from the Crusades, leading to the charming poetical story of his discovery by the minstrel Blondel.

At Trieste is to be taken one of the steamers of the Austrian Lloyds (a corporation which vies with the French Messageries Impériales and the English Peninsular and Oriental Company, in lines running everywhere) through the Grecian Archipelago, to

The Piræus, port of Athens, from which is reached, four miles distant,

ATHENS, capital of Greece, and historically as well as artistically one of the most interesting cities on the globe. Its history is too well known, as connected with science, the arts and letters, to need even the briefest reference; and to those who *do* need such reminder, something more than the few words of the guide-book would be found necessary. Among the most notable of the great architectural remains which make Athens the wonder of the world, are the ruined Parthenon, or Temple of Minerva; the Acropolis; Mars Hill (or the Areopagus), where St. Paul preached to the "too superstitious" men of Athens; the Tower of the Winds; the Arch of Hadrian; the Temple of Jupiter Olympus; etc.; while no one sojourning any time at Athens, should fail to visit the Battle-field of Marathon, in the immediate neighborhood. (Excellent local guide-books, in English, can be purchased at Athens, and for any stay they will be found indispensable.)

From Athens, by steamer, through the loveliest and most noted of the islands of the Archipelago,— by Rhodes, famous as the old seat of the Knights of St. John of Jerusalem; by Patmos, where St. John wrote the Revelation, while in Roman banishment; by Samos, noted in heathen mythology as the birth-place of Juno, and also as the birth-place of the coveted "Samian wine" that Byron ordered "dashed down," in his "Isles of Greece;" by Scio, the largest island of the Levant, and one of the loveliest; by Mytilene, the ancient Lesbos, where "Sappho the Lesbian" had her birth and home; by Tenedos, etc., through the narrow passage of the Dardanelles, into and through the Sea of Marmora, by Abydos (scene of Byron's well-known poem, the "Bride of Abydos"), to

CONSTANTINOPLE, on the European or western side of the Bosphorus (Turkey in Europe), the capital of the Turkish Empire, with nearly or quite a million of inhabitants, and bearing the same relation to the East that is borne by Rome to Western Europe. It was originally "Byzantium," from its Greek founder Byzas; but had little importance until refounded by the Emperor Constantine, and made the capital of the Eastern Empire, in the fourth century. It has filled quite as large a space in history, as even Rome—has been fought over, around and about, nearly as much, even in comparison to time, as the City of Mexico—has been repeatedly besieged, and twice captured: once in 1204, by the Second

Crusaders, and again in 1453 by the Turks, since which time it has been in Mohammedan possession, and supplied the Turkish capital.

Constantinople is considered to be one of the loveliest cities, in situation, on the globe, the Golden Horn (curved branch of the Bosphorus), forming a magnificent harbor, and the shaded suburbs forming a fine background to the tall spires (minarets) of the many mosques which have replaced the Christian churches. Within, however, the city is dirty, ill-laid-out and badly-built. The old walls still exist, with seven of the original forty-three gates; and the suburbs of Pera, Galata and Tophana have a certain beauty, even near—especially the two former, where most foreigners reside.

The leading objects of interest are the Bazaars, where Oriental trade may be seen in all its oddity and shiftlessness; the Sultan's Seraglio (outside); the Mosques of St. Sophia (visited by permission of the Sultan, obtained through the Embassy of the visitor's nation), of Solyman the Magnificent, Sultan Achmet and Mohammed the Second; the Cemeteries, by far the handsomest things connected with the city, etc.

From Constantinople, by steamer, to

SMYRNA, in Asiatic Turkey, the most important commercial city in Asia Minor, where, for the first time, the Orient may be seen in its full glory—the city squalid, the society and trading-community mixed of all Eastern nations, and figs so plenty (Smyrna being the great depot of this fruit) that they become almost a "drug in the market."

From Smyrna, by steamer, to

Beirut (or Beyrout), in Syria, a very old town of no particular present consequence, except as a port, though it has historical recollection as the Greek Berytus, a noted seat of learning, and also in connection with the Crusades.

At Beirut horses and guides will be procured across the Syrian plains, two days, to the mighty and magnificent

Ruins of Baalbec, by far the most ponderous and among the most interesting of the early architectural remains of the East, dwarfing all others in the weight of the single stones and the extent of labor (some of the wall-stones measure each 30 feet long, 15 wide and 13 deep!) thrown together in a limited space, in the Temple of the Sun, that of Jupiter, and the Circular Temple. From Baalbec on, by the same mode of travel, to

DAMASCUS, called the oldest city in the world, and founded by Uz, the grandson of Noah, some 4,000 or 4,500 years ago!—alternately the Syrian capital of the Babylonians, the Persians, the Romans, the Saracens (Arabic Mohammedans) and now of the Turks. It is especially noted for its flat-roofed houses (for sleeping upon), mean without but handsome within—for its beautiful gardens—for its bazaars—and as having for centuries produced the peculiarly-tempered swords known as the "Damascus blades," as well as the artistic work in metal-polishing known as "damascening." It has, of course, a wonderful history, Pagan, Mohammedan (through Mohammed) and Christian (through St.

Paul); and it has an Oriental sleepy magnificence peculiar to its air. There are several mosques, with the Great Mosque principal and said to contain the head of John the Baptist in a gold casket; and there is an old Castle of immense size, with moat, etc., but ruined and dismantled within.

From Damascus, with horses and guides, as before, by Banias (Cesarea Philippi), Safed, Capernaum, Tiberias, Nazareth (birthplace of the Saviour), Jenin, Samaria and Nablous (the ancient Shechem), to

JERUSALEM, the "Holy City," as Rome has been called the "Eternal"—with the places held "Holy" by all Christians—first among them the Church of the Holy Sepulchre, on Mt. Calvary, covering the spot where the body of the Saviour was laid, as also (as alleged) that where He was crucified; the Garden of Gethsemane, the Mount of Olives, the site of Solomon's Temple, and so many other spots and relics connected with sacred history, that a reminder of them would be only an insult. That task may well be left, in detail, to the guides, who will be found quite sufficiently garrulous, in a dozen languages. Outside of and near the city will of course be visited the Valley of Jehoshaphat, the town of Bethany, etc.; and a more extended excursion, occupying three days, will be made to the Dead Sea and the Jordan where it enters that remarkable and thankless lake.

From Jerusalem to the coast, the way will still be pursued with guides and horses, two days' travel (stopping the single night at the Convent at Ramleh), to

Jaffa, on the coast of Syria (eastern end of the Mediterranean Sea). Jaffa has a bad harbor, difficult of landing in rough weather; and it has no other special interest to travellers than the still-remaining (shown) "House of Simon the Tanner," where St. Peter had his vision, instructing him as to what was "uncleanness."

At Jaffa, steamer will be taken to

ALEXANDRIA, in Egypt—at the western mouth of the Nile—the seaport and commercial city of that nation—founded, as the name implies, by Alexander the Great, and splendidly situated between the mouth and Lake Mareotis, while a canal connects it with the Rosetta mouth. It has two ports—the old harbor, on the west, and the new, on the east,—and owes its principal modern importance to the fact of being the landing-place of all the many great lines of steamers on the routes to India and to and from the different ports of the Mediterranean. Of course it has a world of antique history, as the name of its founder recalls, as also the fact that it possessed the celebrated Alexandrian Library, burned by an ignorant tyrant. It has few curiosities, but some of the highest interest, including the celebrated Pompey's Pillar, at the south side, near the walls—erected in honor of the Emperor Diocletian, A. D. 296; the two Cleopatra's Needles, one standing and one fallen and partially covered, at the east side, near the sea —alleged to have been erected in 1495 B. C., and so to be of the ripe age of over 3,360 years; the Pacha's Palace; Catacombs, etc. A very mixed society will be found at Alexandria, but scarcely more oriental

IN EGYPT.

than at Marseilles, and the city may be said to be more than half European.

From Alexandria by rail, some 130 miles up the Nile, to

CAIRO, the chief city and capital of Egypt, with nearly half a million of inhabitants and all the Oriental characteristics exaggerated—no place on earth showing a greater variety in the costume of citizens, and none more oddity in narrow and dirty streets, odd mosques, bazaars, and everything ultra-Mussulmanish. Days may be spent in studying it—the Constantinople of Africa.

One of the first visits, at Cairo, should be paid to the Citadel, to catch the magnificent view of the Nile, the Pyramids, the four hundred mosques of the city, the distant desert, etc. Some of the splendid Mosques will then be visited—especially the new one of Mehemet Ali, the old ones of Taylóon, Sultan Hassan, Sultan Kalóon; some of the Palaces—among others those of Mehemet Ali and Ibrahim Pacha; Joseph's Well, supposed to have been hewn in the rock under the direction of the son of Jacob when ruling in Egypt; some of the fine Gardens surrounding the walls, etc.

The most indispensable of excursions from Cairo is that to the Pyramids, about twelve miles either way—made on donkey-back, with guides. Too much observation and admiration cannot well be bestowed upon the master pile of Cheops, with its two lesser companions and six very much smaller; but there is no law in Egypt to compel the ascent of any one of them, and some sensible people avoid that exercise and its fatigue and extortion. Near the Pyramids is the wonderful Sphynx; and not far distant, on the Nile bank, are the few scattered ruins that remain of the once mighty city of Memphis—all easily embraced in the one day's excursion.

Of course the Nile will receive due attention, as a river and a terrestrial shower. It is from Cairo that all the boating parties start, up the river; but the American short-trip traveller may well content himself with a brief sail or row, and leave the ascent to sleepier or more leisurely people.

Return from Cairo to Alexandria; then take one of the steamers of the English Peninsular and Oriental Company, down the Mediterranean, to

MALTA, the celebrated Mediterranean island of Great Britain, lying about fifty miles southward of Sicily—with a most interesting history, especially in connection with the Knights, driven away from the Crusades, who so long held it against the Turks. Its port, Valetta, has a fine harbor, is splendidly fortified, and shows many remains of the old warlike times; while in the Palace of the Grand Master may be found a splendid collection of old arms and trophies, in the Armory, with many fine pictures by Maltese painters; and these and the Church of St. John, the Grotto of St. Paul (near the town) the Catacombs of St. Paul, etc., would be certain to fill more time than the hurried traveller is likely to have at command.

From Malta to Marseilles, by steamer—ending the route, of which it may be said, in addition, that it may be very hurriedly made, from Trieste to Marseilles, in six to seven weeks, but should properly require ten to thirteen.

Or, as may be easily discovered from the number of steamers and different lines, trips may be arranged to embrace one or another part of it—with or without Constantinople—with or without Jerusalem—with or without Alexandria and Egypt, etc., if something of the East is specially desired and yet the pressure on time or means is too great to admit of all.

XXI.

A FEW USEFUL PHRASES IN FRENCH AND GERMAN.

THE promise was made, in one of the early papers of this volume, that a few words and phrases should be given, at the close, calculated to render an actual assistance in countries of Europe where only French or German should happen to be met. That promise is now to be kept, with the understanding recalled that no attempt is intended at supplying either a "conversation-book" or a glossary—that only those few words and phrases are set down, in both French and German, with a decent understanding of which experience has proved that travel and sight-seeing can be pretty well managed in the countries where those tongues are in use, while without them, to say the least, one gets along badly enough if at all. It is not to be expected that anything here, can render much assistance in understanding replies made: that advantage can only be secured by understanding the languages, or acquired through continued conversations: to be able to ask for things wanted, and direct things necessary to be done, is the only rational immediate hope of the mere English speaker, even assisted by these following pages which seem so incomplete and have yet cost such extended labor.

FRENCH.

A FEW SIMPLE RULES WORTH REMEMBERING.

1st. The French *i* generally sounds like the English *e*.
2d. The French *e* generally sounds like the English *a*.
4th. The French *ll* generally sounds like the English *y*.
5th. The French *en* generally manages to become a cross between *on* and *ong*.
7th. The concluding consonant of a word, in French, is ruthlessly sacrificed when the next word commences with a consonant; but when that next word commences with a vowel, the concluding consonant of the previous word is not sacrificed but carried over and stuck fast to the other.
8th. *Le* (the) is always masculine; *la* is always feminine, and the sex of the words they adjoin is understood by them. *Les*, the plural, however, is both masculine and feminine. The first is pronounced as nearly as posble like the English *luh*, the second like *lah*, and the third *lay*.
9th. *De* (of), *du* (of the), and *des* (of, or of the, plural), are sounded *duh*, *deu*, *day*.
6th. *Eur*, which in English sounds as *ure*, in French leaves out the *u* in sound and is simply *er*.
3d. *E* with an acute accent (*é*) is always pronounced like *a* long, as in "*côté*," where the pronunciation is *kotay*; *e* with a grave accent (*è*) is always pronounced like the English *e* in "met," as in "*caractère*," pronounced "*karackter*," with accent on the last syllable; while *e* with the broad accent (*ê*) is sounded long and broadly, with a cross between English *e* and *a*, as in "*tête*," pronounced *tayt* (nearly).
10th. The French idiom, or arrangement of sentences, is generally the exact reverse of the English; so that when any doubt exists as to which of two adjoining words to place first, it is generally nearest safe to remember what the English would be, and reverse it.
11th. The French noun is not perfect, as the English is, without the article before it: they cannot say *Amérique* (America), but *l'Amérique* (literally *the* America).
12th. Generally, the habit of the French language does not permit words to be *implied*, like the English: they must be *expressed*.
13th. *Re*, concluding a French word, is so lightly used that it is little more than a roll of the *r*, and is sometimes scarcely heard at all, as in *Louvre, quatre*, sounded *Louvrrr, quatrrr*.
14th. The French *qu* generally sounds as *k*, as in *qui* (who), pronounced *ke*.
15th. The more that words are chopped up, mangled, swallowed, and ejected through the nose (like tobacco-smoke by old smokers), the more possibility will exist of their being understood by a Frenchman.

SHORT-TRIP GUIDE.

MONTHS OF THE YEAR AND DAYS OF THE WEEK.

ENGLISH.	FRENCH.	PRONOUNCED.
January,	*Janvier,*	Jhonvay.
February,	*Fevrier,*	Fevray.
March,	*Mars,*	Marrs.
April,	*Avril,*	Ahvreel.
May,	*Mai,*	Myee.
June,	*Juin,*	Jhuan.
July,	*Juillet,*	Jhuelay.
August,	*Août,*	Ah-oo.
September,	*Septembre,*	Septombr.
October,	*Octobre,*	Octobr.
November,	*Novembre,*	Novombr.
December,	*Décembre,*	Daysombr.
Monday,	*Lundi,*	Loondee.
Tuesday,	*Mardi,*	Mardee.
Wednesday,	*Mercredi,*	Mayrcraydee.
Thursday,	*Jeudi,*	Jhudee.
Friday,	*Vendredi,*	Vondraydee.
Saturday,	*Samedi,*	Somdee.
Sunday,	*Dimanche,*	Deemonshee.

NUMERALS AND ORDINALS.

One,	*Un,*	oon.
Two,	*Deux,*	deu.
Three,	*Trois,*	trwa.
Four,	*Quatre,*	Kawtr.
Five,	*Cinque or cinq,*	sankg.
Six,	*Six,*	ziss.
Seven,	*Sept,*	set.
Eight,	*Huit,*	wheet.
Nine,	*Neuf,*	noof.
Ten,	*Dix,*	diss.
Eleven,	*Onze,*	onz.
Twelve,	*Douze,*	dooz.
Thirteen,	*Treize,*	trayz.
Fourteen,	*Quatorze,*	kahtorz.
Fifteen,	*Quinze,*	kanz.
Sixteen,	*Seize,*	sayz.
Seventeen,	*Dix-sept,*	diss-set.
Eighteen,	*Dix-huit,*	diss-wheet.
Nineteen,	*Dix-neuf,*	diss-noof.
Twenty,	*Vingt,*	vant.
Thirty,	*Trente,*	tront.

A FEW USEFUL PHRASES. 301

ENGLISH.	FRENCH.	PRONUNCIATION.
Forty,	Quarante,	karont.
Fifty,	Cinquante,	sankant.
Sixty,	Soixante,	swassant.
Seventy,	Soixante-dix,	swassant-diss.
Eighty,	Quatre-vingt,	kawt-vant.
Ninety,	Quatre-vingt-dix,	kawt-vant-diss.
One Hundred,	Cent,	sawnt.
One Thousand,	Un Mille,	oon meel.
One Million,	Un Milion,	oon meelyong.
First,	Prèmier (e, fem.),	prem-yare.
Second,	Second (e, fem.),	se-kond.
do.,	Deuxième,	dyoozhee-em.
Third,	Troisième,	trwazee-em.
Fourth,	Quatrième,	kawtree-em.
Fifth,	Cinquième,	sawnkee-em.
Sixth,	Sixième,	zissee-em.
Seventh,	Septième,	settee-em.
Eighth,	Huitième,	wheetee-em.
Ninth,	Neuvième,	noovee-em.
Tenth,	Dixième,	dizzee-em.
Eleventh,	Onzième,	onzee-em.
Twelfth,	Douzième,	dooze-em.
Thirteenth,	Treizième,	treze-em.
Fourteenth,	Quatorzième,	katorzee-em.
Fifteenth,	Quinzième,	kanzee-em.
Sixteenth,	Seizeième,	seezee-em.
Seventeenth,	Dix-septième,	dissitee-em.
Eighteenth,	Dix-huitième,	disswheete-em.
Nineteenth,	Dix-neuvième,	dissnovee-em.
Twentieth,	Vingtième,	vantee-em.
Thirtieth,	Trentième,	trontee-em.
Fortieth,	Quarantième,	karontee-em,
	etc., etc., etc.	

A FEW NAMES, OF VERY COMMON OBJECTS AND PERSONS.

(With different prefixes.)

The bread,	Le pain,	leh pan.
The salt,	Le sel,	leh sel.
Some butter,	Du beurre,	deuh berr.
A knife,	Un couteau,	oon cohto.
A fork,	Une fourchette,	oon forchet.
The dish,	L'assiette,	l' ashyet.

ENGLISH.	FRENCH.	PRONUNCIATION.
A napkin,	Une serviette,	oon survyet.
The eggs,	Des œufs,	dez ufe.
Beef,	Le bœuf,	leh beff.
Roast beef,	Rosbif,	r-r-oasbif.
Some potatoes,	Des pommes de terre,	day pom deh tair.
Oysters,	Les huîtres,	lez wecter.
Mutton,	Le mouton,	leh mootong.
Veal,	Le veau,	leh vo.
Some pork,	Du porc,	deuh pork.
Some cherries,	Quelque cerises,	kelke sareese.
The table,	La table,	lah tahble.
Pepper,	Le poivre,	leh pwavr.
Mustard,	La moutarde,	lah mootard.
That church,	Cette église,	set eeglees.
This street,	Cette rue ci,	set reuw sec.
The street-corner,	Le coin de la rue,	leh quan deh lah roo.
A bottle,	Une bouteille,	oon bootyee.
The goblet (glass),	Le verre,	leh verr.
A cup,	Une tasse,	oon tas.
Some coffee,	Du café,	deuh caffay.
A cup of tea,	Une tasse de thé,	oon tas deh tay.
A big fish,	Un gros poisson,	oon gro pwasson.
The little dog,	Le petit chien,	leh paytee sheeon.
My soup,	Mon potage,	mon po-tahj.
Your brandy,	Votre eau de vie,	vootr o devee.
Our cucumbers,	Nos concombres,	no concombr.
A spoon,	Une cuiller,	oon koolyare.
The carriage,	La voiture,	lah vwateur.
The railway,	Le chemin de fer,	leh shaman deh fair.
The shoes,	Les souliers,	lay solyair.
A pair of boots,	Une pair de bottes,	oon piar day boat.
A coat,	Un habit,	oon abbee.
The trowsers,	Les culottes	lay cooloat.
A new vest,	Un gilet nouveau,	oon jelay novo.
The waiter,	Le garçon,	leh garsoon.
The prison,	La prison,	lah pre-zon.
The doctor,	Le docteur,	leh docterr.
do	Le médecin,	leh maydeesan.
The hotel,	L'hôtel,	lotel.
A stairway,	Un escalier,	oon eskalyay.
A bed,	Un lit,	oon lee.
The bed-chamber,	La chambre à coucher,	leh shambr ah cooshay.
A furnished room,	Une chambre garnie,	oon shambr garnee.
A beef-steak,	Un biftek,	oon biftek.
A beef-steak well done,	Un bifted bien cuit,	oon biftek beyon quee.
do rare done,	do saignant,	do saguyong.

A FEW USEFUL PHRASES.

ENGLISH.	FRENCH.	PRONUNCIATION.
Fried potatoes,	Pommes de terre frites,	pom de tayr frete.
A looking-glass,	Un miroir,	oon meerwa.
An umbrella,	Oon parapluie,	oon paraplu.
Thomas's hat,	Le chapeau de Thomas,	leh shappo deh Tomas.
The other horse,	L'autre cheval,	lotr shayvol.
Wine,	Le vin,	leh van.
Some water,	De l'eau,	dello.
The comb,	Le peigne,	leh pine.
The window,	La fenetre,	lah faynayter.
The door,	La porte,	lah poart.
A great house,	Une grande maison,	oon grond miyeson.
The porter,	Le portier,	leh portya.
Breakfast,	Le dejeuner,	leh dejunay.
Dinner.	Le diner,	leh deenay.
Supper,	Le souper,	leh soopay.
A handkerchief,	Un mouchoir,	oon mooshwar.
The watch,	La montre,	lah montr.
A little clock,	Une petite cloche,	oon patee cloash.
A room,	Un appartement,	oon appartmawng.
Our gloves,	Nos gants,	no gawnt.
The shirts,	Les chemises,	la shem-ecse.
A trunk,	Une malle,	oon mal.
My basket,	Mon pannier,	mawng panya.
The theatre,	Le théatre,	lah teeatr.
A theatre-box,	Une loge de theâtre,	oon loaj deh teeatr.
Reserved seats,	Places numérotées	plass numayroatay.
A seat in the theatre,	Un place au théâtre,	oon plass oh tecatr.
A ticket of admission,	Un billet d'entrée,	oon beyea dawntray.
The porter,	Le concierge,	leh consairghe.
A chamber maid,	Une femme de chambre,	von fam deh chambre.
Meats,	Viandes,	vecond.
The baggage,	Le bagage,	leh bahgahzj.
An attendant,	Un valet de place,	oon vallee deh plass.
A body servant,	Un valet de chambre,	oon vallee deh shombr.

QUESTIONS, ANSWERS AND INQUIRIES, OFTENEST USEFUL.

Railway Travelling.

[*To buy a ticket, etc., at the office.*]

TRAVELLER.—*Monsieur, je désire un billet pour Paris.* (*Pronounced:* Jzhe dayseer oon beyea poor Parreese. *English:* Sir, I wish a ticket to Paris.)

TICKET-SELLER.—*Certainement, Monsieur; qu'elle classe voulez vous?* (*Pro.* Sertanmong, Mossiew; kel clahs voolay voo? *Eng.* Certainly, sir; what class will you have?)

TRAV.—*Qu'el est le prix des places?* (*Pro.* Kel ay leh pree da plass. *Eng.* What is the price of places.)

TICKET-S.—*Les premières coutent cinquante francs, et les secondes trente francs.* (*Pro.* La prameyer cootont sankont fronk, ay la segond tront fronk. *Eng.* The first cost fifty francs, the second thirty.) .

TRAV.—*Donnez moi les secondes, s'il vous plait.* (*Pro.* Donneh mwa lay segond, seel voo play. *Eng.* Give me the second, if you please.)

TICKET-S.—*Combien de places, Monsieur?* (*Pro.* Combeyon deh plass, Mossiew. *Eng.* How many places, sir?)

TRAV.—*Une pour moi seulement.* (*Pro.* Oon poor mwa, soolmawng. *Eng.* One for myself only.)

TICKET-S.—*Voici, Monsieur.* (*Pro.* Wahsee, Mossiew. *Eng.* Here it is, sir.)

[*Making Inquiries.*]

QUESTION.—*A qu'elle heure part le train pour Paris?* (*Pro.* Ah kel oor par leh tran poor Parree? *Eng.* At what hour does the train start for Paris?)

ANSWER.—*Le train part à dix heures.* (*Pro.* Leh tran par tah dee soor. *Eng.* The train leaves at ten o'clock.)

QU.—*Où nous arrêterons nous pour dîner?* (*Pro.* Oo noo sarrayteron noo poor denay? *Eng.* Where do we stop for dinner?

ANS.—*A Rouen, Monsieur.* (*Pro.* Ah Ruan, Mossiew. *Eng.* At Rouen, sir.)

QU.—*Combien de temps s'arrête-t-on ici?* (*Pro.* Combeyon deh tom sah-rayteton esee? *Eng.* How long time do we stop here?)

ANS.—*Vingt minutes d'arrêt.* (*Pro.* Vant meenwheet darray. *Eng.* Twenty minutes of stoppage.)

QU.—*A qu'elle heure partirons nous?* (*Pro.* Ah kel oor parteron noo? *Eng.* At what hour do we start?)

ANS.—*Dans quinze minutes, Monsieur.* (*Pro.* Dawn kanz meenwheet, Mossiew. *Eng.* In fifteen minutes, sir.)

QU.—*Est ce le train pour Dijon?* (*Pro.* Ay see leh tran poor Deejhon? *Eng.* Is this the train for Dijon?)

ANS.—*Non, Monsieur; ce train est dix minutes en retard.* (*Pro.* Non, Mossiew; seh tran a dee meenwheet on raytard. *Eng.* No, sir; that train is ten minutes behind.)

ANS.—*Oui, Monsieur; ce train en droit.* (*Pro.* Wee, Mossiew; set tran on drwat. *Eng.* Yes, sir; that train on the right.)

QU.—*Changeons nous à la prochaine station?* (*Pro.* Shonjayon noo ah lah proshain stahshon? *Eng.* Do we change at the next station?)

ANS.—*Non, Monsieur; le premier change est à Bellegarde.* *Pro.* Nong,

Mossiew; leh premya shonje es tah Belgard. *Eng.* No, sir; the first change is at Bellegarde.)

[*Warnings and Demands.*]

GUARD OR PORTER.—*Monsieur a-t-il d'avantage de bagage?* (*Pro.* Mossiew ah teel dah vantahzj deh bahgahzj? *Eng.* Has the gentleman any more baggage?)
TRAV.—*Non, Monsieur—tout le bagage est dans la voiture.* (*Pro.* Nong, Mossiew—too leh bahgahzj ay dawn lah vwahteur. *Eng.* No, sir—all the luggage [American, "baggage"] is in the carriage.)
GUARD.—*Vos billets, Mesdames et Messieurs.* (*Pro.* Vo beyea, Maydam ay Messiew. *Eng.* Your tickets, ladies and gentlemen.)
GUARD.—*En voiture, Messieurs!—en voiture!* (*Pro.* On vwahteur, Messiew!—on vwahteur! *Eng.* Take your carriages, gentlemen!)
GUARD.—*En voiture, de suite, Messieurs, s'il vous plait!* (*Pro.* On vwateur, deh sweet, Messiew, seel voo play! *Eng.* Take your carriages, gentlemen, in a hurry, if you please!)
GUARD.—*Change de voitures, Messieurs!* (*Pro.* Shonjay deh vwateur, Messiew! *Eng.* Change carriages, gentlemen!)

Taking Carriages and Riding.

TRAV.—(*To Cabman, on stand*) *Cocher, ête vous libre?* (*Pro.* Coshay, ettay voo leebr? *Eng.* Cabman, are you free? [disengaged.]
CABMAN.—*Non, Monsieur, j'attends quelqu'un.* (*Pro.* Nong, Mossiew, zjahttond kelkoon. *Eng.* No, sir; I am waiting for some one.)
CABMAN.—*Oui, Monsieur—je suis libre.* (*Pro.* Wee, Mossiew, jeh swee leebr. *Eng.* Yes, sir, I am disengaged.)
TRAV.—*Donnez mois votre carte. Pro.* Donneh mwa voatr cart. *Eng.* Give me your card—*i. e.,* the card of prices which all French cabmen carry with them.)
TRAV.—*Je vous prends à la course.* (*Pro.* Je voo prand ah lah coorse. *Eng.* I engage you for the route to which I wish to go.) Or,
TRAV.—*Je vous prends à l'heure.* (*Pro.* Je voo prend ah loor. *Eng.* I take you by the hour.
CABMAN.—*Où faut-il vous conduire Monsieur?* (*Pro.* Oo fo teel voo condweer Mossiew? *Eng.* Where does the gentleman wish to be taken?
TRAV. *Au Grand Hôtel;* or, *au Boulevard Poissonnière, numero cinquante-huit.* (*Pro.* Oh Gron Dotel; or, oh Boolevard Pwassonyer, numero sankont-wheet. *Eng.* To the Grand Hotel; or, to the Boulevard Poissonière, number fifty-eight.)
TRAV.—*Allez!* (*Pro.* Allay! *Eng.* Go on!)
TRAV.—*Marchez! marchez!* (*Pro.* Marshay! marshay! *Eng.* Faster! faster!)

TRAV.—*Pas si vite!* or, *Allez plus doucement!* (*Pro.* Pah se veet; or allay ploo doosmong. *Eng.* Go more slowly.)
TRAV. (When getting out of the cab, to have it wait)—*Attendez moi ici: je vais revenir;* or, *je reviens dans quelque minutes.* (*Pro.* Je vay rayvaneer; or, je rayveeon dawn kelk meenwheet. *Eng.* Wait for me here I will return; or, I will return in a few minutes.)
CABMAN.—*Mon argent, Monsieur!* (*Pro*. Mong arjong, Mossiew! *Eng.* My money, sir!
TRAV.—*Voici.* (*Pro.* Vwassee. *Eng.* Here it is.)
CABMAN.—*Plus encore le pour boire, Monsieur!* (*Pro.* Ploo sancoar leh poor bwar, Mossiew! *Eng.* More yet, sir; the drink-money!)
TRAV.—*Combien de pour boire?* (*Pro.* Combeyon deh poor bwar? *Eng.* How much drink-money?)
TRAV.—*Ce n'est pas possible de payer rien de plus.* (*Pro.* Ce nay pah posseebl deh paya reeon deh ploo. *Eng.* It is not possible [for me] to pay any thing more.)
TRAV.—*Arrêtez!* or, *arrêtez vous, cocher!* (*Pro.* arraytay; or, arraytay vous, coshay. *Eng.* Stop! or, stop, coachman.)

Eating and Drinking.

ORDERS TO WAITERS.—*Garçon, faites moi servir.* (*Pro.* Gahsoon, fayt mwa sareveer. *Eng.* Waiter, attend on me.) *Je désire dîner.* (*Pro.* Je descer deenay. *Eng.* I wish dinner.) *Donnez moi du potage à la Julienne.* (*Pro.* Donnay mwa deuh potahj ah lah Jzhulion. *Eng.* Give me some soup a la Julienne.) *Du rosbif bien cuit.* (*Pro.* Deuh roosbif beeyon quee. *Eng.* Some roast-beef well done.) *Du rosbif saignant.* (*Pro.* Deuh roasbif sainyong. *Eng.* Some roast-beef rare.) *Du porc roti.* (*Pro.* Deuh pork roatee. *Eng.* Some roast pork.) *Du pain.* (*Pro.* Deuh pan. *Eng.* Some bread.) *Encore un peu plus de beurre.* (*Pro.* Oncoar oon pew ploo deh burr. *Eng.* A little more butter.) *Une tasse de café.* (*Pro.* Oon tass deh caffay. *Eng.* A cup of coffee.) *Un verre d'eau.* (*Pro.* Oon vayr doe. *Eng.* A glass of water.) *Un verre d'eau glacée.* (*Pro.* Oon vayr doe glassay. *Eng.* A glass of ice-water.) *Des pomme de terre.* (*Pro.* Day pom deh tayr. *Eng.* Some potatoes.) *Une bouteille de vin rouge.* (*Pro.* Oon bootye deh van ruzjh. *Eng.* A bottle of red wine.) *Une demi-bouteille de vin blanc.* (*Pro.* Oon daymee bootye de van blong. *Eng.* A half-bottle of white wine.) *Apportez moi un assiette propre.* (*Pro.* Apporteh mwa oon awsyet proapr. *Eng.* Bring me a clean plate.) *Un fricassée de poulet.* (*Pro.* Oon freeasay deh poolay. *Eng.* A chicken fricasee.) *Deux côtelets de veau.* (*Pro.* Deuh cotaylay de vo. *Eng.* Two veal cutlets.) *Du mouton bouilli.* (*Pro.* Deuh mootong boolee. *Eng.* Some boiled mutton.) *Deux œufs frits.* (*Pro.* Deuz ufe freet. *Eng.* Two fried eggs.) *Du poissons bolilli.* (*Pro.* Deuh pwassong boolee. *Eng.* Boiled fish.) *Du pain au sucre.* (*Pro.* Deuh pan o sukr. *Eng.* Some cake.) *Du pâtés de*

A FEW USEFUL PHRASES. 307

fruits. (*Pro.* Denh Pahtay de fruee. *Eng.* Some fruit pies.) *Du sucre.* (*Pro.* Denh soocr. *Eng.* Some sugar.) *Le sel.* (*Eng.* The salt.) *Un autre cuiller.* (*Pro.* Oon otre queclay. *Eng.* Another spoon.) *Une assiette, un couteau, une fourchette, et une serviette.* (*Pro.* Oon awsseyet, oon cocto, oon forshet et oon sairveeyet. *Eng.* A plate, a knife, a fork and a napkin.) *L'addition, s'il vous plait.* (*Pro.* Laddishong, seel voo play. *Eng.* The bill, if you please.)

Greetings.

Bon jour, Monsieur. (*Pro.* Bong joor, Mossiew. *Eng.* Good-morning, sir.) *Bon soir.* (*Pro.* Bong swar. *Eng.* Good evening, when meeting; and good-night, when separating.) *Adieu!* (*Pro.* Ahdeyou. *Eng.* Good-bye.) *Au revoir.* (*Pro.* O rayvwar. *Eng.* Farewell, but to return—literally, good-bye for a little while.) *J'ai l'honneur de vous saluer.* (*Pro.* Sjay lonner deh voo saloocr. *Eng.* I have the honor to salute you.) *Permittez moi de prendre congé de vous.* (*Pro.* Permeetay mwa deh prondr conjay deh voo. *Eng.* Permit me to take leave of you.) *Merci, Madam!* (*Pro.* Mayrsce, Mahdam! *Eng.* Thank you, Madame!) *Mille remerciêments, Mademoiselle.* (*Pro.* Meel raymayrshemons, Madmwasel. *Eng.* A thousand thanks, Miss.) *Je vous remercie, Monsieur.* (*Pro.* Je voo raymayrci, Mossiew. *Eng.* I thank you, sir.)

Inquiries, etc.

Pardon, Monsieur! (*Pro.* Pardong, Mossiew. *Eng.* Beg pardon, sir! [always to be used in accosting any stranger or making apology for any *contretemps.*]) *Je vous prié de m'indiquer cette addresse, etc.* (*Pro.* Sje voo prce deh mandeckay cet address, etc. *Eng.* I beg you to indicate to me that address, etc.) *Dans quelle direction est l'Eglise de St. Roch?* (*Pro.* Dawn kel dereeshon ay layglee de San Roash. *Eng.* In what direction is the church of St. Roch?) *Ou est située cette rue?* (*Pro.* Oo ay seetuay set roo? *Eng.* Where is that street situated?) *Qu'elle est cette maison?* (*Pro.* Kel ay set myeson? *Eng.* What house is that?) *Enface est-ce une maison de modes?* (*Pro.* On fass ay se oon myeson deh moad? *Eng.* Is that the fashion-shop, opposite?) *De quel coté la Bourse, à droite ou à gauche?* (*Pro.* Deh kel cotay lah Boors, ah drwat ou ah goash? *Eng.* Which way is the Bourse, to the right or the left?) *J'ai besoin d'habits.* (*Pro.* Sjay ba-swan dabbee. *Eng.* I desire some clothes [in buying].) *Quel en est le prix, etc.* (*Pro.* Kel on ay leh pree, etc. *Eng.* What is the price, etc.) *C'est trop cher!* (*Pro.* See ay tro share. *Eng.* That is too dear or high-priced.)

Finding Interpreter or Guide.

Je désire un interprète. *Pro.* Sje daseer oon antayrpret. *Eng.* I wish an interpreter.) *Je voudrais un garcon pour me montre les places princi-

pales. Pro. Sje voodray oon garsoon poor montr me lay plass pransee pal. *Eng.* I require a servant to point me out the principal places [of interest.]) *Je désire un valet de place qui parle l'Anglais.* (*Pro.* Je daseer oon vallee deh plass ke parl long-glay. *Eng.* I wish a valet who speaks English.) *Y'a-t-il quelqu'un ici que parle Analais ?* *Pro.* Ee ateel kelkoon esee kee parl Ongglay? *Eng.* Is there any one here who speaks English? *Qui voulez vous qui m'accompagner adjourd-hui?* (*Pro.* Kee voolay voo kee maccompang adjerdwhee? *Eng.* What do you ask, to accompany me during this day?) *Qui demandez vous*, etc. (*Pro.* Kee damandah voo, etc. *Eng.* What do you demand, etc.)

Entering, Finding Persons, etc.

Q. (Knocking or at a door.) *Puis-je entrer?* or, *me permittez vous d'entrer?* (*Pro.* Pweege ontra? or, me permeetta voo dontra? *Eng.* May I come in? or, Will you permit me to enter?) A. *Entrez!* or *Certainement!* (*Pro.* Ontray! or, Certanmong. *Eng.* Come in, or, Certainly.) Q. *Monsieur H., est-il à la maison?* or, *est-il chez lui?* *Pro.* Mossiew H., esteel ah la myesong? or, esteel sha luce? *Eng.* Mr. H., is he in the house? or, is he at home?) A. *Oui, Monsieur, Mons. H. est dans sa chambre.* (*Pro.* Wee, Mossiew, Mossiew H. a don sah shombr. *Eng.* Yes, sir, Mr. H. is in his room.) Q. *Puis-je le voir?* (Pro. Pweege eje leh vwar? *Eng.* Can I see him?) Or, *Demandez lui si'l peut me recevoir.* (*Pro.* Daymanday luee seel peut me raysayvwar. *Eng.* Ask him if he is able to see me.) A. *Non, Monsieur, Mons. H. n'est pas à la maison;* or, *n'est pas chez lui.* (*Pro.* Nong, Mossiew, Mossiew H. neeay pah ah lah myeson; or, neeay pah sha luee. *Eng.* No, sir, Mr. H. is not in the house; or, is not at home.) Q. *A qu'elle heure rentrer a-t-il?* *Pro.* Ah kel oor rontrarateel? *Eng.* At what hour will he return? *Remettez mon carte à Mons. H., s'il vous plait.* (*Pro.* Rametta mon cart ah Mossiew H., seel voo play. *Eng.* Send my card to Mr. H., if you please.)

Language.

Parlez vous le Francais? (*Pro.* Parlay voo leh Fronsay? *Eng.* Do you speak French?) *Parlez vous l'Anglais?* (*Pro.* Parlay voo longglay? *Eng.* Do you speak English?) *Y' a-t-il quelqu'un ici qui parle l'Anglais ?* (*Pro.* Eeeateel kelkoon esee kee parl longglay? *Eng.* Is any one here who speaks English?) *M' entendez vous?* (*Pro.* Mantanday vous? *Eng.* Do you understand me?) *Me comprenez vous?* (*Pro.* Me compranay voo? *Eng.* Do you comprehend me?) *Je vous comprends très-bien.* (*Pro.* Sje voo comprond tray becon. *Eng.* I understand you, very well.) *Je ne vous comprends pas.* (*Pro.* Sje ne voo comprond pah. *Eng.* I do not understand you.) *Qui appellez vous,* etc. (*Pro.* Cappella voo, etc. *Eng.* What do you call, etc.) *Répétez, s'il vous plait;* or, *répétez, je vous prie.* (*Pro.* Raypaytay, seel voo play; or, raypeetay sje voo pree. *Eng.* Repeat, if you please; or, I beg you.) *Je parle mal de Français: parlez plus doucement, je vous prie.* (*Pro.* Sje parl mal deh Fronsay: parlay ploo ducemong, sje voo pree. *Eng.* I speak bad French: speak more slowly, I beg you.)

In Want.

Je suis très pauvre! faites moi du charité, pour l'amour de Dieu! (*Pro.* Sje swee tray poavre: fayt mwa duh charitay, poor lamoor deh Deyoo. *Eng.* I am very poor: do me some charity, for the love of God!) Or, *Pour l'amour de la très Sainte Vierge.* (*Pro.* Poor lamoor deh lah tray Sant Vairj! *Eng.* For the love of the most Blessed Virgin.) *J'ai très faim!* (*Pro.* Sjay tray fam. *Eng.* I am very hungry.) *J'ai très froid!* (*Pro.* S'jay tray frwa. *Eng.* I am very cold.) *J'ai très soif!* (*Pro.* Sjay tray swaf. *Eng.* I am very thirsty.) *J'n'ai pas d'argent!* *Pro.* Je na pah larghong. *Eng.* I have no money.)

In Sudden Sickness or Accident.

Je suis malade. (*Pro.* Sje swee mahlad. *Eng.* I am sick.) *Je suis très malade.* (*Pro.* Sje swee tray mahlad. *Eng.* I am very sick.) *J'ai mal à la tête.* (*Pro.* Sjay mal ah lah tayt. *Eng.* I have sickness in the head.) *Ma jambe est cassée.* *Pro.* Ma jhomb a cazzay. *Eng.* My leg [or my arm—*mon bras*, brah] is broken.) *Je vous prié de me faire conduite immédiatement chez un pharmacien.* (*Pro.* Sje voo pree deh me fair condwee immeedjatemong shez oon pharmahsheeon. *Eng.* I beg you to have me taken at once to a doctor's-shop.) *Conduisez moi immédiatement chez un docteur Anglais, Messieurs, je vous prié.* (*Pro.* Condweesa mwa immeedjatemong chez oon docter Ongglay, Messiew, sje voo pree. *Eng.* Take me immediately to an English doctor, gentlemen, I beg you.)

[For reasons that will be, as the sensational writers say, "obvious to the meanest capacity," no attempt is made at instructing the untravelled American as to any words or formulas of *love-making* in France. Two reasons *might* be adduced, in case of extreme necessity: one, that the writer is totally uninstructed on that special subject; the other, that none of his clients are likely to need much instruction. At all events, he declines to assume any responsibility.]

GERMAN.

The following table of the German vowels and consonants differing in sound from the English, may aid in understanding the spelling of the pronunciation, and insure as much accuracy as is possible by printed characters.

A sounds like *ah* in *ah!* or *a* in *father, party ;* for example, *das glas*, pronounced *dahs glahs*. It should be remembered that in the spelling of the pronunciation, the *ah* is not designed to lengthen the syllable, but simply to represent the sound of the *a*.

E is equal to *ay* in *day*, as *der*, pronounced *dayr*. It has also the sound of the English *e* in *ell*, as *elfte = elf'ty ;* and that of *y* in *twenty*, as *erste = ayrs'ty*.

I sounds like *ee* in *cheer*, as *mir = meer*, and also as *i* in *pin*, as *bin = bin*.

U is equivalent to *oo* in *poor*, as *nur = noor*.

Ae or *ä* equals *ay* in *may*. It is so like the usual sound of *e* that it is seldom distinguished from that letter in the pronunciation.

Oe, or *ö* has no equivalent in English. It is like the French *eu* in *feu*, and approximates very nearly the *i* in *girl*, as *höre=hu'ray*.

Ue, or *ü* is nearly like *u* in *avenue*, or the French *u* in *lu*, as *über = eu'ber*.

Au = ow in *how*, as *haus = howss*.

Eu = oy in *boy*, as *heute = hoy'tay*.

Ei = y in *fly*, or *ey* in *eye*, *mein = meyn*.

B, at the end of syllables, is pronounced like *p*, as *halb = hahlp ; Kalbfleisch=Kahlpfleysh*. Elsewhere like the English *b*.

D, at the end of syllables, has the sound of *t*, as *und = oont ; gesundheit = gay-zoont'heyt*. Elsewhere, like the English *d*.

G = g in *give*, at the beginning of syllables, as *gut = goot*. At the end it has a sound between *g* and *k*. There is nothing like it in English, and is represented in the following pages by *hg*, as *vierzig =fear'tsihg*.

J sounds like *y* in *you*, as *ja = yah ; jäger = yay'ger*.

S, at the beginning of syllables, sounds like *z* in *zone*, as *sein = zeyn*. Elsewhere like *s* in *son*, as *maus = mowss*.

V has the sound of *f*, as *von = fon ; vier = fear*.

W is like *v*, as *wenn = ven ; wasser = vahs'ser*.

Z sounds like *ts* in *rats*, as *zehn = tsayn ; zu = tsoo*.

Ch is pronounced like *k*, at the beginning of syllables, as *chor = kore*. Elsewhere, either like *ch* in the Scotch word *loch*, as *buch = booch*, or, not quite so guttural, as in *ich*.

Sch = sh in *shine*, as *fleisch =fleysh*.

A FEW USEFUL PHRASES.

MONTHS OF THE YEAR AND DAYS OF THE WEEK.

ENGLISH.	GERMAN.	PRONOUNCED.
January,	Januar,	Yah'noo-ahr.
February,	Februar,	Fay'broo-ahr.
March,	März,	Merts.
April,	April,	Ah-pril'.
May,	Mai,	My.
June,	Juni,	Yoo'nee.
July,	Juli,	You'lee.
August,	August,	Ow-goost'.
September,	September,	Zep-tem'ber.
October,	October,	Oc-to'ber.
November,	November,	No-vem'ber.
December,	December,	Day-tsem'ber.
Monday,	Montag,	Moan'tahg.
Tuesday,	Dienstag,	Deens'tahg.
Wednesday,	Mittwoch,	Mit'vohch.
Thursday,	Donnerstag,	Don'ners-tahg.
Friday,	Freitag,	Fry'tahg.
Saturday,	Sonnabend; or	Zon'ah-bent; or
	Samstag,	Zahms'tahg.
Sunday,	Sonntag,	Zon'tahg.

NUMERALS AND ORDINALS.

One,	Eins,	Eyns.
Two,	Zwei,	Tsvy.
Three,	Drei.	Dry.
Four,	Vier,	Fear.
Five,	Fünf,	Feunf.
Six,	Sechs,	Zex.
Seven,	Sieben,	Zee'b'n.
Eight,	Acht,	Ahcht.
Nine,	Neun,	Noyn.
Ten,	Zehn,	Tsayn.
Eleven,	Elf,	Elf.
Twelve,	Zwölf,	Tsvulf.
Thirteen,	Dreizehn,	Dry'tsayn.
Fourteen,	Vierzehn,	Fear'tsayn.
Fifteen,	Fünfzehn,	Feunf'tsayn.
Sixteen,	Sechzehn,	Zech'tsayn.
Seventeen,	Siebzehn,	Zeeb'tsayn.
Eighteen,	Achtzehn,	Ahcht'tsayn.

ENGLISH.	GERMAN.	PRONOUNCED.
Nineteen,	*Neunzehn,*	Noyn'tsayn.
Twenty,	*Zwanzig,*	Tsvahn'tsihg.
Thirty,	*Dreissig,*	Dry'sihg.
Forty,	*Vierzig,*	Fear'tsihg.
Fifty,	*Fünfzig,*	Feunf'tsihg.
Sixty,	*Sechzig,*	Zech'tsihg.
Seventy,	*Siebzig,*	Zeeb'tsihg.
Eighty,	*Achtzig,*	Ahcht'tsihg.
Ninety,	*Neunzig,*	Noyn'tsihg.
One hundred,	*Ein Hundert,*	Eyn Hoon'dert.
One thousand,	*Ein Tausend,*	Eyn Taw's'nt.
One million,	*Eine Million,*	Ey'nay Mill-yohn'.

	M. F. N.	
First,	*Der, die, das erste,*	Dayr, dee, dahs ayrs'ty.
Second,	" " " *zweite,*	" " " tsvy'ty.
Third,	" " " *dritte,*	" " " drit'ty.
Fourth,	" " " *vierte,*	" " " fear'ty.
Fifth,	" " " *fünfte,*	" " " feunf'ty.
Sixth,	" " " *sechste,*	" " " zex'ty.
Seventh,	" " " *siebente,*	" " " see'b'n-ty.
Eighth,	" " " *achte,*	" " " ahch'ty.
Ninth,	" " " *neunte,*	" " " noyn'ty.
Tenth,	" " " *zehnte,*	" " " tsayn'ty.
Eleventh,	" " " *elfte,*	" " " elf'ty.
Twelfth,	" " " *zwölfte,*	" " " tsvulf'ty.
Thirteenth,	" " " *dreizehnte,*	" " " dry'tsayn-ty.
Fourteenth,	" " " *vierzehnte,*	" " " fear'tsayn-ty.
Fifteenth,	" " " *fünfzehnte,*	" " " feunf'tsayn-ty.
Sixteenth,	" " " *sechzehnte,*	" " " zech'tsayn-ty.
Seventeenth,	" " " *siebzehnte,*	" " " zeeb'tsayn-ty.
Eighteenth,	" " " *achtzehnte,*	" " " ahcht'tsayn-ty.
Nineteenth,	" " " *neunzehnte,*	" " " noyn'tsayn-ty.
Twentieth,	" " " *zwanzigste,*	" " " tsvahn'tsihg-sty.
Thirtieth,	" " " *dreissigste,*	" " " dry'sihg-sty.
Fortieth,	" " " *vierzigste,*	" " " fear'tsihg-sty.
Fiftieth,	" " " *fünfzigste,*	" " " feunf' tsihg-sty.

A FEW NAMES OF VERY COMMON OBJECTS AND PERSONS.

(*With different Prefixes.*)

The bread,	*Das Brod,*	Dahs Broht.
The salt,	*Das Salz,*	Dahs Zalts.
Some butter,	*Etwas Butter,*	Et'vahs Boot'ter.

A FEW USEFUL PHRASES. 313

ENGLISH.	GERMAN.	PRONOUNCED.
A knife,	Ein Messer,	Eyn Mes'ser.
A fork,	Eine Gabel,	Ey'nay Gah'b'l.
The dish,	Die Schüssel,	Dee Sheus's'l.
A napkin,	Eine Serviette,	Ey'nay Zer-vyet'tay.
The eggs,	Die Eier,	Dee Ey'er.
Beef,	Rindfleisch,	Rint'fleysh.
Roast beef,	Geröstetes Rindfleisch,	Gay-reus'tay-tes Rint'fleysh.
Some potatoes,	Einige Kartoffeln,	Ey'nee-gay Car-tof'feln.
Oysters,	Austern,	Ows'tern.
Mutton,	Hammelfleisch,	Hahm'mel-fleysh.
Veal,	Kalbfleisch,	Kahlp'fleysh.
Some pork,	Etwas Schweinefleisch,	Et'vahs Shvy'ny-fleysh.
A few cherries,	Einige Kirschen,	Ey'nee-gay Keer'shen.
The table,	Der Tisch,	Dayr Tish.
Pepper,	Pfeffer,	Pfef'fer.
Mustard,	Senf,	Zenf.
That church,	Jene Kirche,	Yay'nay Keer'chay.
This street,	Diese Strasse,	Dee'zay Strahs'say.
The street corner,	Die Strassenecke,	Dee Strahs'sen-ek-kay.
A bottle,	Eine Flasche,	Ey'nay Flah'shay.
The goblet (glass),	Das Glas,	Dahs Glahs.
A cup,	Eine Tasse,	Ey'nay Tahs'say.
A saucer,	Eine Untertasse,	Ey'nay Oon'ter-tahs'say.
Some coffee,	Etwas Kaffee,	Et'vahs Kahf'fay.
A cup of tea,	Eine Tasse Thee,	Ey'nay Tahs'say Tay.
A big fish,	Eine grosser Fisch,	Eyn gros'ser Fish.
The little dog,	Der kleine Hund,	Dayr kly'nay Hoont.
My soup,	Meine Suppe,	My'nay Zoop'pay.
Your brandy,	Ihr Branntwein,	Ear Brahnt'veyn.
Our cucumbers,	Unsere Gurken,	Oon'z'ray Goor'ken.
A spoon,	Ein Löffel,	Eyn Leuf'f'l.
The carriage,	Die Kutsche,	Dee Koot'shay.
The railway,	Die Eisenbahn,	Dee Ey'zen-bahn.
The shoes,	Die Schuhe,	Dee Schoo'ay.
A pair of boots,	Ein Paar Stiefel,	Eyn Pahr Stee'f'l.
A coat,	Ein Rock,	Eyn Rock.
The trowsers,	Die Beinkleider,	Dee Beyn'kley-der.
The prison,	Das Gefängniss,	Dahs Gay-feng'niss.
The doctor,	Der Doktor,	Dayr Doc'tor.
The physician,	Der Arzt,	Dayr Ahrtst.
The hotel,	Der Gasthof,	Dayr Gahst'hof.
A stairway,	Eine Treppe,	Ey'nay Trep'pay.
A bed,	Ein Bett,	Eyn Bet.
The bedchamber,	Das Schlafzimmer,	Dahs Shlahf'tsim-mer.
A furnished room,	Ein möblirtes Zimmer,	Eyn mu-bleer'tes Tsim'mer.

SHORT-TRIP GUIDE.

ENGLISH.	GERMAN.	PRONOUNCED.
A beefsteak,	Eine geröstete Rindfleisch Scheibe,	Ey'nay gay-rus'tay-ty Rint' fleysh Shy'bay.
Meat well done,	Fleisch völlig gar,	Fleysh ful'libg gahr.
Rare meat,	Halb gares Fleisch,	Hahlp gah'res Fleysh.
Fried potatoes,	Gebratene Kartoffeln,	Gay-brah't'nay Car-tof'feln.
A looking-glass,	Ein Spiegel,	Eyn Spee'g'l.
An umbrella,	Ein Regenschirm,	Eyn Ray'gen-sheerm.
John's hat,	Johann's Hut,	Yo-hahn''s Hoot.
The other horse,	Das andere Pferd,	Dahs ahn'd'ray Pfayrt.
Wine,	Wein,	Veyn.
Some water,	Etwas Wasser,	Et'vahs Vahs'ser.
The comb,	Der Kamm,	Dayr Kahm.
The window,	Das Fenster,	Dahs Fens'ter.
The door,	Die Thür,	Dee Teur.
A great house,	Ein grosses Haus,	Eyn gros'sess Howss.
The porter,	Der Pförtner,	Dayr Phurt'ner.
Breakfast,	Frühstück,	Freu'steuk.
Dinner,	Mittagsmahl,	Mit'tahgs-mahl.
Supper,	Abendessen,	Ah'bent-es'sen.
A handkerchief,	Ein Schnupftuch,	Eyn Shnoopf'tooch.
The watch,	Die Taschenuhr,	Die Tah'shen-oor.
A little clock,	Eine kleine Wanduhr,	Ey'nay kly'nay Vahnt'oor.
A pen,	Eine Feder,	Ey'nay Fay'der.
Our gloves,	Unsere Handschuhe,	Oon'z'ray Hahnt'shoo-ay.
The shirts,	Die Hemden,	Dee Hem'den.
A trunk,	Ein Koffer,	Eyn Kof'fer.
My basket,	Mein Korb,	Meyn Korp.
The theatre,	Das Theater,	Dahs Tay-ah'ter. [ters.
A theatre-box,	Eine Loge des Theaters,	Ey'nay Lo'jay des Tay-ah'-
Reserved seats,	Vorbehaltene Sitze,	For-bay-hahl't'ny Zit'say.
A seat in a theatre,	Ein Sitz in einem Theater,	Eyn Zits in ey'nem Tay-ah'ter.
A ticket of admission,	Ein Einlasszettel,	Eyn Eyn'lahs-tset't'l.
A body-servant,	Ein Kammerdiener,	Eyn Kahm'mer-dee'ner.
A chambermaid,	Ein Kammermädchen,	Eyn Kahm'mer-mayd'gen.
The baggage,	Das Gepäck,	Dahs Gay-peck'.

QUESTIONS, ANSWERS AND INQUIRIES, OFTEN USEFUL.

Railway Travelling.

[*To buy a Ticket, etc., at the Office.*]

TRAVELLER.—*Mein Herr, geben Sie mir ein Reisebillet nach Paris.* (*Pronounced.* Meyn Hayr, gay'ben zee meer eyn Rey'zay-bill-yet' nahch Pah-reess'. *English.* Sir, give me a ticket to Paris.)

A FEW USEFUL PHRASES.

TICKET SELLER.—*Ja, mein Herr. Welche Klasse?* (*Pro.* Yah, meyn Hayr. Vel-chay Klahs-say? *Eng.* Yes, sir. What class?)

TRAV.—*Was kosten die Plätze?* (*Pro.* Vahs kos'ten dee Plet'say? *Eng.* What is the price of places?)

TICKET S.—*Die Ersten kosten fünf Thaler, die zweiten kosten drei Thaler.* (*Pro.* Dee ayrs'ten kos'ten feunf Tah'ler, dee tsvy'ten kos'ten dry Tah'ler. *Eng.* The first cost five dollars, the second three.)

TRAV.—*Geben Sie mir gefälligst eins zweiter Klasse.* (*Pro.* Gay'ben zee meer gay-fel'lihgst eyns tsvy'ter Klahs-say. *Eng.* Please give me one of the second class.)

TICKET S.—*Wie viele, mein Herr?* (*Pro.* Vee fee'lay, meyn Hayr? *Eng.* How many, sir?)

TRAV.—*Oh, nur eins für mich.* (*Pro.* Oh, noor eyns feur mich. *Eng.* Oh, one for myself only.)

TICKET S.—*Hier ist es, mein Herr.* (*Pro.* Heer ist es, meyn Hayr. *Eng.* Here it is, sir.)

[*Making Inquiries.*]

QUESTION.—*Um welche Uhr geht der Zug nach Paris ab?* (*Pro.* Oom vel'-chay Oohr gayt dayr Tsoohg nahg Pa-reess' ahb? *Eng.* At what hour does the train start for Paris?)

ANSWER.—*Der Zug geht um zehn Uhr ab.* (*Pro.* Dayr Tsoohg gayt oom tsayn Oohr ahb. *Eng.* The train starts at ten o'clock.)

QU.—*Wo halten wir zum Mittag an?* (*Pro.* Voh hahl'ten veer tsoom Mit-tahg ahn? *Eng.* Where do we stop for dinner?)

ANS.—*In Rouen, mein Herr.* (*Pro.* In Rouen, meyn Hayr. *Eng.* At Rouen, sir.)

QU.—*Wie lange halten wir hier an?* (*Pro.* Vee lahng'ay hahl'ten veer heer ahn? *Eng.* How long do we stop here?)

ANS.—*Zwanzig Minuten.* (*Pro.* Tsvahn'tsihg Min-oo'ten. *Eng.* Twenty minutes.)

QU.—*Um wie viel Uhr gehen wir ab?* (*Pro.* Oom vee feel Oohr gay'h'n veer ahb? *Eng.* At what hour do we start?)

ANS.—*In einer Viertel Stunde, mein Herr.* (*Pro.* In ey'ner fear'tell Stoon'-day, meyn Hayr. *Eng.* In a quarter of an hour, sir.)

QU.—*Ist dies der Zug nach Dijon?* (*Pro.* Ist deess dayr Tsoogh nahg Dijon? *Eng.* Is this the train for Dijon?)

ANS.—*Nein, mein Herr; der Zug geht zehn Minuten später.* (*Pro.* Neyn, meyn Hayr, dayr Tsoohg gayt tsayn Min-oo'ten spay'ter. *Eng.* No, sir, that train goes ten minutes later.)

QU.—*Ist das der Zug?* (*Pro.* Ist dahs dayr Tsoohg? *Eng.* Is that the train?)

ANS.—*Ja, mein Herr; der Zug zur Rechten.* (*Pro.* Yah, meyn Hayr; dayr Tsoohg tsoor Rech'ten. *Eng.* Yes, sir; the train on the right.)

QU.—*Wechseln wir die Wagen an der nächsten Station?* (*Pro.* Vek'seln

veer dee Vah'gen ahn dayr nayk'sten Staht-zyon'? *Eng.* Do we change at the next station?)
ANS.—*Nein, mein Herr; der erste Wechsel ist in Bellegarde.* (*Pro.* Neyn, meyn Hayr; dayr ayrs'ty Vek'sel ist in Bellegarde. *Eng.* No, sir; the first change is at Bellegarde.)

[*Warnings and Demands.*]

GUARD, OR PORTER.—*Hat der Herr noch mehr Gepäck?* (*Pro.* Haht dayr Hayr noch mayr Gay-peck'? *Eng.* Has the gentleman any more baggage?)
TRAVELLER.—*Nein, mein Herr; es ist alles in der Kutsche.* (*Pro.* Neyn, meyn Hayr; es ist ahl'less in dayr Coot'shay. *Eng.* No, sir; it is all in the carriage.)
GUARD.—*Meine Herren und Damen, Ihre Billete!* (*Pro.* Mey'ny Hayrn oont Dah'men, Ee'ray Bill-yet'tay! *Eng.* Gentlemen and ladies, your tickets?)
GUARD.—*Steigen Sie ein, meine Herren!* (*Pro.* Stey'gen Zee eyn, mey'ny Hayrn! *Eng.* Take your carriages, gentlemen!)
GUARD.—*Steigen Sie gefälligst schnell ein, meine Herren!* (*Pro.* Stey'gen Zee ge-fel'lihgst shnell eyn, mey'ny Hayrn! *Eng.* Please to take your carriages quickly, gentlemen!)
GUARD.—*Wechseln Sie die Wagen, meine Herren!* (*Pro.* Vek'seln Zee dee Vah'gen, mey'ne Hayrn! *Eng.* Change carriages, gentlemen!)

Taking Carriages and Riding.

TRAVELLER (*to cabman*).—*Sind Sie unbeschäftigt?* (*Pro.* Zint Zee oon-bay-shef'tihgt? *Eng.* Are you disengaged?)
CABMAN.—*Nein, mein Herr, ich warte auf einen anderen Herrn.* (*Pro.* Neyn, meyn Hayr, ich vahr'tay owf ey'nen ahn'der'n Hayrn. *Eng.* No, sir, I am waiting for another gentleman.)
CABMAN.—*Ja, mein Herr, ich habe nichts zu thun.* (*Pro.* Yah, meyn Hayr, ich hah'bay nichts tsóo toon. *Eng.* Yes, sir, I am disengaged.)
TRAV.—*Geben Sie mir Ihre Karte.* (*Pro.* Gay'ben Zee meer Ee'ray Cahr'tay. *Eng.* Give me your card—*i. e.*, the card of prices.)
TRAV.—*Ich miethe die Kutsche für den ganzen Weg welchen ich zurückzulegen habe.* (*Pro.* Ich mee'tay dee Coot'shay feur dayn gahn'tsen Vehg vel'chen ich tsoo-renk'tsoo-lay'gen hah'bay. *Eng.* I engage the carriage for the whole route I have to go.)
TRAV.—*Ich miethe die Kutsche stundenweise.* (*Pro.* Ich mee'tay dee Coot'shay stoon'den-vey-zay. *Eng.* I engage you by the hour.)
CABMAN. — *Wohin, mein Herr?* (*Pro.* Vo-hin', meyn Hayr? *Eng.* Whereto, sir?)
TRAV.—*Zum grossen Gasthof;* or, *zur Friedrich Strasse, numero acht und fünfzig.* (*Pro.* Tsoom gros'sen Gahst-hof; or, tsoor Freed'rich

A FEW USEFUL PHRASES. 317

Strahs'say, noo'may-ro ahcht oont fenuf-tsihg. *Eng.* To the large hotel; or, to fifty-eight Frederick Street.)
TRAV.—*Fahren Sie!* (*Pro.* Fah'ren Zee! *Eng.* Go on!)
TRAV.—*Schneller!* (*Pro.* Shnel'ler! *Eng.* Faster!)
TRAV.—*Nicht so schnell, fahrt langsamer!* (*Pro.* Nicht zo shnell, fahrt lahng'sah-mer! *Eng.* Not so fast, drive more slowly!)
TRAV. (When getting out of the cab to have it wait.)—*Warten Sie hier; ich komme gleich wieder.* (*Pro.* Vahr'ten Zee heer; ich kom'may gleych vee'der. *Eng.* Wait here; I shall return immediately.)
CABMAN.—*Mein Geld, mein Herr!* (*Pro.* Meyn Gelt, meyn Hayr! *Eng.* My money, sir!)
TRAV.—*Da ist es!* (*Pro.* Dah ist ess! *Eng.* Here it is!)
CABMAN.—*Noch mehr, mein Herr—das Trinkgeld!* (*Pro.* Noch mayr, meyn Hayr—dahs Trink-gelt! *Eng.* More, sir—the drink-money!)
TRAV.—*Ich kann unmöglich mehr bezahlen.* (*Pro.* Ich kahn oon-muhg'-lich mayr bay-tsah'len. *Eng.* I cannot possibly pay more.)
TRAV.—*Halt, Kutscher!* (*Pro.* Hahlt, Coot'sher! *Eng.* Stop, coachman!)

Eating and Drinking.

ORDERS TO WAITERS.—*Kellner, bedienen Sie mich.* (*Pro.* Kell'ner, bay-dee'nen Zee mich. *Eng.* Waiter, attend on me.) *Ich will zu Mittag essen.* (*Pro.* Ich vill tsoo Mit-tahg es'sen. *Eng.* I want some dinner.) *Geben Sie mir Suppe à la Julienne.* (*Pro.* Gay'ben Zee meer Zoop'pay ah lah Sheu-lee-en. *Eng.* Give me some soup à la Julienne.) *Geröstetes Rindfleisch völlig gar.* (*Pro.* Gay-rus'tay-tes Rint'fleysh ful-lihg gahr. *Eng.* Some roast beef well done.) *Geröstetes Rindfleisch halb gar.* (*Pro.* Gay-rus'tay-tes Rint-fleysh hahlp gahr. *Eng.* Some rare roast beef.) *Geröstetes Schweinefleisch.* (*Pro.* Gay-rus'tay-tes Shvey'nay-fleysh. *Eng.* Some roast pork.) *Brod.* (*Pro.* Broht. *Eng.* Bread.) *Noch ein wenig Butter.* (*Pro.* Noch eyn vay'nihg boot'ter. *Eng.* A little more butter.) *Eine Tasse Kaffee.* (*Pro.* Ey'nay Tahs'say Cahf'fay. *Eng.* A cup of coffee.) *Ein Glas Wasser.* (*Pro.* Eyn Glahs Vahs'ser. *Eng.* A glass of water.) *Ein Glas Eiswasser.* (*Pro.* Eyn Glahs ice-vahs'ser. *Eng.* A glass of ice water.) *Kartoffeln.* (*Pro.* Cahr-tof'f'ln. *Eng.* Some potatoes.) *Eine Flasche Rothwein.* (*Pro.* Ey'nay Flah'shay Roht-veyn. *Eng.* A bottle of red wine.) *Eine halbe Flasche Weisswein.* (*Pro.* Ey'nay hahl'bay Flah'shay Veyss-veyn. *Eng.* A half-bottle of white wine.) *Bringen Sie mir einen reinen Teller.* (*Pro.* Bring'en Zee meer ey'nen rey'nen Tel'ler. *Eng.* Bring me a clean plate.) *Ein Hühnerfricassee.* (*Pro.* Eyn Heuh'ner-free-kahs-say.' *Eng.* A chicken fricassee.) *Zwei Kalbscarbonaden..* (*Pro.* Tsvy Kahlps-cahr-boh-nah'den. *Eng.* Two veal cutlets.) *Gekochtes Hammelfleisch.* (*Pro.* Gay-koch'tes Hahm'mel-fleysch. *Eng.* Some boiled mutton.) *Zwei gebratene Eier.* (*Pro.* Tsvy gay-brah't'nay Ey'er.

Eng. Two fried eggs.) *Gekochten Fisch.* (*Pro.* Gay-koch'ten Fish. *Eng.* Some boiled fish.) *Kuchen.* (*Pro.* Koo'chen. *Eng.* Cake.) *Eine Obst Pastete.* (*Pro.* Ey'nay Opst Pahs-tay'tay. *Eng.* A-fruit pie.) *Zucker.* (*Pro.* Tsook'ker. *Eng.* Sugar.) *Das Salz.* (*Pro.* Dahs Sahlts. *Eng.* The salt.) *Einen anderen Löffel.* (*Pro.* Ey'nen ahn'der'n Luf'f'l. *Eng.* Another spoon.) *Einen Teller, ein Messer, ein Gabel, und eine Serviette.* (*Pro.* Ey'nen Tel'ler, eyn Mes'ser, ey-nay Gah'b'l, oont ey'nay Zer-vyet'tay. *Eng.* A plate, knife, fork, and napkin.) *Ich bitte um die Rechnung.* (*Pro.* Ich bit'tay oom dee Rech'-noong. *Eng.* The bill, if you please.)

Greetings.

Guten Morgen, mein Herr. (*Pro.* Goo'ten Mor-gen, meyn Hayr. *Eng.* Good-morning, sir.) *Guten Abend ; gute Nacht.* (*Pro.* Goo'ten Ah'bent ; goo'tay Nahcht. *Eng.* Good-evening ; good-night.) *Adieu!* (*Pro.* Ah-dyu'! *Eng.* Good-bye!) *Auf Wiedersehn.* (*Pro.* Owf Vee'der-zayn. *Eng.* Farewell, till we meet again.) *Ich habe die Ehre Sie zu begrüssen.* (*Pro.* Ich hab'bay dee Ay'ray Zee tsoo bay-greus'sen. *Eng.* I have the honor to salute you.) *Erlauben Sie mir mich zu beurlauben.* (*Pro.* Ayr-low'ben Zee meer mich tsooh bay-oor'low-ben. *Eng.* Permit me to take leave of you.) *Ich danke Ihnen, Madam.* (*Pro.* Ich dahnk'ay Ee'nen, Mah-dahm'. *Eng.* Thank you, Madam.) *Ich bedanke mich tausendmal, mein Fräulein.* (*Pro.* Ich bay-dahnk'ay mich tow-zent-mahl, meyn Froy'leyn. *Eng.* A thousand thanks, miss.)

Inquiries, etc.

Verzeihen Sie, mein Herr ! (*Pro.* Fair-tsey'en Zee, meyn Hayr! *Eng.* Pardon, sir! [always used in accosting a stranger, or apologizing for any accident.]) *Wollen Sie mir wohl den Weg zu dieser Addresse nachweisen ?* (*Pro.* Vol'len Zee meer vohl dayn Vehg tsoo dee'zer Ad-dres'-say nahch-vey'zen? *Eng.* Will you be kind enough to show me the way to that address?) *In welcher Gegend ist die Domkirche ?* (*Pro.* In vel'cher Gay'gent ist dee Dohm-keer'chay? *Eng.* In what direction is the cathedral?) *Wie heisst diese Strasse ?* (*Pro.* Vee heyst dee'-zay Strahs'say? *Eng.* What is the name of this street?) *Was für ein Haus ist das?* (*Pro.* Vahs four eyn howss ist dahs? *Eng.* What house is that?) *Ist das gegenüberliegende Haus ein Modewaarenlager?* (*Pro.* Ist dahs gay'gen-eu'ber-lee'gen-day Howss eyn Moh'day-wah'-ren-lah'ger? *Eng.* Is the house opposite a millinery warehouse?) *Auf welcher Seite liegt die Börse—zur Rechten oder zur Linken ?* (*Pro.* Owf vel-cher Zey'tay leehgt dee Bur'zay ; tsoor Rech'ten oh'der tsoor Link-en? *Eng.* On which side is the Bourse—to the right or the left?) *Ich möchte gern Kleider kaufen ; was ist der Preis ?* (*Pro.* Ich meuch'-tay gern Kley'der kow'fen ; vahs ist dayr Preyss? *Eng.* I wish to buy

A FEW USEFUL PHRASES. 319

some clothes; what is the price?) *Das ist zu theuer.* (*Pro.* Dahs ist tsoo toy'er. *Eng.* That is too dear.)

[Finding an Interpreter or Guide.]

Ich brauche einen Dolmetscher. (*Pro.* Ich brow'chay ey'nen Doll-met'sher. *Eng.* I want an interpreter or guide.) *Ich brauche einen Bedienten um mir die interessanten Plätze nachzuweisen.* (*Pro.* Ich brow'chay ey'nen Bay-deen'ten, oom meer dee in-tay-res-sahn'ten Plet'tsay nahch-tsoo-vey'zen. *Eng.* I require a servant to point out to me the places of interest.) *Ich will einen Diener haben welcher Englisch spricht.* (*Pro.* Ich vill ey'nen Dee'ner hah'ben vel'cher Ayng'lish spricht. *Eng.* I require a valet who speaks English.) *Ist Jemand hier welcher Französisch spricht?* (*Pro.* Ist Yay'mahnt heer vel'cher Frahn-tseu-zish spricht? *Eng.* Is there any one here who speaks French?) *Wie viel fordern Sie mich heute zu begleiten?* (*Pro.* Vee feel for'dern Zee mich hoy'tay tsoo bay-gley'ten? *Eng.* What do you ask to accompany me to-day?)

Entering, Finding Persons, etc.

Qu. (Knocking at a door.)—*Darf ich eintreten?* or, *Erlauben Sie dass ich eintreten darf?* (*Pro.* Dahrf ich eyn-tray'ten? or, Er-low'ben Zee dahs ich eyn-tray'ten dahrf? *Eng.* May I come in? or, will you permit me to enter?) Ans. *Treten Sie ein!* or, *gewiss!* (*Pro.* Tray'ten Zee eyn; or, gay-viss! *Eng.* Come in! or, certainly!) Qu. *Ist Herr H. zu Hause?* (*Pro.* Ist Hayr H. tsoo How'zay. *Eng.* Is Mr. H. at home?) Ans. *Ja, mein Herr, Herr H. ist in seinem Zimmer.* (*Pro.* Yah, meyn Hayr, Hayr H. ist in zey'nem Tsim'mer. *Eng.* Yes, sir, Mr. H. is in his room.) Qu. *Kann ich ihn sehen?* (*Pro.* Kahn ich een zayh'n? *Eng.* Can I see him?) *Fragen Sie ihn ob er mich empfangen will?* (*Pro.* Frah'gen Zee een op ayr mich emp-fahng'en vill. *Eng.* Ask him whether he will see me?) Ans. *Nein, mein Herr, Herr H. ist nicht zu Hause.* (*Pro.* Neyn, meyn Hayr, Hayr H. ist nicht tsoo How'zay. *Eng.* No, sir, Mr. H. is not at home.) Qu. *Wann wird er erwartet?* (*Pro.* Vahn virt ayr er-vahr'tet? *Eng.* When do you expect him?) *Geben Sie ihm meine Karte.* (*Pro.* Gay'ben Zee eem mey'nay Cahr'tay. *Eng.* Give him my card.)

Language.

Sprechen Sie Deutsch? (*Pro.* Spre'chen Zee Doytsh? *Eng.* Do you speak German?) *Sprechen Sie Englisch?* (*Pro.* Spre'chen Zee Ayng'lish? *Eng.* Do you speak English?) *Verstehen Sie mich?* (*Pro.* Fer-stay'en Zee mich? *Eng.* Do you understand me?) *Ich verstehe Sie sehr gut.* (*Pro.* Ich fer-stay'ay Zee zayr goot. *Eng.* I understand you very well.) *Ich verstehe Sie nicht.* (*Pro.* Ich fer-stay'ay Zee nicht. *Eng.* I do not understand you.) *Wie heisst das?* (*Pro.* Vee heysst dahs? *Eng.* What is this called?) *Wiederholen Sie das, wenn ich bitten darf.* (Vee'dayr-hoh'len Zee dahs, ven ich bit'ten dahrf. *Eng.* Repeat that, if you please.) *Ich spreche nur wenig Deutsch; seien Sie so gut und sprechen Sie langsamer.* (*Pro.* Ich spre'chay noor vay'nihg Doytsh; zey'en Zee zoh goot oont spre'chen Zee lahng'sah-mer. *Eng.* 'I speak but little German; be so kind as to speak more slowly.)

In Want.

Ich bin sehr arm! Geben Sie mir ein Almosen, um Gotteswillen! (*Pro.* Ich bin zayr ahrm! Gay'ben Zee meer eyn Ahl'mo-zen, oom Got'tes-vil'len! *Eng.* I am very poor, give me some charity for the love of God!) Or, *Um der heiligen Jungfrau willen.* (*Pro.* Oom dayr hey'lee-gen Yoong'frow vil'len. *Eng.* For the sake of the Blessed Virgin.) *Ich bin sehr hungrig.* (*Pro.* Ich bin zayr hoong'rihg. *Eng.* I am very hungry.) *Mir ist sehr kalt.* (*Pro.* Meer ist zayr kahlt. *Eng.* I am very cold.) *Ich bin sehr durstig.* (*Pro.* Ich bin zayr doors'-tihg. *Eng.* I am very thirsty.) *Ich habe kein Geld.* (*Pro.* Ich hah'-bay keyn Gelt. *Eng.* I have no money.)

In Sudden Sickness or Accident.

Ich bin krank. (*Pro.* Ich bin krahnk. *Eng.* I am sick.) *Ich bin sehr krank.* (*Pro.* Ich bin zayr krahnk. *Eng.* I am very sick.) *Ich habe Kopfweh.* (*Pro.* Ich hah'bay Kopf-vay. *Eng.* I have a headache.) *Ich habe mir das Bein—den Arm zerbrochen.* (*Pro.* Ich hah'bay meer dahs Beyn—dayn Ahrm tser-broch'en. *Eng.* I have broken my leg— my arm.) *Ich bitte Sie, führen Sie mich gleich zu einem Arzt.* (*Pro.* Ich bit'tay Zee, feu'ren Zee mich gleych tsoo ey'nem Ahrtst. *Eng.* I beg you to take me immediately to a physician.) *Führen Sie mich zu einem englischen Doktor.* (*Pro.* Feu'ren Zee mich tsoo ey'nem ayng'lish-en Doc-tor. *Eng.* Take me to an English doctor.)

XXII.

EUROPEAN MONEY IN AMERICAN COIN.

[ONLY two kinds of money (apart from Bank of England notes, drafts, and letters of credit) are likely to be carried over to Europe by Americans. These are English and French gold—English preferable, except on going direct to France, and then quite as convenient. And it so happens that the English and French, extensively used all over Europe (especially the French, on the Continent), are the only ones of the value of which any correct idea can be briefly given, though an attempt will be made to indicate the worth, in dollars and cents (gold) of the more common kinds of German, Italian, etc. American money—even American gold—it is scarcely necessary to say, is not familiarly known in Europe.]

English.

Sovereign (gold)	$4 83
Guinea (calculation—no coin)	5 07
Half-Sovereign (gold)	2 41
Crown (silver)	1 20
Half-Crown (silver)	60
Florin (silver—two shillings)	46
Shilling (silver)	23
Sixpence (silver)	11½
Fourpence (silver)	7¾
Penny (copper)	1⅞
Half-penny (copper)	⅞

NOTE.—English Bank of England notes are equally current with English gold. in France and over much of the Continent.

French.

Double Napoleon (gold)...............................	$7 72
Napoleon (gold).......................................	3 86
Half-Napoleon (gold)..................................	1 93
Five Francs (gold or silver)...........................	95
Franc (silver)...	19
Half-Franc (silver)....................................	9½
Twenty-Centime piece (base)..........................	3⅗
Two Sous (copper)....................................	2
Sou (copper)..	1

NOTE.—The French franc is divided into imaginary hundredths, as the American dollar into cents, and all smaller calculations are made in these hundredths, or "centimes," though there is no coin to represent the unit. The half-franc is of course fifty centimes; the twenty-centime piece is one-fifth of a franc; and the sou is always five centimes; and twenty sous make the franc.

Swiss.

Same in value, and nearly same in appearance, as the French—Napoleons, francs, sous, centimes; but can be readily distinguished from the French coins by the Swiss cross and word "Helvetia," which they bear.

Belgian.

Francs and centimes—same in value and reckoning as in France and Switzerland.

German.

NOTE.—There is such an "infinite variety" and abominable mixture and uncertainty in the German money, that Tom Hood had no way to get out of the trouble, as he crossed from one petty state to another, except always to *throw away his change.* The tourist cannot be expected to practise that costly amusement, but must experience his "little difficulty." No more can be done, here, practically, than to mention a few values, with the countries where the coins originate:

Five Gulden—gold (Baden)............................	$2 06
Crown—silver "	1 10
Florin— "	40
Twenty Kreutzer—base (Baden).......................	10
Ten Kreutzer— " "	05
Double Frederick—gold (Prussia)......................	8 00
Frederick—gold "	4 00
Ten Guilders—gold (Central Germany).................	4 00
Five Guilders " "	2 00
Guilder—silver "	40
Guilder " (Holland).............................	37½
Double Ducat—gold (Germany).......................	4 56

EUROPEAN MONEY.

Ducat—gold (Germany)	$2 28
Thaler—silver (Saxony)	1 00
" " (Prussia)	70
Rix Dollar—silver (Austria and Tyrol)	1 00
Florin " "	50
Ten Thalers—gold (Brunswick)	8 00
" " (Hanover)	8 00
Thaler—silver (Brunswick or Hanover)	80

Italian.

Twenty Lira—gold (Sardinia)	3 80
Ten Lira " "	1 90
Five Lira—silver "	95
Lira " "	19
Half-Lira " "	$9\frac{1}{2}$
Quarter-Lira—base "	$4\frac{3}{4}$
Lira—silver (Venice—larger in proportion)	17
Sequin—gold (Tuscany)	2 30
Scudo—gold or silver (Tuscany)	1 10
Paul—silver (Tuscany—larger and smaller in proportion)	11
Crazia—copper "	$1\frac{1}{4}$
Quatrino " "	$\frac{1}{2}$
Ten Scudi—gold (Rome)	10 00
Scudo—silver or gold (Rome)	1 00
Paul—silver "	10
Grosso—base "	5
Baioque—copper "	1
Half-Baioque—copper "	$\frac{1}{2}$
Ducato—silver (Naples)	81
Piastra " "	95
Carlina " "	$8\frac{1}{4}$
Grano—copper "	$\frac{3}{4}$

Turkish.

Twenty Piastres	1 00
Piastre	5
Five Paras	$0\frac{5}{8}$

ALPHABETICAL PLACE-AND-ROUTE

INDEX.

A

Alexandria to Marseilles, 31.
Arran (Isle of), 70.
Ailsa Craig, 70.
Alderney (Island), 73.
Ayr, 99.
Ardcheanocrochan, 104.
Aberfoil (Clachan of), 104.
Abbotsford, 117.
" route to from Edinburgh, 117.
Ambleside, 138.
Alnwick Castle, 157.
Arques (Castle), 162.
Amberieux, 184.
Aar (river), 197.
Alpnach, 200.
Aix-la-Chapelle, 220.
Antwerp, 223.
Augsburg, 227.
Alps, Across the:
    Mont Cenis Route, 232.
    St. Bernard Route, 234.
    St. Gotthard Route, 238.
    Simplon Route, 241.
Aosta, 236.
Altorf, 237.
Andermatt, 239.
Arona, 242.
ATHENS, 289.
" to Constantinople, 290.
Alexandria, 294.
" to Cairo, 295.
" down the Mediterranean to Malta, 296.

B

Bombay to Suez and Alexandria, 31.
Ballycotton (light), 63.
Bell Buoy (Liverpool), 65.
Beachy Head, 68.
Bute (Island), 71.
Brodick, 71.
Brest, 72.
Blarney Castle, etc., 84.
Bog of Allen (The), 89.
Boyne Water, 93.

BELFAST, 93.
" to Giant's Causeway, 94.
Ballycastle, 94.
Burns Neighborhood, 100.
Balloch, 101.
Ben Lomond, 101.
" Venu, 103.
" A'an, 103.
" Ledi, 105.
Bannockburn, 106.
Ben Nevis, 109.
Berwick, 117, 157.
Bowness, 137.
Birmingham, 142.
Brighton, 152.
British Channel (Crossings), 159.
Bourg, 184.
Bellegarde, 185.
BERNE, 197.
" to Interlaken, 197.
Bernese Oberland, 197.
Brienz, 200.
Brunig Pass, 200.
BÂLE, 202.
" to Strasbourg, 204.
BADEN-BADEN, 206.
" to Heidelberg and down the Rhine, 210.
Black Forest (The), 208.
Bruchsal, 211.
Bingen, 215.
Bonn, 218.
BRUSSELS, 222.
" to Antwerp, 223.
Bruges, 224.
Bregenz, 226.
BERLIN, 229.
" to Hamburg, etc., 229.
Bellinzona, 240.
Brieg, 241.
Brescia, 251.
Bologna, 257.
Bayonne, 278.
Biarritz, 278.
Burgos, 279.
Beirut, 292.
Baalbec, 292.

INDEX. 325

C

Cape Race, 58.
Chebuctoo Head (N. S.), 59.
Cape Clear, 61.
Crookhaven, 62.
Cove of Cork, 63.
Conigsbeg (light), 63.
Cowes, 67.
Cantire (Mull of), 70.
Cumbræ Islands, 71.
Cape La Hogue, 73.
Cherbourg, 73.
Cape Levi, 73.
" Barfleur, 73.
" La Hague, 73.
" La Héve, 73.
CORK, 82.
" to Killarney, 84.
Cloyne, 84.
Charleville, 89.
Carrickfergus, 94.
Cushendall, 94.
Coleraine, 95.
Coilantogle Ford, 105.
Callandar, 105.
Cambuskenneth Abbey, 107.
Crinan Canal, 108.
Crianlarich, 109.
Caledonian Canal, 109.
Craigmillar Castle, 117.
Chester, 121.
Crewe, 123.
Coventry, 143.
Charlecote Hall, 148.
Cheltenham, 152.
Culoz, 185.
Chillon (Castle), 188.
Chamounix (Excursion to), 190.
Colmar, 204.
Carlsruhe, 211.
Coblentz, 216.
COLOGNE, 219.
" to Paris, Route I., 219.
" to Channel, Route II., 221.
Charleroi, 221.
Compeigne, 221.
Civita Vecchia, 262.
Corniche Road (The), 275.
Cordova, 283.
Cadiz, 284.
CONSTANTINOPLE, 290.
" to Smyrna, 291.
CAIRO, 295.
" Excursion to Pyramids, Memphis, etc., 295.

D

Dursey Island, 60.
Daunt's Rock, 62.
Dungeness, 68.
Dover, 68.
Downs (The), 68.
Deal, 69.
Dunoon, 72.
DUBLIN, 89.
" to Holyhead, 92.
" to Belfast, 93.
" Giants' Causeway, 93.
Dargle (river), 92.
Drogheda, 93.
Dundalk, 93.
Doon (river), 100.
Dumbarton Castle, 101.
Dunblane, 105.
Doune Castle, 107.
Dalkeith (Palace), 116.
Dalhousie Castle, 117.
Dryburgh Abbey, 117.
Dee (river), 121.
Doncaster, 156.
Dunbar, 158.
Dover to Calais, 159.
Dieppe, 162.
Dijon, 184.
Drachenfels (The), 217.
Dresden, 228.
" to Berlin, 229.
Domo d'Ossola, 242.
DAMASCUS, 292.
" to Jerusalem, 293.
Dead Sea, 293.

E

Eddystone Lighthouse, 66.
EDINBURGH, 110.
" Castle, 114.
" Excursions from, 116.
" to Berwick and London, 117.
Eaton Hall, 123.
England to Scotland (routes), 154.
Ehrenbreitstein, 216.

F

Fastnet Rock, 61.
Folkestone, 68.
Firth of Clyde, 71.
Fingal's Cave, 108.
Furness Abbey, 140.
Folkestone to Boulogne, 159.
Fontainebleu, 183.
Freybourg, 196.
FRANKFORT-ON-THE-MAINE, 212.
" to Wiesbaden and Mayence, 213.
Fluellen, 238.
Ferrara, 257.
FLORENCE, 259.

FLORENCE, excursion to Vallombrosa, 261.
Fiesolé, 261.

G

Great Orme's Head, 64.
Gosport, 67.
Glengall Head, 70.
Greenock, 72.
Guernsey (Island), 73.
Giants' Causeway (The), 94.
" to Londonderry, 95.
GLASGOW, 97.
" to Ayr, 99.
" to Edinburgh, by the Trossachs, } 101.
" to Edinburgh, by Oban, Caledonian Canal and Inverness, } 107.
Glenfinlass, 104.
Grampians, 109.
Grasmere, 138.
Guy's Cliff, 145.
GENEVA, 185.
" to Chamounix, 190.
" to Berne, etc., 195.
Grindelwald (Glaciers), 198.
Geissbach (Falls), 199.
Ghent, 224.
GENOA, 274.
" to Marseilles, 275.
Granada, 285.
" Alhambra, 285.
" to Malaga & Marseilles, 287.
Gibraltar (Straits), 284.

H

Hong Kong to Bombay, 31.
Halifax Harbor, 59.
Hook Tower (Light), 63.
Holyhead, 64.
Holy Isle, 71.
Havre, 73.
Howth (Hill of), 89.
Hawthornden, 116.
Hastings, 153.
HEIDELBERG, 211.
" to Frankfort, 212.
Hamburg, 229.
Herculaneum, 273.

I

Isle of Wight, 153.
Instrahull, 70.
Innishowen Head, 70.

Inversnaid, 102.
Iona, 108.
Inverness, 109.
INTERLAKEN, 197.
" to Lucerne, etc., 200.
INNSPRUCK, 226.
" to Munich, etc., 227.
Irun, 278.
Isles of Greece (Rhodes, Patmos, Samos, Scio, Mytilene, Tenedos, Abydos, etc.), } 290.

J

Jersey (Island), 73.
Jungfrau (The), 197.
JERUSALEM, 293.
" to Jaffa, 293.
Jordan (river), 293.
Jaffa, 294.
" to Alexandria, 294.

K

Kinsale (Old Head), 62.
Kilbrauna Sound, 70.
Kyles of Bute, 71.
Kinnoul (Mull of), 70.
Killarney (Lakes, etc.), 85.
" to Dublin, 88.
Kildare (Curragh), 89.
Kingstown, 89.
Kew, 131.
Kendal, 136.
Kenilworth, 144.
" Castle, 144.
Kussnacht, 201.
Kehl, 206.

L

Le Have (Nova Scotia), 59.
Liverpool (Nova Scotia), 59.
Lee (river), 63.
Lizard Head, 66.
Lamlash (harbor), 71.
Limerick Junction, 89.
Liffey (river), 91.
Lisburn. 93.
Larne, 94.
LONDONDERRY, 95.
" to Belfast, 96.
Loch Lomond, 101.
Luss, 102.
Loch Arklett, 102.
" Katrine, 102.
" Achray, 104.
" Vennochar, 104.

INDEX. 327

Lanrick Mead, 104.
Leith, 107.
Loch Linnhe, 109.
" Lochy, 109,
" Ness, 109.
LIVERPOOL, 118.
" to Cumberland Lakes, 136.
" to London, 123.
" to Chester, 121.
" to Shakspeare Neighborhoods, 141.
" to Birmingham, 141.
" to Coventry, 141.
" to Manchester and Sheffield, 150.
" to Glasgow, 155.
" to Edinburgh, 155.
" Docks, 119.
LONDON, 123.
" to Paris, 155.
" to Edinburgh, 155.
" Tower of, 127.
" Excursions from, 134.
Lancaster, 136.
Leamington, 149.
Llandudno, 153.
Lausanne, 195.
Lauterbrunnen (Fall), 198.
Lake of Brienz, 199.
LUCERNE (and Lake), 200.
" to the Rhigi, 201.
" to Bâle, 202.
Liege, 220.
Lille, 225.
Liddes, 234.
Lake of the Canton Uri, 238.
Lake Maggiore, 246.
" Como, 249.
" Garda, 251.
Lucca, 261.
Leghorn, 262.
LYONS, 276.
" to Geneva, Paris, etc., 277.

M

Mizen Head, 62.
Mine Head (light), 63.
Margate, 69, 153.
Malta Head, 70.
Moville, 70.
Mallow, 85.
Mucross Abbey, 87.
Melrose Abbey, 117.
Manchester, 150.
Marston Moor, 156.
Macon, 184.
Mont Blanc, 185, 186, 189, 190-195.
Martigny, 191, 234.
Mayence, 213.
Munich 227.

Mont Cenis, 233.
" Tunnel, 233.
Magadino, 246.
MILAN, 246.
" Duomo, 247.
Mantua, 253.
MARSEILLES, 275.
" to Toulon, Paris, etc., 276.
MADRID, 280.
" Excursion to Escorial, 282.
" to Cordova, 283.
Malaga, 285.
" to Granada, 285.
Memphis, 295.
Malta, 296.
" to Marseilles, 296.

N

New York to Panama, 30.
Needles (The), 67.
North Foreland (The), 69.
Nore (The), 69.
Naas, 89.
Newry, 93.
Newbattle Abbey, 117.
Newcastle-upon-Tyne, 157.
Newhaven to Dieppe, 159.
Newhaus, 197.
Namur, 221.
Nuremberg, 227.
Novara, 246.
NAPLES, 270.
" excursion to Pompeii and Herculaneum, 273.
" excursion to Vesuvius, 272.
" Bay of, 272.
" to Genoa, 274.
Nice, 275.
Nile (river), 295.

O

Oban, 108.
Oxenholme, 136,
Ostend, 225.

P

Panama to San Francisco, 30.
Point de Galle, 31.
Point Lynas, 64.
Portland Bill, 67.
Portsmouth, 67.
Portarlington, 89.
Portrush, 95.
Paisley, 99.
Preston, 136.
Peterborough, 156.

PARIS, 165.
" to Geneva, 183.
Pilatus (Mont), 200.
Peschiera, 251.
Padua, 254.
Pistoja, 258.
Pisa, 261.
Pompeii, 273.
Pyramids (The), 295.

Q

Queenstown (harbor), 62.
Queenstown, 81.

R

Roche's Point, 62.
Ramsgate, 69, 153.
Rathlin Island, 70.
Rosslyn (Castle), 116.
Rugby, 149.
Rydal Mount, 139.
Rhyl, 153.
Rouen, 163.
Rhone (river and valley), 184.
Romont, 196.
Rhigi (The), 201, 202.
Rastadt, 211.
Rhine (Down the), 214.
Rolandseck, 217.
ROME, 262.
" to Naples, etc., 270.

S

San Francisco to Yokohama and Hong Kong, 31.
Sambro Head (N. S.), 59.
Skellig Rocks, 60.
Snowdon, 64.
Skerries, 64.
Scilly Rocks, 66.
St. Agnes, 66.
Start Point, 67.
St. Alban's Head, 67.
Solent (river), 67.
Spithead, 67.
Southampton, 68.
St. Catharine's, 68.
South Foreland (The), 68.
Sanda Island, 70.
Stronaclachar, 103.
STIRLING, 105.
" Castle, 105.
" Carse, 106.
Staffa, 108.
Stafford, 123.

Shakspeare Neighborhoods of Warwickshire, route to, 140.
Stratford-on-Avon, 147.
Sheffield, 150.
Scarborough, 152.
Shields, 157.
Seine (river), 166.
St. Cloud, 178.
Sèvres, 178.
St. Denis, 181.
Sallanches, 195.
Scherlingen-Thun, 197.
STRASBOURG, 204.
" Cathedral, 204.
" to Baden-Baden, 206.
St. Michel, 232.
Susa, 233.
St. Remy, 234.
St. Bernard Route, 234.
" Hospice, 235.
St. Gotthard Route, 238.
" Hospice, 239.
Simplon Pass and Route, 241.
" Hospice, 242.
Sion, 241.
Seville, 283.
Smyrna, 291.
" to Beirut (Syria), 292.
Sphynx (The), 295.

T

Tuskar (light), 63.
Tory Island, 70.
Tarbet, 102.
Trossachs (The), 103.
Turk (Brigg of), 104.
Tonnerre, 184.
TURIN, 244.
Toulon, 276.
Trieste, 288.
" to Athens, etc., 289.
Tangier, 285.

U

Ushant, 72.
Unterseen, 197.

V

Versailles, 178.
Valley of the Rhone, 184.
Villeneuve, 191.
VERONA, 252.
" Excursion to Mantua, 253.
Vicenza, 254.
VENICE, 254.
" to Florence, Rome, etc., 257.

Vesuvius (Mt.), 272.
Valladolid, 280.

W

Wicklow Mountains, 64.
Windsor Castle, 130.
Windermere Lakes, 135.
    " route to, 135.
    " to Furness Abbey, 139.
Wigan, 136.

Wolverhampton, 142.
Warwick, 146.
    " Castle, 146.
Wengern Alp, 199.
Weggis, 202.
Weisbaden, 213.
Waterloo (Field of), 222.

Y

York, 156.
    " Minster, 156.

REMINDERS FOR EUROPEAN RAMBLERS.

[IN this department, in subsequent years as well as the present, nothing will be alluded to in any other words than those of the strictest truth,— just as nothing whatever will be taken, in the "announcement" department to which it refers, having the slightest shade of impropriety or that does not commend itself to the best judgment of travellers, when abroad, or after their return to America. It is the intention of the author and publishers, in later editions, to call attention to such hotels and mercantile houses in the leading European cities and at the great European watering-places, as manifest at once their desire to be put more prominently before the body of American tourists, and their fitness to fill the places thus assumed. For the present year, and pending necessary investigations, the brief references here made are exclusively to "things at home."]

In an early paper of the "Short-Trip Guide," some reference was made to the fact that Americans, paying first visits to Europe, would not find *everything better than their own;* and the few words following are to be devoted to citing a few of the instances to which attention has been specially called, and which the New World, where it is not linked with the Old, certainly stands no whit behind it.

On no part of the globe, for instance, can the tourist expect to find hotels supplying both splendor and comfort, to a greater degree than the best of those of New York and some of the other leading American cities. They have long been creditable wonders, in the estimation of travellers and the pencillings of writers.

Of course first among them, as the down-town New York hotel that the people would no more allow to be moved than the City Hall, stands the noble old ASTOR HOUSE, its massive granite outside as commanding as ever, and the unbounded extent of the interior just thoroughly refitted with all the luxury known to modern art; while its location opposite the Park and the new Post Office, at the city-centre, as well as the centre of business and the termini of nearly all the lines of cars in New York, must combine with the life-long reputation of Col. Charles A. Stetson and his sons, Alex. McC. and P. Reddington, to keep it for many a long year at the head of the hotels of the Western Continent and make its reputation as enduring as its material and architecture. Closely linked with this is the splendid new ST. JAMES, on Franklin Square, Boston, just opened under the management of Mr. J. P. M. Stetson, and admitted to be, in every detail, the very perfection of beauty as a building, without and within, and of liberal taste in arrangement and conveniences for the comfort of guests; while still a third, the STETSON HOUSE, Long Branch (New Jersey), supplies the most elegant building on the whole coast, the most complete accommodations shown at any American seaside watering-place, and yet one more proof, in the management of Mr. Charles A. Stetson, Jr., that there is not one of this able family but knows ".how to keep a hotel." Quite the equal of the Astor and its dependencies in importance and popular favor, too, the tourist will remember the splendid up-town hotel, the EVERETT HOUSE, with its unequalled location in full front on Union Square, New York; its proximity to all the more aristocratic places of amusement; the magnificence of its unusually large suites of rooms, in which not a potentate of Europe would not think himself honored in being accommodated; the perfection of its every service; and last, but by no means least, the air of cheerful and elegant comfort which Mr. Borrows and his capable assistants have the faculty of throwing round any house under their management. Nothing beyond these houses (and some of the others which we may have occasion to characterize in our next issue) can be found in Europe; and seldom are they even approached.

Among the attractions which the tourist will find abroad, will of course be *music*. But he will not be long in remembering, listening to it, say in Paris, that a firm of American piano-manufacturers, the Messrs. STEINWAY, won the first prize over all European and American competitors, at the Great French Exposition, after receiving the applause of the finest musicians of the Old World and delighting uncounted thousands with the power and sweetness of their instruments,—and stand, to-day, confessedly at the head of that difficult branch of constructive art, in the whole world. He will see *billiards* played; but he will not be likely to ignore the great masters of the cue whom he has left behind in America, and especially *Michael Phelan*, the "Father of Billiards," in the elevation which he has been the means of giving to that most excellent and gentlemanlike amusement, and the benefactor to the whole billiard-world which he has become, in supplying, in conjunction with his practical partner, *Mr. Collender*, the STANDARD AMERICAN BILLIARD TABLE, matchless on either continent and indispensable wherever amusement has risen to the dignity of an art.

The tourist will deal with European bankers, wisely taking a hint already given and carrying over his funds in drafts or letters of credit, issued by some one or more of the almost royal houses in finance, bearing the honored names of DUNCAN, SHERMAN & Co., of Pine and Nassau Streets, who have supplied exchange, and courteous dealing in effecting it, to half the travelling generation; BROWN BROTHERS & Co., of 59 Wall Street, whose very title suggests Parliament, British solidity married to American thrift, and the Bank of England; JAMES G. KING'S SONS, of 54 William Street, their name, like their reputation, one that the nation has delighted to honor; or JOHN MUNROE & Co., of No. 8 Wall Street, who have not only effected exchange for thousand upon thousand of Europe-bound Americans, but laid them under lasting obligations by care of their letters, free-reading-rooms and general courtesy, at their corresponding banking-house at No. 7 Rue Scribe, Paris.

He will look upon great enterprizes in the Old World; but he must not expect to find any one of them—not even the work of tunnelling the Alps or opening the Suez Canal, at all to be compared with that which the UNION PACIFIC RAILROAD COMPANY are now so rapidly pushing forward to completion, with almost a certainty of finishing it to the Pacific by 1870, and the certainties of rich return for investments, to those who purchase their bonds, such as no other enterprize of the age has dreamed of offering.

He will probably visit some of the great Spa-springs of Europe—Kissingen, or Baden, or Vichy, and drink the health-giving waters; but in the midst of all the gaieties there he will remember the MISSISQUOI SPRING, far away in the Green Mountains of American Vermont, and with agencies for the sale of its waters now established everywhere,—doing every day, in the cure of Cancer, Kidney-diseases, and many others before held incurable, a work astounding the doctors and electrifying the world.

Our tourist, acting upon a previous hint, may and should insure his life before leaving America. Whether or not he selects the EQUITABLE LIFE ASSURANCE SOCIETY OF THE UNITED STATES, 92 Broadway, New York, as the medium of that great justice to himself and his family—one thing is sure, that he will not find, even in life-assuring England, the parallel of that nobly-managed purely-mutual institution, growing faster, and ameliorating the condition of more families, than any other of its class in existence.

He may need jewelry, and fancy, in advance, that he can find it in richer profusion abroad than at home. But if, before he leaves, he should chance to encounter the *griffin* of C. A. STEVENS, the jeweller *par excellence*, of New York Fourteenth St. (a cut of which wonderful animal has been kindly loaned to make this paragraph clearer), then he may find himself amid such a profusion of all that is rich, rare and tasteful, in jewelry, bijouterie, plate and articles of *vertu*, as scarcely to allow him to go to Paris or Geneva with many desires unfilled.

Finally, it scarcely matters on what steamer he may take his way to Europe, he is not likely to es-

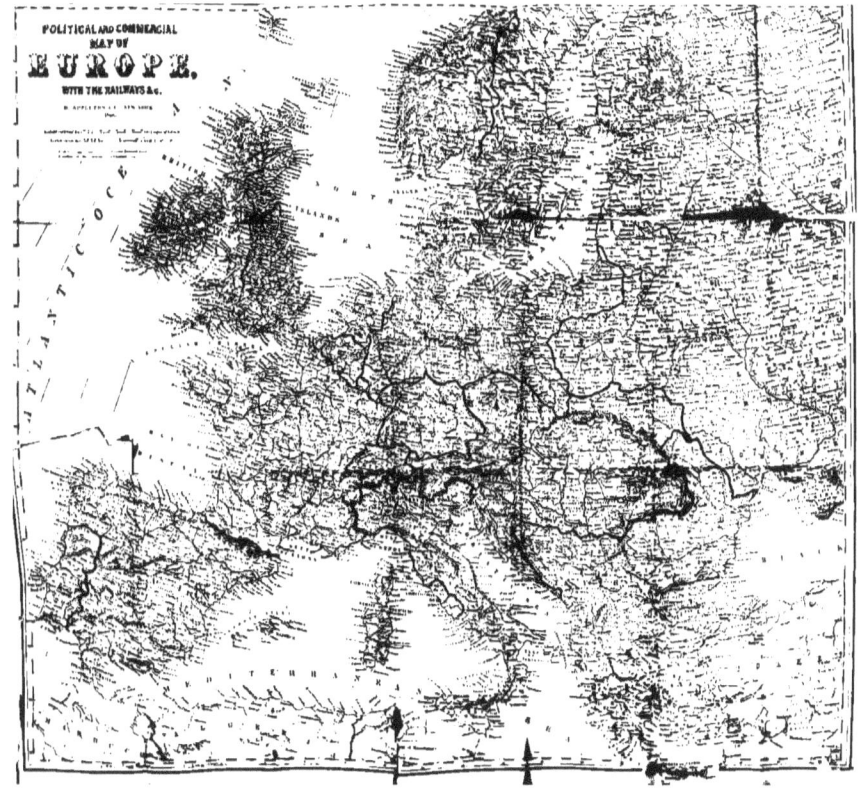

cape admiring his handsome face in a mirror supplied by that prince of dealers in looking-glasses, picture-frames, chromos and other pictures, JOHN S. WILLARD, of Canal Street, who not only manufactures and supplies all that is elegant and excellent in his line, but has (and deserves) a preëmption on all the vessels that carry vain and mirror-gazing humanity over the waters of the world.

THE END.

SHORT-TRIP GUIDE.—ANNOUNCEMENTS.

GUIDE-BOOKS FOR TRAVELLERS,

PUBLISHED BY

D. APPLETON & CO.

I.

Appletons' Illustrated Railway and Steam Navigation Guide,

Containing the Time-Tables of the Railways of the United States and the Canadas. Also, One Hundred Railway Maps, together with Monthly Account of Railways and their Progress, and Anecdotes and Incidents of Travel, etc., etc.

II.

Appletons' Hand-Book of American Travel,

Containing a Full Description of the Principal Cities, Towns, and Places of Interest, together with the Routes of Travel and Leading Hotels throughout the United States and British Provinces. 1 vol., 12mo. Illustrated with Maps.............................$4.00

III.

Appletons' Northern Hand-Book of Travel,

Containing an Account of the Principal Watering Places and Summer Resorts, including Niagara, Trenton Falls, Lake Superior, etc. Illustrated with Maps. 1 vol., 12mo................$2.00

IV.

Appletons' Southern Hand-Book of Travel,

Containing a Complete Account of all the Cities and Towns in the Southern States. Illustrated with Maps. 1 vol., 12mo...$2.00

a

APPLETONS'
(SO-CALLED)

PLUM-PUDDING EDITION

OF THE
WORKS OF CHARLES DICKENS.
Now Complete, in 18 *Vols. Paper Covers. Price,* $5.00.

LIST OF THE WORKS.

Oliver Twist...........172 pp..25 cts.	Bleak House...........352 pp..35 cts.
American Notes........104 " 15 "	Little Dorrit...........343 " 35 "
Dombey and Son... ...356 " 35 "	Pickwick Papers.......326 " 35 "
Martin Chuzzlewit......341 " 35 "	David Copperfield......351 " 35 "
Our Mutual Friend.....340 " 35 "	Barnaby Rudge........257 " 30 "
Christmas Stories.......163 " 25 "	Old Curiosity Shop.....221 " 30 "
Tale of Two Cities......144 " 20 "	Great Expectations.....183 " 25 "
Hard Times, and Additional Christmas Stories ....202 " 25 "	Sketches...............194 " 25 " Uncommercial Traveller, Pictures of Italy, and
Nicholas Nickleby.....338 " 35 "	Reprinted Pieces.....300 " ·35 "

LIBRARY EDITION OF
CHARLES DICKENS'S WORKS,
To be completed in Six Volumes, with Thirty-two Illustrations.
Price, $1.75 *per vol., or* $10.50 *the set.*

D. APPLFTON & Co., Publishers, New York.

SHORT-TRIP GUIDE.—ANNOUNCEMENTS.

APPLETONS' EDITION

OF THE

WAVERLEY NOVELS,

NOW PUBLISHING.

From New Stereotype Plates, uniform with the New Edition of Dickens, containing all the Notes of the Author, and printed from the latest edition of the Authorized Text.

TO BE COMPLETED IN TWENTY-FIVE VOLUMES.

Price, Twenty-five Cents each.

Printed on fine white paper, clear type, and convenient in size.

PRONOUNCED "A MIRACLE OF CHEAPNESS."

ORDER OF ISSUE.

1. WAVERLEY.
2. IVANHOE.
3. KENILWORTH.
4. GUY MANNERING.
5. ANTIQUARY.
6. ROB ROY.
7. OLD MORTALITY.
8. THE BLACK DWARF, and A LEGEND OF MONTROSE.
9. BRIDE OF LAMMERMOOR.
10. HEART OF MID-LOTHIAN.
11. THE MONASTERY.
12. THE ABBOT.
13. THE PIRATE.
14. FORTUNES OF NIGEL.
15. PEVERIL OF THE PEAK.
16. QUENTIN DURWARD.
17. ST. RONAN'S WELL.
18. REDGAUNTLET.
19. THE BETROTHED, and HIGHLAND WIDOW.
20. THE TALISMAN.
21. WOODSTOCK.
22. FAIR MAID OF PERTH.
23. ANNE OF GEIERSTEIN.
24. COUNT ROBERT OF PARIS.
25. THE SURGEON'S DAUGHTER.

The first volume, "Waverley," issued on February 22, 1868. A volume will be published about once a fortnight, until the Series is completed. Any volume mailed, post free, on receipt of price.

For SIX DOLLARS we will send by mail, prepaid, as fast as published, the entire set of WAVERLEY NOVELS, and a copy of a new STEEL-PLATE PORTRAIT OF SIR WALTER SCOTT, suitable for framing.

For TEN DOLLARS we will send by mail, prepaid, a set of DICKENS (in uniform style), 18 volumes, and WAVERLEY, 25 volumes. The cheapest Ten Dollars' worth to be found in the whole range of Literature. Forty-three volumes for ten dollars!

Any FIFTY VOLUMES, selected at pleasure, will be sent to one address (by express at the expense of the purchaser) on receipt of the retail price, *less* 20 *per cent.*

Any ONE HUNDRED VOLUMES, selected at pleasure, will be sent to one address (by express at the expense of the purchaser) on receipt of the retail price, *less* 25 *per cent.*

D. APPLETON & CO.,

90, 92 & 94 GRAND STREET.

1868. **CUNARD LINE.** 1868.

BRITISH AND NORTH AMERICAN
ROYAL MAIL STEAMSHIPS,
Between New York and Liverpool,
CALLING AT CORK HARBOR.
MAIL STEAMERS, CARRYING NO EMIGRANTS.

SCOTIA,	RUSSIA,	CUBA,
PERSIA,	JAVA,	CHINA,
	AUSTRALASIAN.	

From New York, every Wednesday.
From Liverpool, every Saturday.

RATES OF PASSAGE.

From New York to Liverpool, Cabin............ ...$130.00 gold.
" " Second Cabin.......... 80.00 "
" to Paris, Cabin.................. 145.00 "
From Liverpool to New York, Cabin.....................£26.
" " Second Cabin...............£18.

Extra Steamers, carrying First and Third Class.

SIBERIA,	PALMYRA,	TRIPOLI,
SAMARIA,	TARIFA,	ALEPPO,
MALTA,	MARATHON,	MOROCCO,
HECLA,	KEDAR,	SIDON,
	OLYMPUS.	

From New York, every Thursday.
From Liverpool, every Tuesday.

RATES OF PASSAGE.

From New York to Liverpool, Cabin................$80.00 gold.
From Liverpool to New York, Cabin........15, 17, and 21 guineas.

For freight or passage, apply to

IVES G. BATES, Boston; D. & C. MACIVER, Queenstown;
D. & C. MACIVER, Liverpool.

E. CUNARD,
4 BOWLING GREEN & 111 BROADWAY, N. Y.

1 8 6 8.

STEAMERS TO FRANCE DIRECT,
Transit by Railroad, and crossing the English Channel avoided.

THE
General Transatlantic Co.'s
FIRST-CLASS STEAMSHIPS,
Under Government Contract to carry the Mails between
NEW YORK AND HAVRE,
CALLING AT BREST EACH WAY.

Sailing from New York every alternate Saturday.
From Havre every alternate Thursday, and Brest, Saturday.

PEREIRE.	VILLE DE PARIS.
NAPOLEON III.	EUROPE.
ST. LAURENT.	LAFAYETTE.
LAFAYETTE.	WASHINGTON.

The Steamers of this Line do not carry Steerage Passengers.
MEDICAL ATTENDANCE FREE OF CHARGE.

For Freight or Passage, apply to
GEORGE MACKENZIE, Agent,
58 BROADWAY, NEW YORK.
At PARIS, 12 Boulevard des Capucines (Grand Hotel).
At HAVRE, Messrs. WM. ISELIN & Co.
At BREST, Messrs. KERJEGU & VILLEFERON.

The Company's Wharf at New York is at the foot of Morton Street, Pier No. 50, North River.

e

NEW YORK TO LIVERPOOL,
INMAN LINE.

THE LIVERPOOL, NEW YORK AND PHILADELPHIA
STEAMSHIP COMPANY

Will dispatch the following splendid full-powered Clyde-built Steamships, from New York for Liverpool, and
all Parts of Europe,

Every Saturday, at 1 P. M., from Pier 45, N. R.,

Carrying the British and United States Mails.

CITY OF PARIS..Capt. Kennedy.
" ANTWERP................................ " Mirehouse.
" LONDON.................................... " Brooks.
" BOSTON................................. " Roskell.
" BALTIMORE............................ " Leitch.
" BROOKLYN (building).......................

HALIFAX BRANCH.

For Halifax, N. S., and Liverpool, every Alternate Monday.

Carrying the British and United States Mails.

CITY OF NEW YORK...........................Capt. Tibbits.
" WASHINGTON........................... " Halcrow.
ETNA... " Bridgman.

RATES OF PASSAGE.

To Liverpool.............$100 gold. | From Liverpool, $75, $85, $105, gold.
" Halifax............... 20 " | A reduction of ten per cent. allowed on return tickets.

JOHN G. DALE, Agent,

No. 15 BROADWAY, New York.

PHILADELPHIA OFFICE, 411 Chestnut Street.

f

THE
National Steamship Company
(LIMITED)

Dispatch the following Splendid and Commodious Ships of their Line,

FROM NEW YORK TO LIVERPOOL,
CALLING AT CORK HARBOR,

EVERY SATURDAY,

From the Company's Wharf, Pier 47, North River.

FRANCE	Capt. Grace.
ENGLAND	Capt. Thompson.
THE QUEEN	Capt. Grogan.
DENMARK	Capt. Thomson.
HELVETIA	Capt. Cutting.
ERIN	Capt. Hall.
PENNSYLVANIA	Capt. Lewis.
VIRGINIA	Capt. Prowse.
LOUISIANA	Capt. Webster.

Rates of Passage, payable in U. S. Currency.

To Liverpool or Queenstown	$100
London	110
Hamburg	125
Bremen	135
Antwerp	125
Havre	125
Paris	125
Tickets to Liverpool and Return	180
Prepaid Cabin Tickets from Liverpool or Queenstown	90

For further information, apply to

F. W. J. HURST, Manager,
57 BROADWAY.

SHORT-TRIP GUIDE.—ANNOUNCEMENTS.

New York and Liverpool Steamers.

LIVERPOOL AND GREAT WESTERN STEAM COMPANY

Dispatch the following New First-class, Full-power Steamships, sailing as follows:

FROM LIVERPOOL..................ON TUESDAYS.

FROM NEW YORK................ON WEDNESDAYS.

COLORADO........R. C. Cutting..........3,015 tons.
MINNESOTA ......Jas. Price..............2,965 "
MANHATTAN......J. A. Williams.........2,965 "
NEBRASKA..........Jas. Guard.............3,392 "
NEVADA...................................3,000 "
IDAHO....................................3,000 "

STATE-ROOMS LARGE AND WELL VENTILATED.

STATE-ROOMS AND SALOONS ALL ON DECK.

AGENTS.

GUION & Co.............Liverpool.
J. M. CURRIE..........:...Paris and Havre.
A. S. PETRIE & Co ......London.

WILLIAMS & GUION,

71 WALL STREET, NEW YORK.

h

*SHORT-TRIP GUIDE.—ANNOUNCEMENTS.*

NORTH GERMAN LLOYD.
STEAM BETWEEN
NEW YORK AND BREMEN,
VIA SOUTHAMPTON.

The Screw Steamers of the North German Lloyd

AMERICA.........Capt. G. Ernst.	UNION....Capt. H. J. Von Santen.
NEW YORK......Capt. F. Dreyer.	WESER..........Capt. G. Wenke.
HERMANN....Capt. W. H. Wenke.	RHEIN (building).Capt. J. C.Meyer.
HANSA....Capt. K. V. Oterendorp.	MAIN (building).
BREMEN..Capt. H. A. F.Neynaber.	DONAU (building).
DEUTSCHLAND.Capt. H. Wessels.	

Run regularly between New York, Bremen, and Southampton.
Carrying the United States, British, and German Mails.
From Bremen, every Saturday. From Southampton, every Tuesday.
From New York, every Thursday.

PRICE OF PASSAGE.

From New York to Bremen, London, Havre and Southampton.
First Cabin, $120.00; Second Cabin, $72.00; Steerage, $36.00.

From Bremen, London, Havre or Southampton, to New York.
First Cabin, $120.00; Second Cabin, $72.00; Steerage, $40.00.

Price of Passage payable in Gold.

This Company also dispatches regularly, on the first of each month,

FROM BREMEN AND BALTIMORE,
Via Southampton,
The new first-class Steamships,

BALTIMORE.......Capt. Vockler. | BERLIN..........Capt. Undutsch.

Price of Passage from Baltimore to Bremen, Southampton, London, or Havre: Cabin, $90; Steerage, $36. From Bremen, Southampton, London or Havre, to Baltimore: Cabin, $90; Steerage, $40. Payable in gold.

The above vessels have been constructed in the most approved manner; they are of 3,000 tons, and 700 horse-power each, and are commanded by men of character and experience, who will make every exertion to promote the comfort and convenience of passengers. They touch at Southampton, on the outward trip, for the purpose of landing passengers for England and France.

These vessels take freight to London and Hull, for which through bills of lading are signed.

An experienced surgeon is attached to each vessel.

All letters must pass through the post-office.

☞ Specie taken to Havre, Southampton, and Bremen, at the lowest rates.—For further particulars, apply to

The NORTH GERMAN LLOYD, Bremen; OELRICHS & CO., New York; A. SCHUMACHER & CO., Baltimore; KELLER, WALLIS & POSTLETHWAITE, Southampton; PHILLIPPS, GRAVES, PHILLIPPS & CO., London; LHERBETTE, KANE & CO., Paris and Havre.

i

SHORT-TRIP GUIDE.—ANNOUNCEMENTS.

Anchor Line of Steamships
TO AND FROM
NEW YORK AND GLASGOW,
CALLING AT MOVILLE, LONDONDERRY,
To Land and Embark Passengers.

The full-powered Clyde-built Steamships

Steamer.	Captain.	Steamer.	Captain.
EUROPA	J. Craig.	IOWA	J. Hedderwick.
COLUMBIA	G. Carnaghan.	BRITANNIA	J. Laird.
HIBERNIA	R. D. Munro.	UNITED KINGDOM.	
CALEDONIA	J. Macdonald.		J. Donaldson.
CAMBRIA	................(building).		

Sail from Pier 20, N. R., New York,

Every Saturday, at Noon.

RATES OF PASSAGE, PAYABLE IN CURRENCY.

From New York to	Cabins.	Round Trip.	Interm.	Steer.
GLASGOW or DERRY	$90 and $75	$160	$35	$30
LONDON via LEITH	100 "	85..180	40	35
HAVRE " "	110 "	95..200	42	37
HAMBURG "	110 "	95..200	42	37
ROTTERDAM "	110 "	95..200	42	37
ANTWERP "	110 "	95..200	42	37

Cabin Passengers Booked to and from Liverpool at same rates as Glasgow.

Children 1 to 12 years, Half Fare. Infants Free.

Pre-paid Certificates from Glasgow or Derry—Cabins, $90 and $75; Intermediate, $47; Steerage, $37.
From Hamburg, Havre, Antwerp, Rotterdam, etc.—Cabins, $110 and $95; Intermediate, $55; Steerage, $45.

Children between One and Twelve Years......Half Fare.
Infants under One Year.......................$5.00.

HANDYSIDE & HENDERSON, 51 Union Street, Glasgow, or 96½ Foyle Street, Londonderry, or

HENDERSON BROTHERS, Agents,
6 BOWLING GREEN, NEW YORK.

k

Pacific Mail-Steamship Company's
THROUGH U. S. MAIL LINE
TO
California, Japan and China.

Leave NEW YORK from Pier 42, North River, 1st, 9th, 16th and 24th days of each month (except when either day falls on Sunday, then on the preceding Saturday), closely connecting via Panama Railroad with Steamers from Panama for San Francisco. Schedule time, 22 days.

The Steamer leaving New York on the 9th of each month will closely connect with a steamer of the CHINA LINE to leave SAN FRANCISCO for YOKOHAMA the SECOND day after the arrival of the Panama Steamer; except when the designated day falls on Sunday; then on the FOLLOWING DAY.

PROPOSED DEPARTURES FROM SAN FRANCISCO, 1868.

"JAPAN," August 3. | "GREAT REPUBLIC," Oct. 3.
"CHINA," September 1. | "JAPAN," November 2.
"CHINA," December 3.

The same steamer will leave YOKOHAMA two days after arrival, for HONG KONG.

The SHANGHAE BRANCH Steamer will leave Yokohama the day after the arrival of the main Steamer from San Francisco, and will touch at the Inland Seaports and Nagasaki.

THROUGH TICKETS furnished to Ports of CHINA, JAPAN and INDIA, and State-rooms assigned on application. The holder may lie over at Panama, San Francisco, or Yokohama.

250 pounds of baggage allowed, free, to each adult Cabin Passenger for Japan or China; 100 pounds to Passengers for San Francisco or intermediate points.

For Passage Tickets, or further information, apply at the Company's Ticket Office, on the Wharf, Pier 42, North River, foot of Canal Street, New York, to

F. R. BABY, Agent.

Brown Brothers & Co.,

No. 59 WALL STREET,

NEW YORK,

ISSUE

COMMERCIAL AND TRAVELLERS' CREDITS,

FOR USE IN AMERICA AND ABROAD.

LETTERS OF CREDIT FOR TRAVELLERS,

EXCHANGE ON LONDON AND PARIS,

SIGHT DRAFTS ON EDINBURGH AND GLASGOW,

STOCKS AND BONDS BOUGHT AND SOLD

AT THE

NEW YORK STOCK EXCHANGE.

JAMES G. KING'S SONS,

54 WILLIAM STREET, NEW YORK.

Duncan, Sherman & Co.,

BANKERS,

Corner of Pine and Nassau Streets, New York,

ISSUE

CIRCULAR NOTES AND TRAVELLING CREDITS,

Available in all the Principal Cities of the World.

TRANSFERS OF MONEY BY TELEGRAPH TO EUROPE AND THE PACIFIC COAST.

Interest allowed on Deposit Accounts.

John Munroe & Company,

AMERICAN BANKERS,

No. 7 Rue Scribe, Paris, and No. 8 Wall Street, New York,

ISSUE

CIRCULAR LETTERS of CREDIT for TRAVELLERS

In all Parts of Europe, etc.

ALSO,

COMMERCIAL CREDITS.

EVERETT HOUSE,

UNION SQUARE,

NEW YORK.

W. B. BORROWS.

On the European Plan.

MOST CHARMINGLY LOCATED HOUSE IN AMERICA.

SUITES OF ROOMS OF ESPECIAL ELEGANCE,

WITH

FRONTAGE ON THE SQUARE,

AND

All the Details of Luxury.

SHORT-TRIP GUIDE.—ANNOUNCEMENTS.

ASTOR HOUSE,
NEW YORK,
OPPOSITE CITY HALL PARK.
Thoroughly refitted, and with all Latest Improvements.

CHARLES A. STETSON'S SONS.

SHORT-TRIP GUIDE.—ANNOUNCEMENTS.

ST. JAMES HOTEL,
FRANKLIN SQUARE, BOSTON, Mass.
J. P. M. STETSON, Proprietor.
One of the best situated, most elegant, and most commodious Houses in America.

STETSON HOUSE,
LONG BRANCH, NEW JERSEY.
C. A. STETSON, Jr., Lessee.
Most elegant and fashionable House on the best Beach of the American Coast.

STEINWAY & SONS
TRIUMPHANT
AT THE
Universal Exposition, Paris, 1867.

STEINWAY & SONS
HAVE BEEN AWARDED

The First Grand Gold Medal

For American Pianos in all Three Styles Exhibited, viz., Grand, Square, and Upright, this Medal being DISTINCTLY CLASSIFIED FIRST IN ORDER OF MERIT, and placed at the head of the List of all Exhibitors, in proof of which the following

OFFICIAL CERTIFICATE

Of the President and Members of the International Jury on Musical Instruments (Class X) is subjoined: "PARIS, July 20, 1867.

"I certify that the FIRST GOLD MEDAL for American Pianos has been unanimously awarded to Messrs. STEINWAY by the Jury of the International Exhibition. First on the List in Class X.

"MELINET, President of International Jury.
GEORGES KASTNER,
AMBROISE THOMAS,
ED. HANSLICK,   Members of the
F. E. GEVAERT,   International Jury."
J. SCHIEDMAYER,

This *unanimous* decision of the International Class Jury, *indorsed* by the Supreme Group Jury, and *affirmed* by the Imperial Commission, being *the final verdict* of the *only tribunal* determining the rank of the awards at the Exposition, places *The Steinway Pianos* at the head of all others, in competition with over *Four Hundred Pianos* entered by the most celebrated European and American manufacturers.

STEINWAY & SONS
WERE ALSO AWARDED A
FIRST PRIZE MEDAL

At the Great INTERNATIONAL EXHIBITION, London, 1862, for Powerful, Clear, Brilliant, and Sympathetic Tone, with Excellence of Workmanship as shown in Grand and Square Pianos, *in Competition with* 269 *Pianos from all parts of the World.*

STEINWAY & SONS, in addition to the above, have taken THIRTY-FIVE FIRST PREMIUMS, Gold and Silver Medals, at the Principal Fairs held in this country between the years 1855 to 1862 inclusive, since which time *they have not entered their Piano-fortes at any Local Fair in the United States.*

EVERY PIANO IS WARRANTED FOR FIVE YEARS.

Warerooms, First Floor STEINWAY HALL, 109 & 111 E. 14th Street, Between 4th Ave. and Irving Place, NEW YORK.

SHORT-TRIP GUIDE.—ANNOUNCEMENTS.

Diamonds, Pearls, Sapphires, Emeralds, Fine Jewelry, and Watches.

ALSO,

SILVER & PLATED WARE,

FRENCH CLOCKS, FANS,
" BRONZES, OPERA GLASSES,
AND OTHER FANCY GOODS.

A Choice Selection to be found at

C. A. STEVENS & CO.'S,

40 EAST FOURTEENTH STREET,

UNION SQUARE, NEW YORK CITY.

THE STANDARD
AMERICAN BILLIARD TABLE.

This is the best and only reliable Billiard Table manufactured, and is furnished with our

IMPROVED COMBINATION CUSHION,

Patented November 26th, 1867.

• Besides having on hand Tables, Balls, Cloth, Cues, and every article appertaining to Billiards proper, we are manufacturing a

TABLE FOR THE HOME CIRCLE,

Patented April 21st, 1868,

Combining the Library Table, the Dining Table, and the Billiard Table.

For description and price, address

PHELAN & COLLENDER,

Sole Patentees and Manufacturers,

Nos. 63, 65, 67 AND 69 CROSBY STREET, NEW YORK.

550 MILES

OF THE

UNION PACIFIC RAILROAD,

Running West from Omaha across the Continent,

NOW COMPLETED.

THE WHOLE

GRAND LINE TO THE PACIFIC

EXPECTED TO BE

Opened through by 1870.

FIRST MORTGAGE BONDS

PAY

Six Per Cent. in Gold,

And are offered for the present at Par, and accrued Interest at Six per Cent. in Currency, from July 1.

OVER NINE PER CENT. INTEREST.

Subscriptions will be received in New York, at the Company's Office, No. 20 Nassau Street, and by

CONTINENTAL NATIONAL BANK, No. 7 Nassau Street,
CLARK, DODGE & Co., Bankers, No. 51 Wall Street,
JOHN J. CISCO & SON, Bankers, No. 33 Wall Street,

and by BANKS and BANKERS generally throughout the United States, of whom Maps and Descriptive Pamphlets may be obtained.

JOHN J. CISCO, Treasurer,
NEW YORK.

REMARKABLE CURES
BY THE
Missisquoi Spring Water.

CANCER.

Dr. Dixon, an eminent surgeon of the city of New York, and Editor of the *Scalpel*, in a letter describing the effects of this water in a case of glandular cancer, says:

"It is very evident that the use of the Missisquoi Spring Water has raised this lady from a dying condition to comfortable health and strength.
"EDWARD H. DIXON, M. D."

Mrs. Dr. Lozier, Dean of the Faculty of the New York Medical College and Hospital for Women and Children, writes:

"It gives me great pleasure to add my testimony to the healing properties of the Missisquoi Spring Water. I have at present about thirty patients using it. *Three well-defined cases of Uterine Cancer have been cured by it.* . . . As yet I have never prescribed the Missisquoi Spring Water without good effects resulting from it. C. S. LOZIER, M. D.,
361 West Thirty-fourth Street, New York."

Dr. Howard, of Linden, Genesee County, N. Y., writes:

"I wish to inform you of my cure of an internal cancer, in order that those who are similarly afflicted may have the benefit of my experience. . . . I am an object of wonder to those who knew me while suffering with that terrible malady. I owe my life to the Missisquoi Spring Water. I believe it to be a specific for cancer, and, from what I have seen of its effects, I regard it as a great remedy for diseases of the kidneys and all cutaneous disorders. I have advised many to use it, and can bear witness to its wonderful healing powers.
"JONATHAN HOWARD, M. D."

Dr. Hawley, of Syracuse, N. Y., writes in relation to a case of glandular cancer of seven years' standing:

"After the ulceration began it steadily progressed until the summer of 1866, and then it had become fully four and a half inches long by three inches wide, and was surrounded by an angry red margin, from which radiated in every direction bright-red streaks, many of them from six to eight inches long. The ulcer secreted constantly an ichorous watery matter, and frequently bled to an alarming extent. . . . At the same time her general health declined, and the stomach became so irritable as to loath all food and almost reject it as soon as taken. Every symptom presaged an early fatal termination."

After using the MISSISQUOI SPRING WATER, he adds: "In short, her health was renewed. Yours truly, WILLIAM A. HAWLEY, M. D."

DISEASES OF THE KIDNEYS.

In all diseases of the Kidneys and Bladder the MISSISQUOI SPRING WATER acts as a diuretic with marvellous effect. It is a specific in those cases. Hundreds have been cured by it.

IMPURITIES OF THE BLOOD.

The Water is a powerful tonic, and a great remedy for all diseases arising from impurity of the blood.

Pamphlets containing an account of the above and other wonderful cures, attested by eminent physicians, can be had gratis by calling at or addressing a note to

MISSISQUOI SPRINGS,
535 BROADWAY, CITY OF NEW YORK.

SHORT-TRIP GUIDE.—ANNOUNCEMENTS.

John S. Willard & Co.,
MANUFACTURERS OF THE
PRIZE MEDAL MIRRORS,

Dealers in Looking-Glasses, Frames, Mouldings, &c., in all their variety.

Wholesale and Retail, 269 CANAL STREET, NEW YORK.

Always on hand, English, French, and American Chromos.

w

THE GREATEST AMERICAN IDEA

OF A

PROGRESSIVE AND PRACTICAL AGE,

IS THE

AMERICAN SYSTEM

OF

MUTUAL LIFE ASSURANCE,

OF WHICH

The Best Exponent is the

EQUITABLE LIFE ASSURANCE ASSOCIATION,

OFFICE, No. 92 BROADWAY, NEW YORK.

WILLIAM C. ALEXANDER, President.

HENRY B. HYDE, Vice-President.
GEO. W. PHILLIPS, Actuary.
JAMES W. ALEXANDER, Secretary.

Assets—$6,000,000.   Income, $4,000,000.

Policies during 1867—$47,000,000.

All the most desirable and popular kinds of LIFE AND ENDOWMENT POLICIES issued, and every advantage appertaining to the business granted to Policy Holders.

PURELY MUTUAL.

The Charter of the Society requires that all Profits go to the Assured.

DIVIDENDS DECLARED ANNUALLY,

And applied as cash to the reduction of future premiums. Dividends upon the first year's premium may be applied to reducing the second year's premium, and so on annually thereafter.

The Assured have the option annually of applying these dividends in any of the FIVE FOLLOWING WAYS, under the rules of the Society:

FIRST—To the permanent increase of the sum assured;
SECOND—To the increase of the sum assured for one year or a term of years;
THIRD—To the permanent reduction of the premiums;
FOURTH—To the reduction of the premiums for one or more years;
FIFTH—To the reduction of the number of years in which premiums are to be paid.

www.ingramcontent.com/pod-product-compliance
Lightning Source LLC
Chambersburg PA
CBHW020227240426
43672CB00006B/437